# Family
# Theories
### Second Edition

# Understanding Families

*Series Editors:* Bert N. Adams, *University of Wisconsin*
David M. Klein, *University of Notre Dame*

This book series examines a wide range of subjects relevant to studying families. Topics include, but are not limited to, theory and conceptual design, research methods on the family, racial/ethnic families, mate selection, marriage, family power dynamics, parenthood, divorce and remarriage, custody issues, and aging families.

The series is aimed primarily at scholars working in family studies, sociology, psychology, social work, ethnic studies, gender studies, cultural studies, and related fields as they focus on the family. Volumes will also be useful for graduate and undergraduate courses in sociology of the family, family relations, family and consumer sciences, social work and the family, family psychology, family history, cultural perspectives on the family, and others.

Books appearing in **Understanding Families** are either single- or multiple-authored volumes or concisely edited books of original chapters on focused topics within the broad interdisciplinary field of marriage and family.

The books are reports of significant research, innovations in methodology, treatises on family theory, syntheses of current knowledge in a family subfield, or advanced textbooks. Each volume meets the highest academic standards and makes a substantial contribution to our understanding of marriages and families.

# James M. White
*University of British Columbia*

# David M. Klein
*University of Notre Dame*

# Family Theories

## Second Edition

**UNDERSTANDING FAMILIES**

**SAGE Publications**
*International Educational and Professional Publisher*
Thousand Oaks ■ London ■ New Delhi

*For information:*

Sage Publications, Inc.
2455 Teller Road
Thousand Oaks, California 91320
E-mail: order@sagepub.com

Sage Publications Ltd.
6 Bonhill Street
London EC2A 4PU
United Kingdom

Sage Publications India Pvt. Ltd.
M-32 Market
Greater Kailash I
New Delhi 110 048 India

Printed in the United States of America

**Library of Congress Cataloging-in-Publication Data**

White, James M., 1946-
Family theories / James M. White, David M. Klein.--2nd ed.
 p. cm.— (Understanding families)
Includes bibliographical references and index.
 ISBN 0-7619-2064-1 (cloth: alk. paper)
 ISBN 0-7619-2065-X (paper: alk. paper)
 1. Family—Research. 2. Sociology—Methodology.
 3. Sociology—Philosophy. I. Klein, David M. II. Title. III. Series.
 HQ728 .W52 2002
 306.85′01—dc21
                                        2002007263
This book is printed on acid-free paper.

02  03  04  05  10  9  8  7  6  5  4  3  2  1

| | |
|---|---|
| *Acquisitions Editor:* | James Brace-Thompson |
| *Editorial Assistant:* | Karen Ehrmann |
| *Copy Editor:* | Elizabeth Budd |
| *Production Editor:* | Denise Santoyo |
| *Typesetter:* | Siva Math Setters, Chennai, India |
| *Indexer:* | Cristina Haley |

# Contents

# Preface to the Second Edition

It has been 6 years since the original publication of *Family Theories: An Introduction*. This is a relatively brief period of time in terms of how theories develop and change. There have been only modest changes in theories during this brief interval, and we have updated the chapters to incorporate these changes. We have left the Preface to first edition so that our readers may still be guided by what we regard as a very relevant discussion of the format and use of the book.

The biggest changes in this second edition of the book are due to the various types of feedback we have received from the diverse readership. This readership includes academics publishing theoretical papers, as well as students encountering these theories for the first time. We have been excited and humbled by the enthusiastic reception and endorsement the book has encountered. It has been used in both advanced undergraduate courses and graduate seminars with about equal frequency.

The order of authorship for this edition is reversed from the original edition. We did this to symbolize the arbitrariness of the order and to indicate that the work has been a true collaboration.

During the interval since the original publication, we have used the book in our teaching, assisted other classes via e-mail and Internet, and discussed the book at scholarly conferences. We have also undertaken a yearlong process of surveying some of our users regarding their suggestions for the second edition.

As a result of these dialogues we have made some notable changes from the original version. The first chapter now includes all the material (previously in Chapters 1 and 2) on generic theory and philosophy of science. This discussion has been shortened and clarified. We have added a chapter on feminist theories. We have also added to and clarified the chapter on ecological theories. Last, we have removed the metatheoretical discussion from the last chapter and focused more on future directions and theory construction. We feel the reader, regardless of level, will be better served by this new edition as a result of these changes.

Adding the chapter on feminist theories was difficult because some felt it does not constitute a theoretical but an ideological stance; others felt that feminist theories, although rightfully theories, are not theories about marriage and families but about gender and sex. Although we understand these arguments, we also think that feminist theories have had a strong effect on contemporary theoretical thinking about families and not to introduce these views would be a disservice. Therefore, we have added a chapter on feminist theories that approaches them in the same dispassionate way that we approach the theories in the book. We lay out the basic assumptions, concepts, and propositions. We discuss applications and relevant criticisms. We do not take an "insider" perspective on any of these theories but attempt to follow the same protocol throughout our treatments. We think such an even-tempered treatment is the best way to expose readers to a diversity of approaches and allow readers to compare groups of ideas for themselves.

We are excited to release this second edition to our students and colleagues. We, of course, continue to welcome your thoughtful feedback and comments. It is our hope and intent that the world of ideas this book opens for you shall enrich your lives and those of your families.

James M. White
David M. Klein

# Preface to the First Edition (revised)

## For Everyone

In this preface, we want to set the stage for reading this book. We see our intended audience as diverse. First, our academic colleagues constitute an audience that will be served by the unique approach we have taken. Second, we expect that students, especially advanced undergraduate and graduate students, will acquire this book as part of a university or college course on the family. As a result, we also expect our colleagues in the teaching profession to read this book. Our subject will undoubtedly interest many others, such as family practitioners and anyone else interested in explaining family life.

This preface is divided into three parts. The first part is aimed at the various readers of this volume. The second part is directed at undergraduate and graduate students using the book. Finally, the last part is aimed at our colleagues using the book for instruction in their classes. We do not mean to be exclusionary. On the contrary, we encourage all readers to examine each part. Yet we feel that there are some things we need to bring to the attention of students and other things we want to say to those instructors using this book for teaching purposes.

### WHICH FRAMEWORKS AND THEORIES?

One question that we expect to arise is, Why did we choose to emphasize a particular set of six theories? As with all academic works, we are building on the shoulders of those who have preceded us, such as Boss, Doherty, LaRossa, Schumm, and Steinmetz (1993); Burr, Hill, Nye, and Reiss (1979); Christensen (1964); Nye and Berardo (1966/1981); and Winton (1995). The authors of all of these books organized their treatment of family theories in a way similar to ours. Yet the theories covered in these books are never identical. Each of the major surveys has viewed the topography of family theories differently, although not radically so. Indeed, the number of theories surveyed has ranged from 4 to 16. Theories that are notably absent in one survey reappear in another and disappear again in a third; the number included does not simply increase over time.

The way we have selected theories for inclusion in our work is different. Because we want to limit the number of basic ideas for students to learn, we have attempted to cover only what we regard as the major theoretical frameworks. A theoretical framework is identified by its basic theme or metaphor. For example, exchange theories share the basic view of humans as rational economic actors, conflict theories share the view that conflict rather than harmony is the major social process, and family development theories share the metaphors of change and maturation. We deal with the variations within each theory to point out that the landscape is more complex than any set of six theoretical frameworks could accommodate. This approach should keep the number of new concepts and arguments at a manageable level but still allow us to present the richness and diversity of ideas contained in the variations.

Whenever choices like ours are made, questions arise about missing frameworks or theories. For example, some scholars might argue that functionalism is not sufficiently addressed in our chapters. We believe that theories often evolve into new forms with new names. In the case of functionalism, the basic form of the functional argument survives within some variants of the ecological framework and some variants of other theories. We do not see functionalism as a family theoretical framework that could stand on its own, even though others in the past have argued otherwise.

In the final analysis, the reader must accept the organizing decisions we have made as one among many possible and defensible ways to divide up the territory. We believe that the theoretical frameworks identified in this volume recommend themselves on the basis of clarity and efficiency of presentation.

ORGANIZATION OF THE BOOK

The first chapter of this book provides a general introduction to the topic of family theory and theory in general. In chapter 2, we discuss one of the major purposes of theory explanation and trace the history of theoretical explanations of the family.

The following six chapters covering theoretical frameworks are organized in the same manner. We now briefly examine the subheadings used to organize these chapters. Each theoretical framework is introduced by a brief fictional account or vignette about some aspect of family life. These accounts serve to focus the reader on the particular form of behavior and interaction that the theoretical framework is intended to explain.

The first subheading the reader encounters in these six chapters is Intellectual Traditions. This section introduces the reader to a brief and nonexhaustive historical perspective on the ideas in the theoretical framework. This section should be especially valuable for assisting students to integrate this material with material they encounter in other courses in the social sciences and humanities.

The second subheading to be encountered is Focus and Scope Assumptions. All theories contain basic assumptions, but most important among these are the assumptions that set the boundaries for the theory. Each theoretical framework sets boundaries on explanations and, just as important, focuses on some particular elements or processes in families. Understanding the focus and scope of a theoretical framework assists in understanding the explanatory power of a theory.

The third subheading is Concepts. Concepts are the building blocks of any theory. In theories, concepts are used to provide meaning and to help classify phenomena. Meanings are provided by formal definitions. Classification is achieved by placing a particular act or event in the broader category of a concept. Concepts also assist explanation when they are used in propositions.

The fourth subheading is Propositions. In this section, a modest and nonexhaustive list of theoretical propositions gives the reader a simple idea of how an explanation might proceed.

The fifth section is Variations. In this section, a small set of theoretical variations is discussed. These variations are selected to capture the range of differences that the theoretical framework may accommodate.

The sixth subheading is Empirical Applications. One or two examples are discussed, and the more general theoretical framework or one of its variations is used to explain and interpret an empirical research finding or small set of findings in a topical area. The principal goal here is to demonstrate how the theory interacts with research.

The seventh subheading is Implications for Intervention. Every theory about families contains some practical implications for therapists, educators, practitioners, and policymakers. Although the critical scientific tests for a theory are based on empirical research, practical implications reveal meanings and shed light on aspects of the theory that otherwise might be overlooked.

The eighth subheading is Critiques and Discussion. This section covers the major flaws or weaknesses of the framework. Our treatment is aimed at enhancing the student's depth of understanding of the theory rather than to encourage rejection of the theory.

A Conclusion section provides a brief synopsis of the major thrusts of the theory and our perspective on the theory. Suggested Readings are included in all chapters of the book.

The final chapter of the book presents a typology for analyzing and comparing the six theoretical frameworks. This chapter also takes stock of where we are in the field and offers directions for theory construction we would like to see developed in the future.

### For Students

Combined, we have been teaching family theory to undergraduates and graduates for 40 years. Our students have often challenged us to make theories approachable and to cut through what many students view as scholarly obfuscation. It's difficult to forget some experiences we have encountered, such as the time a student asked why theorists would use an old English word *limn* when the contemporary word *illuminate* would serve very well. The student went on to ask, "If these guys are interested in communicating to others, why would they revert to language that is archaic and remote?" In this case, the instructor could not muster a good response.

Undergraduate and graduate students are not necessarily different from each other in their backgrounds or developed talents. In some years, our best undergraduate student may be more sophisticated than our best graduate student. The one uniform impression we have from our classes is that by the time our students reach the family theory course, they are generally well prepared. We believe the biggest mistake we could make in this book is to write down to them. This would be a disservice to the students as well as to the theories. What we have chosen is an interesting series of compromises. Of course, we cannot write at a level that is just right for everyone. We have aimed at a level that will stretch the understanding of many undergraduate readers and some graduate students, but most of this stretch will concern the intellectual heritage of the theories. We have made every attempt to keep our discussion of the current theories as clear and approachable as possible. We have, however, nowhere sacrificed plausibility to clarity.

We both recall our own student experiences and have witnessed many cohorts of students sharing similar experiences. Students may read a chapter just before the midterm or final exam. But students may not always read the chapters before their instructor discusses them. For many of you, the ideas, although not inherently difficult, will require both concentration and some absorption time. We think that you should at least begin the course by reading the chapters in advance of lectures and discussions and, if possible, give yourself a few days to think about the ideas.

As an entering graduate student, one of us sat through an hour-long orientation lecture suggesting that the most effective learning was achieved by guided small-group discussions. As polite and somewhat intimidated graduate students, we waited the entire hour for the question period and then asked, "If group discussion is most effective, why did we just get an hour-long lecture?" The lecturer was embarrassed. Even so, we have come to realize that, when covering massive amounts of material, lectures are sometimes the only way. It would be helpful, however, if you could discuss the ideas in this book with other students in your class and with some who are not taking the course. Even if you have class time for discussion, do not place all the burden of your learning on those 3 hours a week.

There is an old and probably untrue anecdote about a university teacher who said "sex" whenever student attention waned. Neither of us has yet had to resort to this. We attribute our lack of need for this crutch to the fact that we have a tremendous enthusiasm for theories. There is little doubt that if your instructor is really passionate about the ideas he or she is teaching, this enthusiasm will help to make the subject interesting to students. We hope we have captured some of our enthusiasm in the pages of this book. Moreover, we have confidence that your instructor shares our enthusiasm.

This book is full of robust, subtle, powerful, and magnificent ideas. Whether they are wrong or right, true or false, is immaterial to your enjoyment of the life of ideas. We think the ideas in this book can open a treasure chest of intellectual riches that will enrich your life both now and with the passage of time.

## For Instructors

Those who teach courses in family theory come from diverse backgrounds. Some are from academic disciplines such as sociology or psychology. Others are from professions such as nursing, social work, and home economics. And a growing number of instructors have received their training from the newer departments of family and child studies or family science. Both of us are familiar with students from these diverse areas. Between us, we have taught students in family science, sociology, home economics, social work, and nursing. In addition, we have worked on various projects with colleagues from all of these areas. Thus, we have experience with the diversity of readership that this book might receive.

Although we expect a diverse student audience, we also see several common elements that link and unify the interests of this audience. First, all these students are concerned with families. Second, these students are all taking a course in which the subject matter provides some degree of intellectual challenge. In our experience, students rate research methods and theory as the two most challenging types of courses. We expect many of your students to share this experience of being challenged, regardless of diversity among disciplines and professional programs.

The third common element we see for this diverse readership is that most of the courses in which this book might be used will be required courses for the undergraduate or graduate student's program. As with any required course, you will be challenged to discriminate between the basic and more specialized aspects of the topic that you want your students to learn.


DEPTH AND BREADTH

Because students are likely to bring some degree of anxiety and uncertainty to this often abstract area of family studies, we have attempted to present the theories in the clearest and most succinct manner without sacrificing the necessary depth. The variations within each framework are attempts to show the range of thinking within the framework. Although we do not include all of the variants, we do try to choose those that demonstrate the breadth and range within the theory.

We believe that our coverage of the six major theoretical frameworks is sufficiently generic to allow instructors to include additional readings on variants and applications they deem to be especially important. For example, there are many other versions of feminist theory besides the Marxist-feminism of Shulamith Firestone (1970). Indeed, Firestone may be one of the more radical versions. We are trying to show the range of the conflict theoretical framework, however, rather than to exhaust the possibilities. A few suggested readings are provided at the end of each chapter. Although some are more appropriate for advanced students, we hope that you can use these or others familiar to you to complement our coverage and to expose your students to other points of view.

It is possible to argue that one or more of the variants we cite do not properly belong to the theoretical framework in which we have placed it. For example, life course analysts might argue that they should not be subsumed under the family development framework but deserve their own framework. Our argument in all such cases is uniform: If a theoretical variant identifies the same key concepts and basic processes as does the theoretical framework, then we feel it should belong as a variant. Returning to our example, life course analysts believe that systematic patterns in the life course are explained by social norms and that individuals develop both ontogenetically and sociogenetically with families. Life course analysts share these assumptions with other family developmentalists.

Another way our approach departs from other authors is the way we see the variants within each of the frameworks. For instance, communication theory is subsumed under the systems theory framework, phenomenology is subsumed under the symbolic interaction framework, feminism is subsumed under the conflict framework, and both demography and sociobiology are subsumed under the ecological framework. Although we have done this with the student in mind, we may eventually discover that such a scheme promotes theoretical unification and cross-fertilization in ways previously unappreciated.

Of course, we have not included everything possible in this introductory survey. We have not included postmodernist thought (or some of its earlier predecessors, such as critical theory and deconstructionism) as a major framework. Several components of this movement, such as deconstructionism and phenomenology, appear as variants of other theoretical frameworks. Throughout this volume, we focus on theories that are either about the family or that have received major scholarly application to the family. For example, communication theory was not expressly developed to study families, yet it has become one of the major variants of the general systems framework applied to family communications. We are not able to make a similar claim for postmodernist thought. As interesting as it is, postmodernism has not yet contributed a theory about the family. The same principle can be cited for other omissions.

We occasionally take the liberty of propositionally formalizing theoretical frameworks that have not previously been formally developed. Recasting theoretical arguments is an ongoing process, and you may find that you or your students will benefit from giving additional attention to this.

## LIMITATIONS

Although every book has limitations, those of our book will be more sharply felt depending on the level of the course and the students' backgrounds. We have tried to write with the advanced undergraduate in mind. Such a student is likely to have taken courses in history, philosophy, general science, and other social sciences, in addition to family courses. The sections on intellectual traditions in each theoretical framework will call on this general knowledge base and allow the student to locate and integrate these theories within the history of social thought. Because of differences in student backgrounds, we have left it to instructors to fill in whatever gaps in preparation might exist.

Another limitation of this book will emerge when the volume is used with graduate students. It is our experience that graduate students vary greatly in their preparation for graduate-level family theory courses. Naturally, the most advanced of these graduate students might find our book to be of assistance in reviewing what he or she already knows before moving on to more detailed expositions of the theories. For the many graduate students who come to the family area from other disciplines, our book might provide their first introduction to family theory. In the last analysis, we expect that the use of this book in graduate coursework will vary from program to program and from student to student.

## ORIENTATION

We feel it is especially important that we explain our general orientation to presenting social science theories. Our orientation is different from some other recent surveys of family theories (e.g., Boss et al., 1993). In the past few decades, historians of science such as Kuhn (1970) and scholars concerned with the sociology of science have emphasized the importance of the social context in which theories develop. Both of us have participated in this way of thinking about theories, but we stress that theoretical ideas cannot be adequately judged by such a perspective. For example, it is deceptively easy to dismiss theoretical ideas as coming from a racist, sexist, or other social context. Some philosophers of science have pointed out the sharp division between the context of discovery for ideas and the justification of ideas. Ideas may be discovered in many ways: deductively, inductively, or haphazardly.

There is no correct way to develop a theory. The justification of a theory involves the rigorous testing of predictions and explanations against our common and shared experiences, regardless of a theory's source or creator. Of course, we do not deny that the nature of theoretical arguments, viewed as textual products, and the attitudes that others have of them are dependent on the social contexts of authors and consumers. All we are saying is that truth or falsity (or even probability and plausibility) does not rest with where or how the ideas originated but rather with what and how the ideas predict and explain.

In science, there is a long and important tradition that hypotheses and theories are to be investigated and judged by evidence rather than how we feel about their authors or their social situations. In the end, most racist and sexist theories are wrong not because they were developed from biased perspectives, but because they fail to predict and explain phenomena. After all, every author of every theory has some biases. If the biases of theoreticians were cause for rejecting a theory, all theories would be rejected out of hand.

We find the history and sociology of science endlessly interesting and often they illuminate the ideas in a theory. We supply a modest discussion of intellectual traditions with each theoretical framework for context but not to judge the ideas. We believe that it is our job to provide a clear exposition of the assumptions, concepts, and propositions, thereby allowing students to understand and apply the theories to the evidence provided by their own experience and the data they have gathered from their courses.

David M. Klein
James M. White

# Acknowledgments

We express our gratitude to our students and numerous colleagues for their support and encouragement. In particular, we would like to thank Dr. Richard Bulcroft, Dr. Wes Burr, Christopher Butler, Michelle Janning, and Dr. Gary Peterson. Special thanks goes to Darnell Coote, MD, for her reading and comments on the feminism chapter as well as the anonymous reviewers who reviewed an earlier version of Chapter 7. We would like to thank the reviewers of the first edition for their critical comments and constructive criticism. Finally, we would like to express our deepest gratitude to Bert Adams and Jim Brace-Thompson for their patience and unwavering support of this project.

We acknowledge and express appreciation to the University of British Columbia for granting Professor White a study leave (2001) so that he could undertake the writing of the new feminism chapter and, in collaboration with Professor Klein, undertake revisions to all other chapters in the book.

# 1

# What Is a Theory?

Generally speaking, theories are abstract and general ideas that are subject to rules of organization (see Box 1.1). These qualities may be why the study of theory is often difficult for students. All of us are more likely to be interested in concrete experiences, our own or those of others. Theories are not the facts or data of experience, but they are connected to those facts or data.

One complication in linking ideas and data is that the very same data can be organized in different ways. As a result, different theories can be used to make sense of the same set of facts. For example, how are we to interpret the fact of a relatively high divorce rate? One answer might be that the family as an institution is being threatened, perhaps even disappearing. A different answer is that divorce weeds out less viable marriages, thereby preserving the family institution. To evaluate the merits of the two arguments, one must see what other relevant facts are operating and how the entire argument is organized into statements at a more abstract level.

One useful way to understand theoretical arguments is to examine their basic components. We start with the idea that a theory is a systematic collection of concepts and relations. This is consistent with all four of the quotes in Box 1.1. Because there is an endless variety of ways to organize ideas, we will limit ourselves to the requirements for a *scientific* theory. Such theories contain systematically related propositions that are empirically testable (Rudner, 1966). Thus, there are several components that we need to discuss in further detail: (a) concepts, (b) relations between concepts, (c) propositions, (d) relations between propositions, and (e) connections between propositions and the empirical world of observation. Before we look at each of these components, we must distinguish between ideas and data.

### Box 1.1    What Is a Theory?

"A scientific theory might be likened to a complex spatial network: Its terms are represented by the knots, while the threads connecting the latter correspond, in part, to the definitions and, in part, to the fundamental and derivative hypotheses included in the theory. The whole system floats, as it were, above the plane of observation and is anchored to it by rules of interpretation. These might be viewed as strings which are not part of the network but link certain points of the latter with specific places in the plane of observation. By virtue of those interpretive connections, the network can function as a scientific theory: From certain observational data, we may ascend, via an interpretive string, to some point in the theoretical network, thence proceed, via definitions and hypotheses, to other points, from which another interpretive string permits a descent to the plane of observation." (Hempel, 1952, p. 36)

"A theory is nothing—it is not a theory—unless it is an explanation. One may define properties and categories, and one still has no theory. One may state that there are relations between the properties, and one still has no theory. One may state that a change in one property will produce a definite change in another property, and one still has no theory. Not until one has properties, and propositions stating the relations between them, and the propositions form a deductive system—not until one has all three does one have a theory. Most of our arguments about theory would fall to the ground, if we first asked whether we had a theory to argue about." (Homans, 1964, p. 812)

"Deductive theory can be described briefly as an attempt to increase human understanding by providing explanations of why certain things occur. It provides this explanation by having a set of propositions and then deducing that, if these propositions are true, and if certain other conditions are met, certain specific and observable events occur. The more specific events are then 'explained' by the more general propositions that have been used as premises in deducing that the specific events occur. The explanation is only as valid as the propositions and logic that are used in the deduction, but one of the goals of science is to gradually eliminate invalid propositions and increase the number of useful, valid ones." (Burr, 1973, p. 3)

"Theorizing is the process of systematically formulating and organizing ideas to understand a particular phenomenon. A theory is the set of interconnected ideas that emerge from this process." (Doherty, Boss, LaRossa, Schumm, & Steinmetz, 1993, p. 20)

## Ideas and Data

Science is fundamentally concerned with ideas, data, and relationships between them. Theory exists in the realm of ideas. Research takes place in the realm of data. A science advances to the extent that its theories and its studies (i.e., its empirical research) are productive and mutually reinforcing. For knowledge to be scientific, scientists must explain empirical observations by ideas or theory. Theories explain by treating particular facts or observations as examples of general principles or processes. For example, there may be certain conditions, such as first intercourse, that encourages dating couples to become more serious and less casual about their relationship. This would constitute a hypothesis or testable conceptual proposition if data have not yet been examined in this regard. If, however, we have a great deal of data suggesting that first intercourse has a specific effect on couples' "probability of marriage," then that generalization is what we often regard as a scientific fact.

The linkages between ideas and data can be organized in different ways. If research produces empirical generalizations, the data might *inductively* lead to the development of a new theory, or the data might be interpreted in terms of an existing theory. When the process goes from data to ideas, we think of it as being *inductive*. Sometimes, a researcher starts with an existing theory, derives expectations about the data (i.e., hypotheses), and then makes observations to see how well the data fit. When the process goes from ideas to data, we think of it as being *deductive*. Theoretical ideas in science are developed both inductively and deductively. In either case, the ideas and the data must fit together in a meaningful way for the theory to be judged adequate.

We caution against too rigid a distinction between ideas and data. Sometimes, ideas can themselves be data. If the dating persons in our example have ideas or beliefs about what might propel their relationship to marriage, these ideas might be measured and become part of the data. The ideas that people have may be beliefs, attitudes, or preferences. These ideas might even be theories or explanations that people have about such things as why couples have children at certain times in a marriage. Thus, the ideas held by the people we study are often part of our data. Even more important is the fact that our measures and observations are founded on theories about the world and how we can know and measure the world. So in many ways, scientific data are constructed from ideas. We will have more to say on this point shortly.

This book is mostly about theoretical ideas that supply plausible explanations about families. Over the years, family scholars have offered many such explanatory ideas. We cannot call attention to or restate every single such idea. Instead, we focus on the clusters of ideas, or frameworks, that seem to be the most significant and popular now at the beginning of the 21st century. New theories about the family will be developed in the future. Some will build on one or more of the currently existing theories, but others may have features that cannot now be anticipated.

The question "From whom or where do theories and propositions originate?" is important because it leads to a basic distinction regarding theory. This distinction is between the "context of discovery" and the "context of justification" (Kaplan, 1964). The answer to the question about the origins of theory is simple: Theories and propositions can come from anyone and anywhere. We might find a possible theory in the writings of ancient scribes, a newspaper cartoon, or the observational work of a research scientist. There should not be any restrictions on the creative insight that might lead to fruitful theory building. This is the "context of discovery," and creative insight and thought are its hallmarks. Grounding in the research literature and an understanding of logic might be helpful, but they are not necessary conditions for the development of theory. As a corollary, it follows that we should not judge the usefulness or fruitfulness of a theory by its origin. For example, if there are two proposed theories to explain " adolescent bed-wetting," one from an esteemed research scientist in the area and the other from your grandmother; we cannot decide on which is better based on the status of the originator. Indeed, it is a hallmark of the context of discovery in science that we do not judge theoretical propositions by whether they originate with a political leader, a grandmother, or a respected scientist.

The context of justification, on the other hand, is the context in which theoretical propositions are put to the test. Here, we see if the theory is justified in its claims. In science, this is a twofold process. The first criterion applied is *logical coherence*. We ask, "Is this set of theoretical propositions logically consistent with itself, and then is it logically consistent with other well established theories in the area?" The second criterion is the *empirical adequacy* of the theory. At this point, we ask, "Do the deductions from the theory fit with our empirical measures of phenomenon?" It is this step that many people identify with "science." However, during the evolution of a discipline or area of study, it is obvious that the production of ideas (context of discovery) must precede the testing of those ideas (context of justification). Therefore, it is not unusual to find multiple approaches and both qualitative and quantitative research strategies in areas that are still developing basic theory.

This book will assist you in estimating the current status of theoretical ideas about families. In the remainder of this chapter, we cover the main ingredients that go into any scientific theory and then suggest what makes theories about the family unique among scientific theories. The next seven chapters separately cover the principal theoretical frameworks that are important in family science today. Finally, in the concluding chapter, we compare the major frameworks and look forward to the future of theory in family science.

## Scientific Theory

PHILOSOPHIES OF SCIENCE

The term *philosophy* can refer both to the values and way of thinking of a person and to an academic discipline. Both meanings are important in understanding the emergence and growth of family studies, but for the moment we focus on the importance and relevance of academic philosophy, especially the academic philosophy of science, for scientific theories.

The methods of philosophy are logic and other forms of discursive reasoning. Philosophers do not use the empirical methods of science to establish the credibility of their ideas. Some philosophers, known as philosophers of science, examine the principles by which scientists work through reconstructing the logic of scientific processes. Whereas sociologists of science systematically study the behaviors and thoughts of scientists and the social organization of the sciences, philosophers of science explore what science should or could be like in terms of abstract ideas. There are several ways in which this philosophical study is important.

The discipline of philosophy was historically prior to the scientific disciplines. The ancient Greek philosophers, among others, had many creative ideas about human affairs and the workings of the natural world. It was out of the Enlightenment philosophy of the 18th and 19th centuries that the modern sciences in the Western world were born. During this period, it was common for individual scholars to be both philosopher and scientist at the same time or to easily shift back and forth between the two. It has only been during the 19th and 20th centuries that the various scientific disciplines have branched into special fields to which a person could devote an entire career.

The historical legacy of philosophy as a precedent to the sciences has meant that philosophy, as a formal discipline, has influenced all sciences. Many of the influences have been indirect. The so-called physical sciences, such as physics and chemistry, emerged first. Between 1850 and 1900, the philosophical principles embedded in these earlier sciences spilled over into the biological sciences, such as botany and zoology, and the social sciences, such as psychology and sociology. During the 20th century, as family science emerged as a subspecialty within several of the social sciences, the philosophical underpinnings continued to operate. Now, near the start of the 21st century, we are able to think of family science as a distinct field with an interdisciplinary character or even as a unique discipline in its own right.

In philosophy as in other academic disciplines, new ideas are constantly being proposed and debated. A particular philosophy of science may be popular at a given moment, but later it may be challenged and some other philosophy may take its place at or near the top of the heap. Scientists, including family scientists, frequently turn to the literature produced by philosophers to see what the current issues are. When scientists need to justify the basic principles guiding their search for answers to important questions, they sometimes seek guidance from philosophers of science or from other philosophers.

It is now often asserted that there are different, if not rival, philosophies of science. This is apparent in professional philosophy itself and, more important for this book, among family scientists as well. The philosophies we adopt influence the way we conduct our scientific practice, including the theories we create and our attitudes toward the theories of others. We sketch below a few of the central philosophical views that may help to distinguish family theorists and other family scholars from one another.

Key elements of three philosophies of science appear in Box 1.2. We have called these *positivistic, interpretive,* and *critical* philosophies of science (e.g., Neuman, 1994). We do not claim that these are the only three alternatives in family science. Indeed, we discuss other alternatives, such as feminism and postmodernism, in subsequent chapters. At this juncture, we present Box 1.2 to illustrate the nature of philosophical assertions. To further illuminate the issues involved, we focus now on truth claims and values.

A group of philosophers working in Vienna in the early part of the 20th century argued that knowledge claims are either true or false and that the job of scientists is to verify the true claims. Another philosopher, Sir Karl Popper, disputed this view. Popper (1959) argued that knowledge claims could be shown to be false but that there is no way to prove them to be true. Popper's position has become influential among not only philosophers but also practicing social scientists. Whether or not family scholars have read Popper, his ideas have indirectly influenced family theorizing, helping to usher in what is sometimes called a postpositive era in the philosophy of family science (Thomas & Wilcox, 1987).

## Box 1.2    Three Philosophies of Science,
## Applied to Family Studies

**POSITIVISTIC View of Knowledge. There are objective truths, processes, or realities to be discovered about families.**

**Values:** Family science can and should be value neutral if not value free.

**Criteria for Evaluating Family Theories:** Good theories should be rationally constructed (e.g., internally consistent, simple, coherent, clear, explicit, general, abstract). Good theories also should be empirically relevant (e.g., testable, fit well with data).

**Goals:** Explanation and prediction.

**Scholarly Style:** Analytical, causal, deductive or inductive, deterministic or probabilistic, factual, logical, materialistic, mathematical, mechanistic, observant, planful, precise, quantitative, structural, etc.

**INTERPRETIVE View of Knowledge. Truth is subjective, and all knowledge about families is created by interpreting actors engaged in conversations with one another.**

**Values:** Family science is value relevant, and family scientists should become aware of and open about their own values.

**Criteria for Evaluating Family Theories:** Good theories should have literary qualities (e.g., elegance, imagination, narrative power). Good theories also should be based on data grounded in the experiences of family members.

**Goal:** Understanding.

**Scholarly Style:** Artistic, evocative, existential, hermeneutic, humanistic, intuitive, metaphorical, phenomenological, postmodern, processual, self-reflective, sensitive, speculative, spontaneous, symbolic, etc.

**CRITICAL View of Knowledge. Truth is imposed by those with the power to shape knowledge.**

**Values:** Family theories are value laden. All values should be exposed and challenged to create opportunities for change.

---

**Box 1.2   (continued)**

---

**Criteria for Evaluating Family Theories:** Good theories contextualize phenomena and allow for pluralism. Good theories also are emancipatory, prescribe changes, display the theorist's ethical stance, and fit well with the theorist's personal experiences.

**Goals:** Emancipation or empowerment of oppressed people and social groups.

**Scholarly Style:** Constructivistic, dialectical, feminist, liberal or radical, macroscopic, pluralistic, postmodern, processual, relativistic, etc.

---

A central difference between positivism and other philosophies of science is their perspective on values. It should be obvious that no human behavior is valueless in an absolute sense. Indeed, all of the philosophical arguments we are considering are themselves evaluative. To say that science should be without values is to value "valueless-ness." To value something is simply to hold and to express a conception of a desirable state of affairs.

One of the key reasons that science emerged historically as a way of thinking and working that is somewhat different from the arts, religion, and politics was concern about the distortions in knowledge along with considerable human suffering that seems to result when reasonableness, fairness, and facts are devalued. Science is not without its faults, just as no individual human being or social organization is faultless. The "value neutrality" sometimes advocated by scientific positivists is similar in at least some ways to value tolerance or respect for value diversity. But this is a matter of degree, and the value-relevant and value-laden positions push further the ideals of tolerance and diversity, sometimes to the extreme point of complete relativism.

Writing several decades ago about science as a vocation, sociologist Max Weber made some interesting comments:

> Today one usually speaks of science as free of presuppositions. Is there such a thing? All scientific work presupposes that the rules of logic and method are valid. Science further presupposes that what is yielded by scientific work is important in the sense that it is worth being known. In this, obviously, are contained all our problems. For this presupposition cannot be proved by scientific means. It can only be interpreted with reference to its ultimate meaning, which we must reject or accept according to our ultimate position toward life. (quoted in Gerth & Mills, 1946, p. 143)

More recently, Christensen (1964) provided an analysis of the value issue in family science. His assessment was quite Weberian.

Christensen advocated neither the rejection nor espousal of non-scientific values by theorists and other scientists. Rather, he advocated the identification and separation of nonscientific values from scientific values. This may continue to be the most common view among family scientists, but it is not the only view. According to the critical philosophy in Box 1.2, for example, scientific facts are inseparable from the values that scientists have about their subject matter.

What we have just said about values applies as well to ideologies. The notion of ideology has three major meanings: (a) a set of beliefs; (b) the systematic study of a set of beliefs, their nature, and their origin; and (c) visionary speculation, often about ideals and with an action agenda for achieving the ideals. There is no question that systems of belief about families can be part of a family theory or that carefully studying those beliefs might improve a family theory. There is also no doubt that beliefs about family science can affect family theories. Even visionary speculation has creative potential for theories. Our caution is only that ideologies among family scholars that are philosophical or political may be usefully connected with a particular family theory, but they are not within or constitutive of the theory itself. So if a scientific theory argues that X causes Y, the truth of this does not depend on whether we like or dislike X or Y. The theory may suggest how to change Y if the direction of change is consistent with our values and ideology, but scientific theory should be equally useful for someone with exactly the opposite values and ideology.

To summarize, philosophical ideas establish principles that help frame the ways that family theories and other aspects of scholarship are created and used. Philosophical ideas are themselves foundations for scholarship, but they cannot be scientifically proven true or false. In many ways, scholars either consciously or unconsciously adopt a particular philosophical stance in regard to research by the way they do their research. Those who attempt not to use their research as a vehicle for their own values, the values of their religion, or their political values would be clearly identified as "positivist." Although those holding interpretive and critical philosophies have criticized this perspective, the positivist approach remains the hallmark of scientific work and scholarly accountability. Indeed, the public expects family scientists to present their research findings independent from their religious and political beliefs. In science it is expected that any research finding can be replicated by other researchers regardless of whether they have the same or different political and religious beliefs. This is as close as we may be able to get to scientific "objectivity."

PARTS OF A THEORY

All scientific theories use the same basic building blocks. These building blocks are concepts, relations, and propositions. The section below discusses each of these central ideas.

*Concepts* are abstractions. A concept is not the thing but stands for the abstract class of things, ideas, or entities. Concepts are essential to theories because they enable us to organize experience. We do not invent a new concept every time we refer to a unique event. For example, we do not need a new term for marriage or a new meaning for the event called marriage every time a wedding takes place. Instead, we think of getting married in a more abstract way. We say that all weddings have certain defining properties. If we want to distinguish different kinds of weddings, we might establish categories. We could distinguish elopements from formal weddings and church weddings from civil wedding ceremonies. The categories remain abstractions, however, in that they all refer to occasions of a particular type, not to specific instances of weddings.

Social actors construct concepts for the purpose of communicating meaning, whether the social actors are family members or family scientists. So all concepts are "constructs." However, we do not whimsically invent concepts but rely on the common stock of terms and definitions that already exist in common usage. Sometimes we alter meanings or the words used for important ideas. Even dictionaries do not change whimsically, but they do evolve.

In science, however, the more explicit the definition for a concept, the better we can determine when it applies and when it does not apply. A scientific concept can mean only what a community of interacting scientists agrees that it means. Although scientists sometimes argue about the "proper" meaning of concepts, a theory tends to gain a footing in the scientific community once scholars settle on meanings for the time being. Many concepts in scientific theories refer to states of affairs with fairly stable properties. For example, we cannot have a coherent theory about the distribution of housework responsibilities if the meaning of *housework* changes every time we use this word.

Many but not all concepts can correspond to a set of empirical measures. A *variable* is any measure that can have two or more values such as yes or no, strongly agree to strongly disagree, or even a range of values such as the Centigrade scale of temperature. For example, we may measure housework by hours of work within the house or by a specified set of tasks such as doing laundry, toilet cleaning, and so on. Variables that might measure housework could be the hours a person spent doing the work, the economic value of the work, and so on.

*Relations* play the role of verbs in a theory. To relate concepts to each other, we need connecting relations asserting how the concepts are related. All relations have properties (symmetry, reflexivity, and transitivity). So for example, we could use the same concepts but with different relations, and the truth of the statement will change completely.

John is a relative of George.
George is a relative of Bill.

Therefore

John is a relative of Bill.

Or

John is the father of George.
George is the father of Bill.

Therefore

John is the father of Bill.

In these two cases, one relation is transitive (is a relative of), and the other is not transitive (is the father of). This simple difference in the properties of relations makes all the difference in the validity of the final statement. Relations can often be formalized in simple terms such as *greater than* or *less than,* and definitions are signified by identity or equals. As we shall see shortly, this fact provides a key link between theory and research.

*Propositions* exist when a concept is linked in a meaningful way by a relation to another concept. So we could say that among dual-earner couples, *the social class status of the husband is positively related to the amount of housework he performs.* This would be a theoretical proposition. The first concept is *social class status of the husband.* The second concept is the *amount of housework.* The relation in this proposition says that the greater a husband's social class status (relative to other husbands), the greater the husband's amount of housework. This relation can be mathematically expressed (modeled) as a function:

$$Amount\ of\ housework = f\ (Social\ class\ status).$$

As we shall see shortly, our first approximation of this functional relation ($f$) between a husband's social class status and amount of housework is usually a straight line with either a positive or negative slope. When a proposition asserts covariation between variables, the relation between concepts includes a sign (positive or negative), indicating that increases either occur together or go in opposite directions. When a relation asserts causal influence, the relation also makes clear which variable (independent) is influencing which other variable (dependent).

DEFINING THEORY

Earlier in this chapter, we defined a scientific theory as "a set of systematically related propositions that are empirically testable" (Rudner, 1966). Now that we have the building blocks in place we can discuss the meaning and implications of this definition in greater detail.

*Systematically related propositions.* A theory usually comprises several propositions. Indeed, one proposition alone would not constitute a theory but would simply be a conceptual "hypothesis." Not only must a theory have at least two propositions, but these two propositions must be systematically linked by relations. The way we link one theoretical proposition to another is by logical form. Although there are many mathematical and logical systems at our disposal, we will use simple syllogisms to show what we mean by form and relations. Note that the mini theory below is used only for an example of logical form and should not be regarded as empirically adequate.

Imagine that we have two propositions, but they may at first appear unrelated. For example, from a set of propositions about the intergenerational transmission of social class, we find the following:

> *The greater the family of orientation's value on education, the greater the son's social class status.*

If we combine this with our previously discussed proposition, we get a mini theory with two related propositions. Furthermore, we can deduce a third, new and interesting proposition from these two.

> *The greater the family of orientation's value on education, the greater the son's social class status.*

> *The greater the husband's social class status, the greater the amount of housework performed.*

*Therefore, the greater the family of orientation's value on education, the greater the amount of housework performed by the son (husband) in his family of procreation.*

Now the above mini theory is in the form of a syllogism. These deductive arguments are constructed so that if the first two propositions (called premises) are true, then the deduction, called the conclusion, is necessarily logically true (although not necessarily empirically true). Much more important is that if the conclusion is false, then we know that at least one or both of the premises are also false. These properties hold only if the correct form is followed. In regard to syllogisms, the correct form is that the middle term $B$ (below) must appear at the end of the first premise and at the beginning of the second premise. This is called the rule of distributed middle.

$$A \rightarrow B$$
$$\underline{B \rightarrow C}$$
$$A \rightarrow C$$

Regardless of whether these ideas are in the correct form, what we want to know is if our theory as a whole is accurate. In logic, if we showed that our conclusion is true, that would not mean that the two premises are also true. Indeed, when we make such an assertion, it is called the "fallacy of affirming the consequent." In reality, we have to work backward. What we try to do is to disprove our conclusion. If we show that our conclusion is false, then we also know that at least one of the premises is false. We get much greater intellectual power out of using this reverse logic (*modus tollens*). This is one of the major theoretical reasons we use the null hypothesis in testing our theories.

*Empirically testable.* For a set of propositions to qualify as a scientific theory rather than religious or literary or political, it must be capable of being empirically tested. That does not mean that all our scientific theories have been empirically tested but that a theory that is incapable of being empirically tested is *not* a scientific theory. Now we turn to the question "What does it mean to say that a theory is capable of being empirically tested?"

The proposition in the conclusion of our mini theory used above can be used as an example. It states that the degree to which the husband's family of orientation values education is related to the amount of housework the husband will perform in dual-career couples. This concluding proposition will now become our research focus. When we decide to research a particular proposition, it becomes the "conceptual hypothesis" in addition to being the deduced conclusion of a theoretical argument.

The first thing we must do to research this "conceptual hypothesis" is to find ways to measure its components as variables. That means that we must find or develop measures for the first concept, husband's family of orientation's value on education, and the second concept, amount of housework performed. Finally, we must not forget that we must find a way to demonstrate (or operationalize) the relation between these concepts. We might operationalize or measure the family of orientation's value on education by asking the husband several questions about his perception of his mother and father's values about education and how much financial assistance they offered for his education. Both of these measures would have problems of validity and reliability because of faulty recall, halo effects, and so on. We might measure amount of housework by either the number of hours spent on various household tasks or the economic value of tasks performed by the husband. Both of these measures would have problems. Which tasks should we list? Would the husband inflate his estimate of the time spent? If we had the husband list the tasks and then assigned the economic value at the cost of a plumber for plumbing jobs, a babysitter for child care, and so on, would we find that this correlates poorly with the measure of amount of time spent on household chores? Indeed, there are always problems and questions regarding how accurately our empirical operationalizations measure our concepts in our conceptual hypothesis.

The last component of our conceptual hypothesis to be operationalized is the relation. As we indicated previously, we hypothesize that amount of housework is a function of family's values on education. What is this function? In most social research, the first functional form that we test is that of a straight line. You may recall the slope-intercept formula for a straight line ($y = b [x] + a$). Indeed, this simple mathematical model is the basis for much of our analysis of relations in the social sciences. The formulae for a straight line is a *mathematical model* and it has a corresponding *statistical model* expressed in the formula ($Y = a + b [X] + e$). Basically, the application of the statistical formula in the analysis of the data allows us to examine the linear relation between amount of housework ($y$) and the family's value on education ($x$). The strength and direction (positive or negative) of that relation will be given by the regression (correlation) coefficient ($b$).

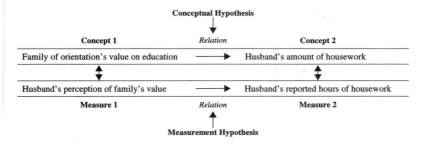

**Figure 1.1**     Conceptual and Measurement Hypotheses

Once all of the measures are in place, we have in effect two hypotheses. Our theoretical proposition represents the *conceptual hypothesis,* and our measures and the relation between them represents the *measurement hypothesis.* The architecture of the empirical test of a theory is portrayed in Figure 1.1.

Finally, if we were to conduct our study on husbands in dual-career couples, we would have to control for several variables that might account for the relationship, such as number of children, maid service, wife's level of housework, and income level. After we analyze the results, we might find that there is no relationship between the variables we measured. If we can satisfy our critical colleagues that we have valid and reliable measures of the concepts and relations in the conceptual hypothesis, then we could conclude that the theoretical proposition is false. Because this is a deductive system (syllogism), we would also know that at least one of our premises is also wrong. As a result, it would be time either to recast and modify the theory significantly or even to discard it completely.

On the other hand, what if our results are supportive of the conceptual hypothesis? If we can satisfy our colleagues regarding the validity and reliability of our measures and procedures, then we might want to say that the theory is true. However, as we said previously, this would be committing the fallacy of affirming the consequent. If the proposition seems to hold, it does not mean that the other propositions (premises) are true because it is logically possible to deduce the conclusion from several other sets of premises. We can never determine which possible set of premises might be true. As a result, science and theory achieve a great deal by disproving hypotheses and theoretical propositions rather than ever proving anything. All our scientific knowledge is tentatively held until we disprove it. Scientist are not true believers, but skeptics.

FUNCTIONS OF THEORY

Scientific theories serve many purposes. Here, we emphasize how they contribute to understanding. It is widely recognized, however, that knowledge for its own sake is not the only worthwhile goal in life. We all want to do something with our knowledge. In our preceding example, if we had some confidence in our theory about housework, a young woman searching for a helpful mate might want to examine the educational values of the family of orientation of prospective spouses. More seriously, for those in one of the helping professions, theories about the family may provide knowledge to improve their services as therapists, program evaluators, or social policy advisers. For those who are political activists, agitators for modest or revolutionary causes or the reduction of major social problems, or even staunch defenders of the world as it is or once was, theoretical knowledge about families can be put to fruitful use. Without meaning to diminish the importance of any of these practical uses of theories, we concentrate here on the ways in which theories contribute to the immediate goals of science.

1. *Accumulation.* Theories assist in the accumulation and organization of research findings. Much of the pursuit of knowledge involves the collection and analysis of empirical facts, filtered through the lenses of researchers. A body of empirical knowledge, however, is just a pile of findings. Theories tell us how to select and arrange research findings into meaningful groupings. If no existing theory is available for this purpose, new theories can be constructed from findings through a process of tentative generalization.

2. *Precision.* Theories articulate ideas in more carefully specified ways than everyday language allows. Thinking theoretically forces one to clarify what concepts and relations really mean and what they include and exclude. This precision facilitates communication, so long as the communicators are trained in the language of science.

3. *Guidance.* Theories direct researchers to develop and test measurement hypotheses (i.e., empirical statements about what the data are expected to look like). Because theoretical ideas entail abstract, plausible, and tentative arguments, they must be checked against the empirical evidence for confidence in them to grow. Theories point to new kinds of relevant evidence for which findings do not currently exist. It is relatively easy to find or create evidence in support of a theory that one likes, however. Theories, therefore, also promote a critical spirit of inquiry. Efforts are made to refute theories, not just to support them. If a field contains two or more theories that yield

incompatible hypotheses, it may be possible to design a study or a series of studies that help to decide which theory is better.

4. *Connectedness.* Theories demonstrate how ideas are connected to each other and to other theories. Theories are systematic sets of ideas. The parts of a theory fit together in a coherent way. Knowing what the parts are and how they fit together helps to distinguish one theory from other theories. This also helps us to see what two or more theories share or how they could be connected or combined by bringing together elements of each.

5. *Interpretation.* Theories help to make sense of how the phenomena they cover operate. There are at least two aspects of sensibleness in interpretation. One is essentially descriptive: A theory should enable a good description of the subject matter with which it is concerned. This does not necessarily mean that the theory must fit our intuitive judgments of the way things work. In fact, a theory may challenge many intuitions or commonsense views of the world. Rather, to enable us to describe a subject, a theory provides a plausible picture of structures or processes that we can accept as reasonable given the assumptions in the theory. The other feature of interpretation is that theories evoke or promote stories about the way things work. If we can visualize concrete or even general scenarios of how things work, the theory is providing an interpretation.

6. *Prediction.* Theories point to what will or can happen in the future. If a theory helps us understand what has happened in the past or is happening now, this is of course desirable. To continue to be useful, however, a theory must contain propositions equally applicable to future events and experiences. This does not mean that any theory accurately foretells the future, only that it should make some relevant propositions regarding future outcomes. If we know what a theory predicts, this can contribute to the guidance function mentioned earlier. If a theory predicts something that is subject to human intervention and alteration, future actions may invalidate the theory. Normally, however, a theory is expected to hold up in the future to the extent that its predictions are confirmed. Even if predictions are not confirmed, the theory may be basically correct, and only the conditions under which it works may require revision.

7. *Explanation.* Theories provide answers to "why" and "how" questions. As the quotes in Box 1.1 from Burr (1973) and Homans (1964)

suggest, explanation is often considered the single most important function of a theory. Because explanation is so central to the functioning of theories and because it has a variety of different meanings, we need to address this topic in more detail. Without theories, we cannot determine why and how things happen the way they do. In our everyday lives, we may be satisfied by saying that one specific event, say, a divorce between two friends, happened because of one or more other events that took place before the divorce. Such reasoning captures some of what goes into a scientific explanation, but it overlooks the most important aspect. Scientific theories explain by relying on deductive arguments. Specific events and the connections between them must be derived from more general statements for us to say that the events and the connections between them have been explained.

Explanation is provided by a general statement (sometimes called a "covering law") that includes (or covers) the specific instance we want to explain. So for example, if you drop this book and it falls to the floor, we could ask you to explain why it fell. You would simply cite the law of gravity as explaining why the book fell. This is to say that the particular phenomenon is part of a generally understood pattern we call "gravity." Now this is not to say that in reality our understanding of gravity is simple; indeed, it involves complex theories of electromagnetism, mass, space, and time. But the "law" derived from these complex theories covers the specific phenomenon of the falling book. Thus, to explain why someone got divorced (a particular instance) would be to provide the general theoretical propositions (covering laws) explaining divorce.

It is crucial to remember that although functions or goals like those we have listed represent ideals, this is no guarantee that a particular theory will fulfill such ideals. In fact, we can use the seven listed functions as standards against which to measure the performance of a theory at any stage of its development. A theory may perform well in some respects but less well in others. Determining such facts helps us decide where our energies need to be directed to improve the theories that we have or invent better ones.


## Family Theory

Ideas about human families can come from many sources, including scientific disciplines concerned with the study of entities that are not families, as well as personal experiences with our own families. No potential source should be dismissed, although we should be aware that those sources selected likely will affect key features of the theory that emerges. Most of the family theories that exist today draw on ideas from external sources. Family theories are not insulated sets of ideas, and family theorists do not merely talk to each other about family ideas.

For a theory to be about families, there must be at least one family concept in the theory. We cannot decide what a family concept is, however, unless we first decide what a family is. Let us, therefore, begin by thinking of a family as a social group. We need to identify the distinguishing features of this group. Following are some of the major ways that families differ from such groups as associations of coworkers and networks of close friends.

1. *Families last for a considerably longer period of time than do most other social groups.*

Of course, some relationships in families are not enduring. Marriages can be broken by divorce or death fairly soon after they are formed. Yet we normally think of our own families as lasting throughout our lifetimes. We actually are born into a family that already exists. Our parents remain parents even after we become adults. We add members to the family when we marry and become parents. Our siblings remain siblings throughout our lifetimes. Although it is possible for coworkers and close friends to maintain relationships for long periods of time, families are the only groups that virtually require lifetime membership, even though some members are added and subtracted along the way. Belonging to a family is involuntary in the sense that we do not choose which parents are going to give birth to us. Other groups tend to be much more voluntary, in that we have some choice about joining them in the first place.

2. *Families are intergenerational.*

Through the act of giving birth, families include people who are related as parents and children. If elders live long enough, we have ties to grandparents, and maybe even to great-grandparents and great-great-grandparents. At some point, we ordinarily have living members of both older and younger generations, and we may eventually become grandparents or great-grandparents ourselves. Other kinds of groups may include people with fairly large age differences, but families are the only groups that virtually guarantee this.

The fact that the human infant at birth is a helpless creature and cannot approach self-sufficiency for almost 20 years means that the intergenerational bond is particularly crucial to human survival. Every child needs some sort of caretaker and caregiver, whether it is a biological parent, an adoptive or foster parent, or somebody else who takes the responsibility for providing nurturance during the early years of life. It is no accident that our image of family includes an intergenerational component.

   3. *Families contain both biological and affinal (e.g., legal, common law) relationships between members.*

It is the biological act of birth that creates the fundamental family tie. This act also means that we share at least some inherited characteristics or proclivities with family members that are directly or indirectly related to us by birth. At least until humans perfect the cloning of adults, and perhaps even then, the process of becoming a person will be based to some degree on biology. Families are in the business of producing and sustaining persons and personhood. Even though work groups or friendship groups may sometimes contain biologically related members, such groups tend to have other purposes.

There is also a social side to this process of creating persons. No society leaves the biological act of birth or the rearing of children to chance. Personhood is achieved through a process of socialization. That socialization is subject to secular and religious rules about how the process should be carried out. Pursuant to these rules, family members have rights and obligations, which tend to be codified in both laws and informal agreements.

Aside from adoption, the major legal provision about families concerns marriage. We may not think of a marriage in itself as constituting a family, but we recognize marital relationships as part of families. Some families are conjugal, in that they contain one or more marriages. It might even be argued that if humans didn't have families they wouldn't need marriages, although families may often function well without marriage. In any case, marriage itself involves rights and obligations under the law, and it also creates family ties in law. Some of our family members join and leave the group either because of our own marriages and divorces or because of the marriages and divorces of other family members.

Other kinds of groups are subject to regulation by laws (e.g., contracts) and informal agreements, of course. Such regulations may exclude as well as include people in work and friendship groups, and they govern proper conduct within such groups. What such groups do not have, however, are relationships anything quite like, for example, cousins or aunts and nephews, which arise because our mother's sister is married.

*4. The biological (and affinal) aspect of families links them to a larger kinship organization.*

It follows from what we already have said that families are not just small groups of closely related individuals who live together or interact on a frequent basis. Families extend outward to include anybody sufficiently related to us by blood, marriage, or adoption. This kinship group may have the identifiable boundaries of a clan, or it may be loosely organized and diffuse. Everybody stops counting distant relatives as family members at some point along the periphery. Nevertheless, the ties of kinship create the potential for lineages and collateral (i.e., within generation) family relationships that can become quite extensive. Through kinship, families are tied to history, tradition, and multiple generations of group members. In some societies, these kinship groups are major features of the social, cultural, political, and economic landscape. Work and friendship groups tend to be much more temporally and spatially encapsulated.

To answer the questions in Box 1.3, we likely will find ourselves asking other questions. Do we visualize the people listed in each example as all being part of one family, or do they belong to two or more different families? Are the listed persons the only ones in the family or could there also be others (i.e., is this a whole family or just part of one)? Should we think of these persons as members of an actual family, or are they a family in either a symbolic sense or in the way they function in their relationships? Are we thinking of how common or uncommon a grouping is in a particular society, either in frequency or in what is expected as normal, natural, and acceptable by law or custom? And are both affinal and consanguineal relationships identified as family relationships?

We could discuss additional arguments about the distinctive features of families as groups. For example, we could draw attention to certain qualities of social interaction that are commonly found in families but not elsewhere. One of these is that family members supposedly care about one another as whole persons (cf. Beutler, Burr, Bahr, & Herrin, 1989). Whichever criteria are considered, however, the distinctiveness of family groups tends to be only a matter of degree. Nonfamily groups, such as networks of friends or coworkers, usually have some family properties but fewer of these properties or in less obvious amounts.

It also is worth noting that we can conceptualize the family not only as a concrete group or social organization but also as a social institution. As an institution, family includes all of the beliefs and practices of and about all of the families in a particular society or

---

### Box 1.3    Which of These Is a Family?

A husband and wife and their offspring.

A single woman and her three young children.

A 52-year-old woman and her adoptive mother.

A man, his daughter, and the daughter's son.

An 84-year-old widow and her dog, Fido.

A man and all of his ancestors back to Adam and Eve.

The 1979 World Champion Pittsburgh Pirates (theme song: "We Are Family").

Three adult sisters living together.

Two lesbians in an intimate relationship and their children from a previous marriage of one woman and a previous relationship of the other woman with a male friend.

Two children, their divorced parents, the current spouses of their divorced parents, and the children from previous marriages of their stepparents.

A child, his stepfather, and the stepfather's wife subsequent to his divorce from the child's mother.

Two adult male cousins living together.

A 77-year-old man and his lifelong best friend.

A childless husband and wife who live 1,000 miles apart.

A widow and her former husband's grandfather's sister's granddaughter.

A divorced man, his girlfriend, and her child.

Both sets of parents of a deceased married couple.

A married couple, one son and his wife, and the latter couple's children, all living together.

Six adults and their 12 young children, all living together in a communal fashion.

---

geopolitical context. It also includes the ways in which different families are connected to each other and to other social institutions. For example, in most modern and well-developed societies, families tend to have a private character, each one walled or fenced off from other families and from public view much of the time. There also are expected and experienced linkages between families and schools, families and the workplace, families and governments, families and the mass media, and so on. Because members of families often share economic resources and collaborate in both productive labor and the consumption of resources, it is also useful to consider families as being involved in a society's system of social stratification. Thus, some families have more wealth, power, and status than do other families.

With an idea of the meaning of family, we can begin to envision what counts as a family concept. Some of these concepts describe the composition, or size and configuration, of family membership. Some describe the structures and processes of interaction that take place between family members. Some describe the ways that families relate to their environments. Some will describe the whole family as a group, the family as an institution, or the nature of the ties between two or more members within the family group.

We believe that for a theory about human relationships to be a family theory, one or more ideas (concepts or variables) about families must be included in the theory. The family idea may appear in either or both of two places: (a) as part of the explanation (e.g., parental discipline helps explain juvenile delinquency), (b) as the phenomenon to be explained (e.g., the state of the economy in a country helps explain the divorce rate in that country), or (c) both (e.g., marital communication styles help explain marital satisfaction).

Thus, we can distinguish two general kinds of family theories, those that are "about the family" or explaining how families work (b and c above) and those that consider family ideas to be useful explanations (a and c above). Of course, a wide variety of ideas, some familial and some not, may be needed in combination to adequately explain family life (e.g., marital affection plus the economy influence the odds of divorcing). Likewise, the forces that help explain family life may also help to explain other things (e.g., the state of the economy may influence stock prices as well as the divorce rate). When assessing the family theories of others, or when creating one yourself, it helps to locate where the family ideas are or at least where you think they belong.

## A Brief History of Theory in Family Studies

Each theory in family science has its own historical legacy, as we discuss further in subsequent chapters. Our focus here is on major themes and examples of how family theory has been important to scholarship throughout history. We refer to several useful accounts of this history and recommend them for greater depth of coverage.

Adams and Steinmetz (1993) surveyed contributions of the classics, which encompass ideas up to the 20th century. Early philosophers were often interested in prescribing ways of living according to their own values. Adams and Steinmetz called attention to this infusion of ideology, and they noted that it sometimes was accompanied by efforts to describe families in more dispassionate ways. Only scattered references to family life per se are contained in the classical works, with little resemblance to the kind of scientific explanation we have now come to expect of scholarship.

Much of the early work centered on attempts to find the origins of marriage as an institution and to trace its evolution as societies moved toward a more modern form (Adams & Steinmetz, 1993, pp. 76–78). Some scholars searched for the ultimate purposes of marriage or the family. Some saw progress or at least the adaptation of family life to changing social circumstances. Some lamented the declining importance of the family, especially as industrialization and urbanization gripped the Western world in the 19th century. Adams and Steinmetz (1993, p. 86) conclude that the closest these social philosophers came to a real theory was a model of parental socialization that resulted in positive outcomes for children and the meeting of needs for both generations when parents became elderly. For the most part, however, and whether obvious or subtle, ideology in the classics, Adams and Steinmetz (1993) found, is seldom totally absent, although its presence makes a theory neither right nor wrong (p. 93).

Howard (1981) examined the history of U.S. family sociology from 1865 to 1940. He also noted the early emphasis on evolutionary thinking, as well as the interest of "moral reformers" in doing something about the problems families seemed to be facing because of the industrial revolution. Howard considered the period between 1890 and 1920 a progressive era. Even as moral reformers and charity workers expanded their initiatives, the idea that families could adapt to changing environments became popular. An emphasis on the psychosocial interior of family life took hold, and educational programs to foster the socialization of children seemed promising. If families were sometimes struggling and disorganized, it was because they were caught between two conflicting value systems, one emphasizing traditional images of the family and the other based on the requirements of the modern democratic and capitalistic state.

The years 1920 to 1940 constitute the latest period Howard described in detail. In these years, the key theme in family scholarship shifted from ecology to interaction among family members, with the goal of personal adjustment. In 1924, the American Sociological Society (now the American Sociological Association) established its

Family Section, and at about the same time, Ernest Groves developed the first systematic college course in family life education at Boston University. Howard also noted as a counter-theme during this period a renewed emphasis on the institutional level of analysis, with studies of families in a community context and attention to cultural diversity on a broader scale. In a chapter published with Howard's book, van Leeuwen (1981) noted that European family scholars remain more interested in the institutional, or macroscopic and historical, levels. On both continents, however, the norm developed that family scholars should refrain from moral and political evaluations as they increasingly relied on empirical data collected through fieldwork (van Leeuwen, 1981, p. 133).

Reflecting on much of the same body of work mentioned above, Christensen (1964) concluded that systematic theory building in the family field did not begin until about 1950. Concepts and rough orientations were taking shape in the first half of the century, along with a growing industry of empirical research, but without formalized explanations meeting the requirements of propositional theory. Although not highlighted in any of these historical accounts, an upswing in scholarly interest about families within many academic disciplines appeared before 1950, with contributions by sociologists, anthropologists, psychologists, home economists, and social workers, among others. Yet Christensen's designation of 1950 as a turning point seems to be basically correct. An inspection of the *International Bibliography of Research in Marriage and the Family, 1900–1964* (Aldous & Hill, 1967) shows that of almost 4,000 entries before 1950, only 7 contain theory or a cognate term in their titles. Of the 12,000 entries for the 1950–1964 period, 93 entries contain such terms. By comparison, for the 2-year period from 1991 to 1993, 264 of 7,600 entries in a subsequent inventory (Touliatos, 1994) pertain to family theory. Interestingly, the largest proportion of theoretical works before and during the 1950s dealt with courtship and mate selection. This was the first topic to receive systematic and cumulative theoretical treatment.

Aside from the increasing attention to family theory in the scholarship of the field since 1950, the last half of the century can be subdivided into three stages, each with its own set of themes.

CONCEPTUAL FRAMEWORKS: 1950–1966

The single most prominent theme in family theorizing during the 1950s and early 1960s was an emphasis on identifying conceptual frameworks. This emphasis is evidenced by a series of works devoted to the topic (Christensen, 1964; Hill, 1951; Hill & Hansen, 1960;

Nye & Berardo, 1966/1981). The number and character of the particular frameworks varied, but the basic idea remained the same. As research on family life accumulated, most analysts attempted to give explanations for their findings. The explanations often were narrowly focused, and it was difficult to see how various studies fit together. The attempt to identify frameworks was a search for under- lying principles that might help in the construction of general theories for the field. It was not claimed that such theories already existed, nor was it often assumed that a single integrated theory would be prac- tical. Rather, the idea was that by comparing the currently fragmented works with respect to the concepts and assumptions they used, schol- ars might be able to work toward the building of family theories in a more coordinated way.

Christensen (1964) captured the spirit of this period well in the closing remarks of his introductory essay in the *Handbook of Marriage and the Family*:

> As has been said several times, there is urgent need for better theory. Critics of family research have described it as being amateurish, trivial, scattered, often sterile, and sometimes moralistic. . . . There is still need for correcting what Goode (1959, p. 186) spoke of as a hornet's nest of conceptual and terminological problems. There is still need to isolate and then integrate, insofar as seems feasible, the theoretical frameworks which can guide the discipline. And there is still need to find and then specify the relationships among empirical generalizations in order to constitute true theory. (pp. 29–30)

### FORMAL THEORY CONSTRUCTION: 1967–1979

A change in tone characterized the next several years of work on family theory. Following Hill's (1966) address after receiving the first Burgess Award for a career of scholarly achievement in the family field, attention turned toward methods of deductively and inductively creating theories, using a clearly delineated propositional format. Many examples of this type of work emerged. Nye and his colleagues presented a propositional theory of family stability (Nye, White, & Frideres, 1969), followed by a propositional theory of age at marriage (Bartz & Nye, 1970). Goode and his colleagues published a massive volume listing hundreds of propositions relevant to scores of family topics (Goode, Hopkins, & McClure, 1971).

The most important works of this period, however, were those spearheaded by Burr (Burr, 1973; Burr, Hill, Nye, & Reiss, 1979, Vols. 1 & 2). In his 1973 volume, Burr applied the principles of deductive, propositional theory building provided by philosophers and sociologists to 11 topical areas of research. In the first volume of Burr, Hill, et al. (1979), Burr and his colleagues applied the same procedure to twice as many areas, involving experts in those areas as chapter authors. In Volume 2, Burr, Hill, et al. (1979) focused on five general theories that were not substantively limited. The editors noted that the second volume was not comprehensive in its coverage of general theories, and they acknowledged difficulties in linking the two volumes. Inductively integrating materials from the first volume proved difficult because of the lack of semantic equivalence across domains, the complexity of models in the first volume, and the lack of a way to bridge macro- and microlevel propositions (Burr, Hill, et al., 1979, Vol. 2, pp. xii–xiv).

Organizational developments within the National Council of Family Relations (NCFR) also were important during this period. In his Burgess address, Hill (1966) had called for the creation of a Theory Section to parallel the existing Research Section. Although his initiative was defeated, by the late 1960s NCFR had created the joint Research and Theory Section that continues today. Hill did not relent in his effort to give visibility to theorizing as a major professional activity, however. With the help of Nye and others, he created the Workshop on Theory Construction, which began with meetings at the NCFR annual conference site just before the regular NCFR conference. The workshop served as a training ground for both students and more advanced family scholars, allowing them to nurture and demonstrate their talents in theory building. In 1975, the name of the workshop was expanded to Theory Construction and Research Methodology. This workshop also survives today. In its first 24 years, more than 560 papers were presented, and more than 730 participants appeared on its programs. It is interesting that both the section and the workshop evolved to combine theoretical and research interests. This symbolizes the extent to which family scholars see the two enterprises as fundamentally connected.

PLURALISM: 1980 TO THE PRESENT

It is always difficult to gain perspective on developments in a field when they are still swirling and the next major turning point is unforeseen. Lacking the distance afforded by time to reflect backward, we tend to see the present as chaotic or transitional. Of course, this perception also may mean that our tendency to periodize the past is an oversimplification, and all moments of intellectual history (and even family history) are fuzzier and more complex than they appear in retrospect. Nevertheless, the publication of the two edited volumes by Burr and colleagues (Burr, Hill, et al., 1979) seems to represent the high-water mark, if not the culmination, of the theory construction movement.

The pluralism of the most recent decades has several possible interpretations. It can be seen as a continuation of the quantitative growth of contributions by scholarly participants in family theory and research. It can also be taken to be a furthering of fragmented and specialized interests. Or it can be viewed as a new respect and tolerance for diverse philosophies, theories and theory-building methods, and research strategies.

Doherty et al. (1993) provide a cogent summary of nine main trends, although they gave these developments somewhat more recent origins than we would. We excerpt their list from a more detailed discussion:

1. The impact of feminist and ethnic minority theories and perspectives

2. The realization that family forms have changed dramatically

3. The trend toward greater professional (multidisciplinary) inclusiveness

4. The trend toward more theoretical and methodological diversity

5. The trend toward more concern with language and meaning

6. The movement toward more constructivist and contextual approaches

7. An increased concern with ethics, values, and religion

8. A breakdown of the dichotomy between the private and public spheres of family life and between family social science and family interventions

9. Greater recognition by family scholars of the contextual limits of family theory and research knowledge (pp. 15–17)

To be sure, Doherty et al. (1993) see challenges posed by, and potential problems with, these emergent developments, but their basic posture is laudatory and optimistic. Nonetheless, any idealistic hope on the part of some leaders in the field that we would eventually converge around one grand theoretical scheme to explain everything about families has now been completely dashed and discarded. What we see is the continuing proliferation of theories, the eclectic combination of elements from different theories, and variations and transformations within existing theories. It is as common now, if not more common than ever before, for theorizing to be narrowly focused on particular topics and issues. Countless mini theories, middle-range theories, and models of mostly causal processes, all closely linked to Hempel's (1952) plane of observation, characterize the literature, particularly in professional journals and in the proceedings of conferences and workshops.

The other main trend in recent years has been a vigorous questioning of the philosophical foundations in the field (cf. Osmond, 1987; Thomas & Wilcox, 1987). The result has been a turn toward interpretive and critical philosophies (see Box 1.2) and away from at least some elements of the positivistic philosophy. It is important to remember, however, that the entire scholarly community does not move in unison in any one direction. Some theorists attempt to blend and integrate, whereas others find one philosophy or even one theory compelling and the others inadequate. The current scene is a curious and shifting mixture of consensus and conflict over theories and theory-building methods.

In light of the current situation, a precaution is in order as we prepare to explore in some detail seven of the currently important theoretical frameworks in the family sciences. Our own map of the alternatives is not the only possible one, nor is it necessarily complete and otherwise adequate. In 1950, only the symbolic interactional perspective, among the theories we cover, would likely have been widely recognized. Until the mid-1960s, three other perspectives that we do not cover as distinctive were commonly identified (structure-functional, institutional, and situational). By this time, the developmental perspective had gained recognition, but several others were either widely rejected or absorbed into other points of view. When Nye and Berardo (1966/1981) attempted to comprehensively cover conceptual frameworks at the end of this period, they even added six more, each roughly representing an academic discipline (i.e., anthropology, psychoanalysis, social psychology, economics, legal studies, and Western Christian studies). When Broderick (1971) reviewed the theoretical developments of the 1960s, he saw several new possibilities. Of these, the exchange and systems perspectives have continued to thrive, and they are represented in our following chapters. By the end of the 1970s, a similar review by Holman and Burr (1980) added conflict, behavioral, ecological, and phenomenological perspectives as being of at least secondary importance. Of these, we give major attention only to the conflict and ecological perspectives. When Nye and Berardo (1966/1981) reissued their 1966 book, they added exchange, systems, and conflict theories in their introduction, as well as "social individualism" and "transactional analysis," neither of which seem to have progressed thereafter. Finally, the most recent comprehensive treatment includes more than a dozen chapters on distinct theoretical perspectives (Boss et al., 1993), with the notable addition of feminist theory.

In a study (Klein, 1994) of more than 100 family scholars, the participants were asked to rate 11 alternative theories as to how favorably disposed they were toward them. Of those we emphasize in this book, their ranking, in descending order was as follows: symbolic interactional, developmental and systems (tied for second place), exchange, conflict, and ecological. In general, however, the participants indicated dislike for very few, and most were favorably disposed toward several. Furthermore, the scholars nominated dozens of others that they liked, although the nominations seldom coincided. We conclude from this pattern of findings that no single scheme focused on only a small number of general theoretical perspectives would be universally accepted.

A fruitful typology of theories is only partially in the eye of the beholder. Some threads seem to be common to the various alternative classifications, and some reflect historical changes in the field regarding the popularity and promise of the alternatives. Nevertheless, each mapping of the territory is at least somewhat dependent on the purposes and viewpoint of the author. In our case, we aim for relative simplicity to meet the needs of readers. We capitalize on the existing complexity mainly by covering some of the varying and more recent emphases within the broader traditions. We use an organizational concept throughout this book: that of "theoretical framework." What we mean by theoretical framework is that there exists in each scientific field a core of theoretical assumptions and propositions. We do not simply refer to these as theories, because although they are theories, they also are sufficiently general to have given rise to a number of theoretical variants. In this one sense, these theoretical frameworks are like families, with the core theory providing sufficient richness for the development of offspring. After exploring these various frameworks, we return in chapter 9 to the problem of fitting the theories into a coherent overall picture.

## Suggested Readings

Adams, B., & Steinmetz, S. (1993). Family theory and methods in the classics. In P. Boss, W. Doherty, R. LaRossa, W. Schumm, & S. Steinmetz (Eds.), *Sourcebook of family theories and methods: A contextual approach* (pp. 71–94). New York: Plenum.

*This is an excellent historical overview of the development and evolution of family theory.*

What Is a Theory? 31

Beutler, I., Burr, W., Bahr, K., & Herrin, D. (1989). The family realm: Understanding its uniqueness. *Journal of Marriage and the Family, 51,* 805–816.
*This is a bold attempt to identify the distinguishing characteristics of families. The commentaries by scholars that follow on pp. 816–829 indicate the controversy surrounding the proposals of Beutler and his colleagues.*

Burr, W. (1973). *Theory construction and the sociology of the family.* New York: John Wiley.
*This book, despite its age, remains an excellent introduction to theory construction and philosophy of science. The first chapter is outstanding.*

Thomas, D. L., & Wilcox, J. E. (1987). The rise of family theory: A historical and critical analysis. In M. B. Sussman & S. K. Steinmetz (Eds.), *Handbook of marriage and the family* (pp. 81–102). New York: Plenum.
*This provides a solid historical picture from the perspective that the field is moving to a less positivistic approach.*

# 2

# The Social Exchange and Choice Framework

Kevin and Sarah have been dating seriously for about 6 months. Both agree that they have a close relationship with a lot of warmth and support. After going to a romantic movie, Kevin and Sarah go back to Kevin's apartment and are in the middle of some pretty serious petting when Sarah says, "Kevin, if we are going to do it, I want you to use a condom. I have one in my purse." Kevin says, "Gosh, honey, are you serious? Don't you trust me? I mean, it's not as though I have AIDS or something." Sarah seems to be caught off guard and pauses for a moment before responding. "Kevin, I know how you feel about me, and I trust you, but a condom makes good sense because it is easy for anyone to pick up a sexually transmitted disease. Some of these diseases are hard to detect and even harder to cure, especially for women. I don't want to end up not being able to have children when I am ready to as a result of carelessness." Kevin quickly blurts, "But these things are so plastic. You know, Sarah, a guy doesn't feel anything if he wears one of those!" Sarah's voice carries a tinge of anger or bitterness. "Kevin, I wanted to make love with you, but now I feel you are just after your own pleasure and don't really care about the possible consequences for me. I'm the one who could get pregnant, I'm the one who has to get an abortion or carry the baby for 9 months, and in the end I am now the one who has to ask for a commonsense preventive measure that would protect both of us." Kevin's tone becomes disappointed but still angry. "Come on, and I'll take you home."

This sketch of Kevin and Sarah's interaction provides us with an illustration of two people pursuing their self-interests. Kevin's self-interest is to maximize his sexual pleasure. Sarah's self-interest is to avoid the costs associated with unprotected sex. From this standpoint, often called *utilitarianism,* both Kevin and Sarah are acting rationally, but they are operating on different values. The essence of utilitarianism is that individuals rationally weigh the rewards and costs associated with behavioral choices. They choose those activities that maximize their rewards.

Utilitarianism is a philosophical perspective that has heavily influenced exchange theories in the social sciences. The central focus of exchange theory is on motivation. Human beings are viewed as motivated out of self-interest. What does it mean to say that utilitarianism focuses on motivation? Motivation is what induces a person to act. The focus, therefore, is on the person and what propels that person to choose a particular action. Theories inspired by utilitarian thinking are based on the assumption of individual self-interest. This in turn means that we as social scientists can understand a person's actions by understanding the individual's interests or values. These interests allow the individual to account for both costs and rewards and make choices that maximize the actor's utility or profit. The basic notion, then, is that rational actors choose a course of action that produces the greatest benefit.

Exchange theorists usually explain the existence and endurance of social groups such as the family by their appeal to the self-interest of individual members. Individuals come together in groups so as to maximize their rewards. Of course, membership in social groups may also necessitate compromise and even costs to the individual member. If the costs of group membership exceed the rewards, then membership in the group is no longer a rational choice. Thus, the family group is usually conceptualized as a source of rewards for the individual members.

## Intellectual Traditions

Utilitarian thinking refers to several varieties of theory. Some examples of utilitarian thinking are the ethical utilitarianism of the Epicureans and later Jeremy Bentham and John Stuart Mill, psychological hedonism, and the ideal utilitarianism of G. E. Moore. A complete picture of all the variants of utilitarian thinking would require volumes rather than pages. We direct our attention to the forms of utilitarian thinking found in the social sciences, particularly in the area of family studies.

Among the varieties of philosophical utilitarian thinking are voluntaristic, or interest, theories of value. In these variants, great emphasis is placed on the unfettered choice of individuals. One of the originators of this perspective, Adam Smith, held an economic view of humankind based on the belief that people act rationally to maximize benefits, or utility. When choice was externally controlled or determined, however, actors could not make rational choices. This view was the basis for laissez-faire economics and, in addition, much of the utilitarian theory in the social sciences today.

In current social science, utilitarian thinking is quite obvious in microeconomic theory of the family (Becker, 1981), social psychology (Emerson, 1976; Homans, 1961; Nye, 1979), organizational sociology (Blau, 1964), and rational choice theory (Coleman, 1990; Hechter, 1987). There are major differences of emphasis among these authors, especially in how they unite individual motivation to macroscopic processes of reciprocity and social change. The focus of all these theories is on the rational utilitarianism of the individual, however.

Many of these theories have been termed *exchange theories*. This has led to some confusion with a group of theories that are structural and not at all focused on individual motivation. For example, the French anthropologists Claude Levi-Strauss (1969) and Marcel Mauss (1954) are often called exchange theorists, but their focus is on the institutional norm of reciprocity and the social functions of exchanges in terms of group solidarity and the formation of group alliances. Other theorists, such as John Scanzoni (1970) and Randall Collins (1975), have a conflict–resource orientation; they only marginally fit into our characterization of utilitarianism because of their additional emphasis on macroscopic structures. In the study of the family, utilitarian thinking is generally referred to as exchange theory, and we follow this convention. However, it is certainly possible to argue that patterns of human motivation are responsible for the emergence of social structures to regulate those motivations.

In the contemporary study of the family, Ivan Nye (1978, 1979, 1980) has been a foremost proponent of exchange theory. Nye's (1979) formal propositional statement of exchange theory relied heavily on the social-psychological approach of his predecessors from psychology, Thibaut and Kelley (1959). Although Nye's (1979) version of utilitarianism does include the norm of reciprocity and group-level exchanges, these macrosocial concepts are not well integrated with the social-psychological utilitarianism that is his principal focus. Nye (1979) titles his chapter "Choice, Exchange, and the Family," thus emphasizing the voluntarist assumption guiding his version of utilitarianism. To date, Nye's statement of utilitarianism applied to the family is the most thorough and ambitious. Although there have been more recent summaries of exchange theory (Sabatelli & Shehan, 1993), our characterization of the core of the theory takes into account the thoroughness and completeness of Nye's vision.

## Focus and Scope Assumptions

*The individual is real.* The assumption that the individual is real is technically referred to as *methodological individualism.* This assumption implies that group phenomena, social structure, and the normative culture are constructed by the actions of individuals. Thus, if we understand the actions of individuals, we will also understand these macrosocial phenomena. In regard to the family, this is an important and perhaps tenuous assumption. In exchange theory, the family is viewed as a collection of individuals. But we are all aware that mate selection, parenting, and many other family matters are regulated by both formal norms (laws) and informal ones. Regarding mate selection, for example, laws in some jurisdictions forbid certain degrees of consanguinity, such as marriage with one's dead sister's husband (e.g., Province of Manitoba). Clearly, these laws are unjustified by contemporary scientific understanding in genetics. How can these laws be understood solely as the result of the self-interest of individual actors and their self-interested behavior? This is the task set by the assumption of methodological individualism. James S. Coleman (1990), in the first chapter of his book *Foundations of Social Theory*, tackles this question from a utilitarian, or exchange, perspective. We recommend his discussion as supplying one of the best direct confrontations with the challenges of methodological individualism for the study of social groups and institutions.

*Prediction and understanding come about by understanding the individual actor's motivation.* Many theorists who assume methodological individualism do not attempt to understand individuals' actions through motivation. Those who hold utilitarian and microexchange perspectives usually do, however. Although these theorists acknowledge that individuals are always constrained in their choices, within these constraints any choice can be understood as based on the actor's motivation rather than exogenous forces or constraints. In this sense, exchange theory is a voluntaristic theory in the same way in which Adam Smith's theory was voluntaristic. This insight led Nye (1979) to state that the basic theory is about choice (p. 4). Because families are a relatively long-lasting social group, the voluntaristic assumption leads exchange theorists to assume that families are rewarding to individual members. The fact that children do not voluntarily choose their parents may provide some difficulties for the theory, however.

*Actors are motivated by self-interest.* Even with the assumption that the actor's motivation explains behavior, a theorist could still assume that motivation is multidimensional or not conscious (as in the

concept of subconscious) or founded on inherent drives such as those
that Freud proposed. But microutilitarian exchange theories usually
include the assumption that individuals are unilaterally motivated by
self-interest; individuals seek things and relationships they regard as
beneficial for themselves. The notion of self-interest raises some interesting questions regarding what we commonly know as altruism.
Even some variants of ethical utilitarianism have been based on the
assumption that we should act to accrue the greatest good for the
greatest number. But for family exchange theorists such as Nye
(1979), collective interests and altruism are derived and explained by
the self-interests of individuals. So, although self-interest is not necessarily the hallmark of all forms of utilitarian thinking, it is a basic
assumption in regard to exchange and choice theory.

*Actors are rational.* It is easy to agree with the assumption that actors
are rational. All of us like to think that we are rational human beings.
But how often do we stop and think about what it means to be
rational? This is a more complex assumption than we initially might
have thought.

To be rational is to have the ability to calculate the ratio of costs
to rewards. This is an analytic ability. One crucial dimension of rationality is that it is the same for all actors. Any two rational actors in
identical situations with identical values and identical information
would necessarily reach the same result in their calculations and thus
pursue the same behavior. This assumption of rational actors is as
important for microeconomics as it is for choice and exchange theory
because it allows the interchangeability of actors and the concept of
general rational actors captured in notions like "the consumer."

The idea of rational actors evolved from the rationalist philosophies of the Age of Enlightenment. Many students will recall that the
Enlightenment was characterized by a newfound confidence in the
ability of humans to reason. What was meant by reason was deduction or analytic thought. Such analytic thinking was believed to be
independent of experience or sense data. Many philosophers, such as
the French philosopher René Descartes, believed human rationality
provided unequivocal knowledge that was true (*quod erat demon-
stratum*). Indeed, the view of humans as rational actors originating in
the work of Enlightenment philosophers such as John Locke provides
much of the rationale for our current legal system. For example, juvenile offenders are treated differently from adults because they are
believed to have not yet fully developed the ability to calculate
rewards and costs. The rational assumption also provided the basis
for much of the economic theory of Adam Smith.

It is easy to confuse rationalism with other words that share the same root but have very different meanings. For instance, *rational* is not interchangeable with *rationalization*. A rationalization is an attempt to provide an apparently rational justification for one's behavior after the behavior occurred; it is not proof of a choice but rather a fabrication after the fact. Later, we further discuss the ex post facto nature of rationalization, which critics of exchange theory raise as an objection.

## Concepts

### REWARD AND COST

A reward is anything that is perceived as beneficial to an actor's interests. A simple way to conceptualize cost is as the inverse of reward. It is possible to conceptualize "costs" as the negative dimension of rewards. It is also important, however, to include as costs or negative rewards the opportunities for rewards that might be missed or foregone that are associated with any specific choice. It would be naive to assume that the concepts of costs and rewards are unique to utilitarian theories. Certainly, Watsonian and later Skinnerian psychology emphasizes rewards and punishments. Although the basic notions are similar, the theories differ because the assumption of rationality is largely absent from these psychological theories. Indeed, behaviorists deny that conceptual processes need to be included in explanations of human behavior and posit that only behavioral patterns of stimulus and response need be examined. This view is at odds with the emphasis in exchange theory on rationality.

Microeconomics is focused on economic rewards and costs. Exchange and choice theorists view rewards and costs as being formulated from a much broader array of values than is used in economic theory. For example, Nye (1979), Blau (1964), and Foa and Foa (1980) each list six sources of rewards and costs, although each list includes some different sources. We consider these general sources of costs and rewards in greater depth below.

When we examine the basic concept of rewards more deeply, we find definitions referring to things or relationships that bring pleasures, satisfactions, and gratifications. Such definitions come uncomfortably close to a naive hedonistic calculus weighing pleasure and pain. Such a hedonistic view falls apart rapidly when the complexities of decisions are examined. For example, one may climb a mountain because it is gratifying, but it also involves risk and hardship. Indeed, it is doubtful that mountain climbers would find the task as gratifying if it did not contain the risk and hardship. Many of our most gratifying experiences are gratifying in part because not everyone is willing to undertake the hardship or risk.

PROFIT OR MAXIMIZING UTILITY

The notions of reward and cost alone do not explain behavior. If one attempts to explain that an actor behaves in a certain way because it is rewarding, the resulting explanation is overly simplistic and fails to account for the many elements that were rationally calculated by the actor. Indeed, reward and cost alone supply us with little other than a form of behaviorism.

It is the concept of profit, or utility, that allows the theory to avoid such criticisms. Profit is defined as the ratio of rewards to costs for any decision. Actors rationally calculate this ratio for all possible choices in a situation and then choose the action that they calculate will bring the greatest rewards or the least costs. Thus, the mountain climber weighs the rewards of climbing a mountain, such as the social approval of other climbers and the aesthetic enjoyment of the climb, against costs such as the risk of being killed or injured in a rockfall or avalanche. From this example, you can see that it is the notion of rational calculation of profit that makes exchange theory more than naive hedonism.

COMPARISON LEVEL (CL) AND
COMPARISON LEVEL FOR ALTERNATIVES (CL+)

In complex situations, the evaluation of profit available to an actor may be divided into two comparison levels. The first is the comparison (CL) of what others in your position have and how well you are doing relative to them. The second comparison (CL+) is how well you are doing relative to others outside of your position but in positions that supply an alternative or choice. For example, if instructors at your university were given a 3% raise in salaries, they might ask how well they are doing relative to instructors at other universities (CL). The second comparison they might make is how well they are doing relative to others in private enterprise and government with equivalent education and training (CL+).

The role of comparisons in the evaluation of choices has mainly been emphasized by Thibaut and Kelley (1959) and Nye (1979). This perceptual orientation is especially useful for family researchers wanting to explain phenomena such as timing of children or the decision to divorce. The decision to divorce provides a good illustration of the two comparison levels. For example, a husband may compare (CL) his profit ratio for his marriage with what he perceives other husbands he knows are receiving in their marriages. The second level of comparison (CL+) would be to compare his profit as a husband with the profit he perceives in other possible, unmarried positions, such as divorced and remarried husbands. According to the theory, if he were to calculate greater profit for an alternative position, he is more likely to choose a divorce.

For family researchers, evaluation levels represent one of the more attractive components of the theory because they allow us to understand changes of marital and family status. Comparison levels can be used to understand a choice such as divorce, and they can also be used to understand the degree of satisfaction or gratification an actor associates with an outcome. Sabatelli and Shehan (1993) propose that the notion of comparison level could help us understand why young couples with children experience lower marital satisfaction than couples in other stages of family life (e.g., Rollins & Feldman, 1970). Sabatelli and Shehan (1993) point out that couples with young children are in a period of family life that follows a stage (early marriage) marked by high satisfaction, thus constituting a high comparison level. Demands and expectations associated with child rearing take time and energy away from fulfilling the high marital expectations in the way they were satisfied before children. Hence, the comparison of present rewards with what one has previously received is linked to greater dissatisfaction with marriage.

RATIONALITY

We have previously discussed rationality as a basic assumption necessary for the calculation of the ratio of rewards to costs. If you think about things and relationships that you find rewarding in your life, however, you will probably notice that the value of these rewards changes with time and situation. In addition, you would surely note that not all rewards are equally weighted. For example, you might be thirsty and want a drink, but not all liquids that would quench your thirst are equally valuable (as any cola commercial attests). Furthermore, the value of a reward may decrease as you gain more of it (marginal utility); a dollar to a rich person has less value than a dollar to a poor person. To deal with the changing value of rewards and costs, it is necessary to add the idea of the importance, salience, or weight of alternatives. To understand any actor's choice as rational, we need to know what the person considers rewarding and costly, and, in addition, we have to know the relative weights (or salience) for each of the rewards and each of the costs.

A simple example might clarify this idea. Imagine that your family is trying to decide on a destination for a summer vacation. You have narrowed the choices down to backpacking in the backcountry near Jackson Hole, Wyoming, or visiting the campgrounds along the Oregon coast. To reach this stage, each family member has to compare the possible alternatives, such as taking individual vacations rather than a joint vacation. This is similar to the second comparison level, or what Thibaut and Kelley (1959) called the comparison level for alternatives. Is it a reward or cost to go on a family vacation? Do you enjoy being together, or is it more valuable to spend some time away from family members? After there is agreement that a family vacation is more valuable, the next step is to decide on the destination. Do you value hiking in the mountains or walking miles of uncluttered beaches? Do you want the adventure of backpacking or the more placid contentment of watching the Pacific Ocean? Are there activities for all family members in both spots? Each value, such as adventure and diversity of opportunities for other family members, is weighted by the importance or salience of this for you. Finally, you make a choice based on the maximization of profit for you. Of course, your family as a whole might choose the other alternative.

This example raises a critical question. How could a researcher ever examine the complex decisions of family members in one family, let alone a large sample of families? Certainly, the theory appears too cumbersome for a detailed accounting of rewards, costs, and relative weights for each individual, for every decision in each and every family. Exchange theory can be used in such investigations by making two assumptions. One assumption we have already discussed: Because actors are rational, they are interchangeable. This assumption means that given the same rewards, costs, and weights, any actor would make the same choice as any other. The second assumption is one we have not discussed in any detail. It is the assumption that for large numbers of actors, we can assess the rewards, costs, and weights as those that would be held by a modal, or average, actor. In other words, we assume that for most people in a social group or social system, rewards, costs, and weights are relatively uniform. There may be variation in how people look at rewards and costs, but there is great overall uniformity and little systematic variation.

EXCHANGES AND EQUITY

The rational weighing of costs and rewards in an unconstrained environment seldom happens in reality. Usually, we live in a social system characterized by social interdependencies; some of the rewards we may desire are dependent on the cooperation of others, or we may need to trade with others something we have of lower value in exchange for something of higher value. This is an economic view of society. In most instances, maximizing profit entails exchanges with others. Social relationships that last over some period of time do so in part because they offer profits. A rational person is willing to incur some losses to maintain such profitable relationships. Marriage may be one such relationship, in which inequities at one point in time are tolerated because of the expectation of future rewards from the relationship. Certainly in families, vacations are planned not so as to optimize the profit for any individual but rather to distribute fairly and equitably rewards to all family members.

In a few exchange perspectives (Scanzoni, 1972; Sexton & Perlman, 1989; Walster & Walster, 1978), the principle of equity is viewed as being central to the maintenance of social relationships and groups. After all, siblings play together because of a set of negotiated and agreed-on exchanges perceived by them to be a fair exchange. Families decide on a vacation spot based not on any one individual's profit but on an equitable distribution of rewards for all members. Husbands and wives can be viewed as in a fair exchange situation, and when the situation becomes unfair or imbalanced, we expect divorce or separation. As we shall see later, marriages are seldom exactly equitable at any point in time, and some people may be so committed to marriage that inequity is not an issue. Indeed, if equity generally operated in marriage, we would not have so much literature on division of household labor in the family (e.g., Pina & Bengtson, 1993).

It is useful to keep in mind two precautions. First, equity can be defined as "fairness" or "justice," and relations do not need to be exactly equal to be fair or just but can be perceived to be so. Social norms in a given place and time may require inequality, such as women being expected to subordinate their self-interests for the good of men and children. So, it is possible that an unequal division of household labor is viewed as fair or equitable. Second, rationality may not be uniform across social actors. A person cannot know how rewarding or costly something is to others in a group, or what comparison levels other group members have, without adequate information and experience.

GENERALIZABLE SOURCES OF REWARDS

The concept of a set of general rewards and costs for actors in a specific social system is absolutely necessary if exchange theory is to be applied to groups and large numbers of people and families. Of course, some of the most interesting research questions are not about one family or person but about why people in general behave in a certain way. For instance, we may want to know why married couples delay childbearing or why people wait until their late 20s to get married. Examining why one person, say, Martha Jones, delayed marriage would not give us the answer we seek. Martha was hospitalized with a major disease from her 20th birthday until she was 30 years old. We doubt that this explains why most people delay marriage. The answer to our question would usually come from representative survey research using large numbers of respondents. If we attempt to explain our respondents' choices by maximization of profit, then the question arises as to how we can compute the ratio for all of these actors in our sample.

The notion of general sources of costs and rewards enables us to compute a general accounting of saliencies, costs, and rewards and to establish a general choice that would be most profitable for actors in a social system. Indeed, the relative stability of general costs and rewards in a social system allows actors to make rational decisions. Various theorists have proposed different general sources of rewards and costs. Homans (1961) originally emphasized social approval as the most general source of rewards and costs. Other theorists have felt a need for the inclusion of other sources. Blau (1964) proposed the social rewards and costs of personal attraction, social acceptance, social approval, instrumental services, respect, and power. Foa and Foa (1980) proposed love, status, services, goods, information, and money. Nye (1979) proposed social approval, autonomy, predictability/ ambiguity, security, agreement, and equality of resources. Nye makes the claim that many of these sources are culture free and may be used anywhere in the world, but he fails to tell us which ones have such universal generalizability. None of the exchange theorists have spent their energies addressing general salience weights for these general costs and rewards, but in specific applications they usually make an argument as to why one set of rewards or costs is more salient than another. Because salience may change dramatically with the situation, the question is perhaps best left open at the general theoretical level.

Because most social exchange theorists identify social approval as a reward or cost, we can use that source for a general example. Let's return to the question "Why do people delay marriage?" and see what kind of answer we can formulate according to exchange theory, using the broad category of social approval for rewards and costs. We must first postulate the profit linked to marriage. In North America, most people marry at least once. According to exchange theory, a rational actor would marry to maximize profit. We must all agree that marriage is socially approved more than alternative forms of relationships such as cohabitation, singlehood, and so on. Our parents, religious institutions, and political institutions view marriage as the appropriate relationship between coresident heterosexual adults.

It is not difficult to make the argument that social approval is one of the major reasons we marry. Why are young people delaying marriage? Very simply, marriage roles and responsibilities (especially pregnancy and child care) interfere with the social approval attached to other early life course expectations such as finishing education and getting started in a career. Today, as opposed to only a few decades ago, these educational and work expectations apply to both men and women as sources of social approval. Thus, young men and women delay marriage so that they may first achieve these other socially approved statuses. After all, most of us had parents, teachers, and clergy who advised us to finish our education and get a job before getting married. Although there are many gaps in our explanation, it nonetheless serves to illustrate the way in which general sources of reward might be used to explain social patterns such as delay of marriage.

## Propositions

Exchange theorists explain individual and family phenomena by identifying general propositions that seem to cover the particular phenomenon of interest. This is, of course, the procedure for all deductive theories. In the case of exchange theory, the number of general propositions required for any explanation are few. According to theory, social phenomena can be explained with little conceptual and propositional baggage. When a theory leads to successful explanations with very little baggage, we call it *parsimonious*. This simplicity is seen as an asset in comparing competing theories. Let's examine the propositions called for in exchange theory.

*Actors in a situation will choose whichever behavior maximizes profit.*

The simplest and most powerful proposition in exchange theory is simply that an actor will choose the course of action that offers the greatest rewards relative to costs. One implication of this proposition is that actors may not necessarily choose options that provide the greatest rewards if the costs are high relative to costs associated with other choices. A less rewarding option may be selected because the costs are lower. This fact should caution us that unlike the case in behaviorism, in exchange theory profit rather than reward determines behavioral choices.

> *Actors in a situation in which there are no rewards seek to minimize costs (principle of least costs).*

Some of you might ask, What if there are only potential costs in a situation and no rewards? The theory actually incorporates this concern but in an implicit rather than explicit way. Implicit in exchange theory is the concept of reward and cost being interchangeable because of the notion of calculation of profit. If profit is the ratio of rewards divided by costs, then clearly a fraction results when costs exceed rewards. Because division is the same operation as subtraction (the dividend is how many times you can subtract the denominator from the numerator), we can see that costs are mathematically equivalent to negative rewards. Indeed, a cost is a negative reward. Implicitly, then, the proposition regarding maximization of profit becomes the minimization of costs. This rule, or proposition, about minimization of costs can then be applied to the special case in which there are zero rewards but different costs associated with choices.

One of the more vexing problems for exchange theory has been the computation of long-term costs and rewards versus short-term costs and rewards. We give up many immediate rewards to achieve long-term rewards. For example, those who believe that a university education has the purpose of getting a good job might sacrifice 4 years of income while they are in a university, and many other immediate rewards, for what they perceive as higher rewards after they graduate. In a marriage, one spouse might pass up the satisfaction of making an angry response to an affront from the other spouse for the marriage to last over the longer term.

Compared with school groups and work groups, families are relatively lengthy in duration. The analysis of long-term rewards and costs is essential to understanding the behavior of its members. We can extrapolate two general propositions in this regard from Nye (1979, p. 6):

> *When immediate profits are equal, then actors choose according to which alternative provides the most profit in the long term.*

and

> *When long-term profits are equal, then one chooses the alternative that provides the most profit in the short term.*

These two propositions allow us to gain some perspective on the calculation of profit by interjecting time as a complicating variable. We still have to add the relative salience to the actor of immediate rather than deferred gratification. And of course, these propositions tend to provide guidelines for analysis rather than predictions, as it is doubtful that we would often encounter situations in which profits are equal.

The propositions in this section suggest that exchange theory is deterministic. If we knew all of the values and salience weights composing an actor's calculations, we could accurately predict the actor's choice and behavior in any given situation. The only obstacle to such accurate predictions would be errors in our measurements, which might lead us to speak in probabilities rather than necessities. Nonetheless, this is a causal perspective in which the actor's perceptions, values, and calculation of profit compose the causal variables and the actor's choice and behavior are the effect variables. As a result of this strongly deterministic view, exchange theorists might, for example, argue that those actors who choose to get married calculate that marriage is more rewarding than remaining single.

If people are basically selfish (motivated by self-interest), how is social order possible? In particular, how can family members cooperate, live in harmony, and invest themselves in each others' welfare? Exchange theorists tend to argue that individuals learn to increase the profits of others in order to increase their own profits. Thus, relationships become bargaining processes, each party exchanging rewards valued by other parties. Bargaining can eventually lead to "contracts," or promises by each to mutually reward the other at acceptable costs to both. Over time, trust and commitment develop out of fair exchanges. We trust that the rewards we give to others will be reciprocated in due course, and we commit to enduring investment costs for the moment with the assurance that relationship partners will repay our investment. When a group such as a family has a stabilized pattern of exchanges, such that commitment, trust, and profit are operating to the mutual benefit of all, then a spokesperson for the group can engage in exchanges with spokespersons of other groups. So macroexchanges can be viewed as the bargaining process between or among groups.

## Variations

We have been following Nye's (1979) version of exchange theory, but it is important to note the diversity within exchange theories. We classify the many variants on the basis of whether they are microsocial or macrosocial. You may recall that a microsocial theory includes the assumption that the individual is the active unit of analysis, whereas in macrosocial theories the active unit of analysis is the social group or institution. Although all theorists would like to think that they have successfully bridged the chasm between micro- and macroperspectives, there are in reality few theories for which one can confidently make such a claim. Individual exchange theories usually involve simply adding up all the individual motivations and calling that group motivation or developing a "great man" theory whereby one actor is responsible for social change and therefore only one motive need be analyzed (Homans, 1967). Macroexchange theories examine the exchanges between groups and the resulting social solidarity and alliance formation. Individuals are largely lost in the larger social group and in most ways unidentifiable and unrecoverable as part of an explanation.

MICROEXCHANGE THEORIES

In our characterization of exchange theory, we have followed the microsocial perspective associated with Nye (1979), Levinger (1982), Lewis and Spanier (1979), Sabatelli (1988), Thibaut and Kelley (1959), and Sabtelli and Shehan (1993). There are other variants of this microsocial perspective, but these have not been developed as family theories. For example, Coleman (1990) and Hechter (1987) have both authored variations on a type of utilitarianism referred to as *rational choice theory*. Both of these authors take the individual as the basic unit of analysis and attempt to construct macrosocial applications through a notion that some rewards can only be achieved by groups and social organization. There have been attempts at applying parts of the Coleman approach to the study of the family using the concept of "social capital" (e.g., Teachman, Paasch, & Carver, 1997). This is a concept added to the concepts of human and economic capital that evolved from an earlier work by the Nobel-prize-winning economist Gary Becker (1981), whose work *A Treatise on the Family* presented a rational actor economic theory of the family. Becker (1981) and his followers have met with considerable criticism that their approach is both too focused on economic motivation and too individualistic. Despite these criticisms, economic theories of the family and family behaviors such as mate selection and divorce tend to be widespread in the economic literature. In addition, following the pioneering work of Kahneman and Tversky (1979) on the seeming irrationality of human choices, there has been and continues to be critical questioning of the ideas of "choice" and "rationality" within microeconomics and psychology (Khaneman & Tversky, 1984; Laibson & Zeckhauser, 1998). We have more to say about these criticisms of exchange theories in the next section.

Another example of a microexchange variant is the theoretical work of Emerson (1976), dealing with the *relative balance*, or ratio, of rewards in social relationships. His unit of analysis is the relationship rather than the individual. His microsocial approach might be suitable to the study of the family, but there has as yet not been any research applications of his work directed specifically at studying families.

One of the more important variants of exchange theory used to study family relationships is *equity theory*. Although equity theory is directly derived from exchange theory propositions, it contains the additional proposition that fair exchanges are more profitable to relationships than are unfair exchanges. If A and B are in an unfair relationship, then the social norm of reciprocity is not maintained, and the relationship is likely to be discontinued by one of its members. Thus, whenever a relationship provides profitable outcomes, it is essential for the maintenance of the relationship that exchanges be equitable. One can immediately see how equity might be applied to exchanges between marital partners and in family relations. Indeed, family scholars have used equity theory to study such longer-term family relationships (e.g., Scanzoni, 1972; Sexton & Perlman, 1989; Walster & Walster, 1978). It is interesting to note that several investigators of equity in marriage (e.g., Pina & Bengtson, 1993; Sexton & Perlman, 1989) have concluded that, at best, equity appears to have restricted explanatory value for marital relations.

MACROEXCHANGE THEORIES

As we said in our introductory remarks to this chapter, we are mainly concerned with presenting the microsocial exchange perspective, because that is the perspective generally applied to the study of the family. We do not want to leave the impression, however, that macrosocial exchange theorists have totally ignored the study of the family. You may have noted that our previous discussions of microexchange theories focus mainly on the individual's choices and decision making. Certainly such decision making can be applied to decisions such as the selection of a mate or the choice between divorce and staying married. Macroexchange theories tend to be focused more on the group or organization, however.

The transition from a microexchange to a macroexchange perspective is achieved by the addition of several concepts to those we have already reviewed. First, most macroexchange theorists identify two types of exchanges: *restricted* and *generalized* exchanges. Restricted exchanges take place at one point in time and involve little trust. For example, when you buy something in a store, you hand money to the salesperson, who then gives you the item you have selected. On the other hand, generalized exchanges take place over a longer period of time and therefore require more trust. An example of a generalized exchange is lending money to a friend or relative and trusting that repayment will be made at some future date. The trust required in generalized exchanges is buttressed by the *norm of reciprocity* as discussed above in regard to equity theory. That individuals find the relationships in a family group profitable is in part because the family group maintains profitable exchanges with other social organizations such as schools, churches, and the economy. The essence of macroexchange perspectives is the view that these group and organizational exchanges are more central than individual decision making.

In structural exchange theories, the individual's choices are viewed as being determined by the macroexchanges between group and organizations. Note that this is just the opposite of the view in microexchange theories such as rational choice theory that the individual's decisions determine the group's exchanges.

Perhaps the best example of macroexchange thinking applied to the family is provided by the work of the French structuralist Claude Levi-Strauss (1969), who developed a theory that the fabric of societies is constructed by norms that require generalized social exchanges between groups. At the heart of these generalized exchanges are the exchanges between kin groups and clans. Prescriptive mating norms require the formation of alliances between groups through the exchange of mates. For example, in a moiety, or two-clan system, if you are a member of the Bear clan and want to form a political, social, and economic alliance with the Eagle clan, you could create a mating rule such as, Bear women must marry Eagle men. The strongest expression of this alliance rule would be a totemic incest taboo, for example, forbidding an Eagle man to marry an Eagle woman. Levi-Strauss's (1969) work has been criticized as not being applicable to voluntary mate selection systems such as our own, but his work has led to some interesting applications, such as Harrison White's (1963) book examining mathematical models of kinship. In general, the more macrosocial utilitarian theories have not been applied to the family as a unit of analysis but rather to larger kinship groups such as clans. As a result, North American family scholars have tended to favor the more microsocial variants of utilitarian thinking.

It should be useful to remember that exchanges need not be dyadic (between two people). In groups with three or more members, such as most families, the interests of all members need to be accommodated so that no member's personal interest dominates. Also, in groups with three or more members, the exchanges may be indirect. For example, I may help my wife, who helps her mother, and her mother may then do something nice for me because I helped her daughter. Or, various groups of in-laws may take turns hosting holiday celebrations. And, as we know from even casually thinking about inheritance patterns, the accumulated benefits of one generation may be passed along to the next generation ad infinitum. I may be eligible for inheritance not by promising to pay back my parents, but by assuring my parents that I won't break the chain and will pass on inheritance myself to my parents' grandchildren (Ekeh, 1974).

## Empirical Applications

One way to understand a theory is to apply it to some examples. In this section, we apply exchange theory to two areas of research in the study of the family: divorce and sexual relations.

### DIVORCE

Over the past half century, divorce in North America has increased dramatically. The past two decades have seen a slowing and stabilizing of divorce rates, but the risk of divorce is sometimes estimated to be as high as one divorce out of every two marriages. Divorce means difficult and painful adjustments for children as well as the husband and wife in a family. It is not surprising, then, that the explanation of why partners separate and divorce continues to occupy the attention of a significant number of family scholars.

Among the many possible explanations of divorce, exchange theory appears to offer one of the more promising roads to understanding. Briefly, according to exchange theory, each spouse analyzes the marriage by using the two comparison levels. First, a spouse compares profits relative to other marriages. If he or she feels deprived relative to other marriages, then the marital satisfaction of that spouse would be low, creating a motive for choosing separation and divorce. As Lewis and Spanier (1979) have aptly pointed out, however, many unhappy spouses remain married because of other constraints. Exchange theorists view these other constraints as costs associated with divorce. In the second comparison level, the spouse calculates the rewards and costs (profit) associated with possibilities other than marriage, for example, being single and divorced. Among the possible costs to this alternative would be child support, alimony, peer disapproval, the church's disapproval, kinship group disapproval, sexual deprivation, loss of interaction with one's children, role loss, and so on. Some of the possible rewards might be finding a more compatible partner, freeing family members from a confrontational and conflict-ridden home life, and freeing oneself from family responsibilities. The computation of the perceived alternatives to marriage depends on a diversity of variables, such as the gender ratio of the community in which one lives and the ages of one's children.

George Levinger (1965, 1966) assessed the likelihood of divorce in terms of "attractions," "barriers," and "alternatives." If attractions to one's spouse and barriers to divorce are both low, and if alternatives are attractive, then divorce is more likely. Because all three factors are important, it is not sufficient to explain divorce in terms of any one of them alone. This application should remind us that it is important to know if the subjective calculations of both partners must be taken into account. Is divorce more likely if only one partner perceives a "poor deal" by staying married, or must both partners be getting a "poor deal"? In some societies, it may not be possible for one partner to end the relationship unilaterally if the other partner is unwilling to do so. Thus, when applying the exchange perspective to divorce, we need to specify the conditions under which miserable spouses can be expected to stay married.

One of the major stumbling blocks for successfully applying this exchange theory explanation to divorce is that the rewards and costs in the two comparison levels seem to change over the life span of the individual. This is evident in the paradoxical finding pointed out by White and Booth (1991) that the great bulk of divorces (30%–40%) occur in the first 5 years of marriage, the very point in the life span that is associated with the highest marital satisfaction. Furthermore, as marital satisfaction declines over the life course, so does the risk of divorce. It seems a paradox that we should find the greatest number of divorces when marriages are the happiest! However, the comparison levels for happiness are highest early in a relationship, and it is easier to become disappointed when expectations are not fulfilled.

White and Booth (1991) explain this paradox by proposing that as marriages proceed through the spouses' life course, the importance of marital happiness tends to decline; in addition, longer-duration marriages have relatively high costs for dissolution (*barriers*). White and Booth (1991) proposed that longer marriages with high costs for dissolution require high levels of marital unhappiness to propel spouses to divorce, whereas early marriages with few costs to divorce require greater levels of marital happiness to keep them together. Thus, the life course changes in salience and the ratio of rewards and costs explain the paradox. Lewis and Spanier's (1979) model of marital stability has been challenged by a competing exchange model offered by Thomas and Kleber (1981), who propose that regardless of marital quality, marital stability will be high when there are few alternatives and high barriers to dissolution. White and Booth (1991) feel that in addition to solving the paradox between high divorce rates and marital satisfaction, their data resolve the debate in favor of Lewis and Spanier's (1979) model. We believe grounds remain for further research on these competing models.

GENDER DIFFERENCES IN SEXUAL BEHAVIOR

Our second application of exchange theory is drawn from propositions presented by Nye (1979) regarding sexual behavior, although we focus not on the formal propositions but on what the explanation would look like. But first, what is it that we want to explain about gender differences in sexual behavior? In most, if not all, cultures, sex seems more actively sought after by males than females. Although there may exist a biological answer to why this is the case (see Chapter 8), most authors assume that the biological drive is malleable in how it is satisfied. Furthermore, many of the behaviors that could be associated with a higher sex drive in one gender, such as prostitution, are usually labeled social rather than biological problems.

Nye (1979) argues that males are more likely to exchange rewards (especially money or marriage) for sexual access. Because exchange theory is essentially a motivational theory, Nye posits that sex is more profitable for males than it is for females. Nye is not assuming a more vital sex drive for males than females. Such an assumption would place the entire explanation on the shoulders of the biological importance, or salience, of sex for males over females. As a social scientist, Nye seems to assume that the biological drive for the two genders is equal and he therefore searches for a social explanation.

First, Nye argues that in all cultures women take the major responsibility for the children they bear. Unwanted pregnancy is thus more costly to women than it is to men. Even in the most modern societies, paternity is still difficult and expensive to prove. Contraceptives can be used to prevent the potential outcome of unwanted pregnancy, but contraception also is usually left to the female partner. These are real and potentially high costs to intercourse. A second differential is that men for the most part report better outcomes from sex than do women. Men are more likely to achieve orgasm than are women, and women are more likely to experience frustration from sexual relations.

The result of these differential costs and rewards is that relative to women, men, in general, find that sex offers greater rewards and fewer costs. As a result, men must either have sexual relations with those who find it as rewarding as they do (homosexuality) or they must increase the rewards for women. Nye says that the usual ways in which these rewards are increased for women is for men to offer either money or the probability of marriage. Other rewards, such as status and security, might be more salient at various points in the life course.

Nye's application of exchange has great scope and breadth. For example, it could explain female adornment as a sexual attractor that functions to increase the value of the exchange. Because married persons have already struck a bargain, we would expect much less difference between men and women in postmarital sexual relations. This prediction is consistent with the fact that a difference of less than 10% exists between male and female extramarital affairs (Blumstein & Schwartz, 1983). Furthermore, we can make some general predictions, such as that when the costs of contraception (inconvenience and medical complications) are equally distributed among both genders and sexual knowledge is shared among both genders so that both genders enjoy the same level of outcome, then we would expect less sexual bargaining with marriage and money. Keep in mind that Nye's (1979) theory remains to be tested and must be shown to provide a better explanation than competing theories, but this example does illustrate exchange theory's potential breadth of explanation.

## Implications for Intervention

Exchange theory has numerous implications for family policy, treatment, and intervention. We can only sketch a few of these to give the flavor of the richness of this theory for application to family issues.

One of the most influential applications of the theory is in the area of intervention and prevention in marital and parent–child interactions. This application has largely been constructed on the view that parent–child and husband–wife relations represent behavioral exchanges. Gerald Patterson and his associates at the Oregon Research Institute pioneered this approach (Patterson & Reid, 1970). Currently, many scholars and practitioners use the behavioral exchange approach. For example, Bagarozzi (1993) suggests that in designing behavioral contracts with spouses, therapists should focus on increasing positive or rewarding behaviors and decreasing negative behavioral exchanges.

Clearly, such an intervention would increase the profitability of the marital relationship. Markman and his colleagues developed the Prevention and Relationship Enhancement Program for enhancing marriages and decreasing divorce based on the notion that distressed couples seem to enter a reciprocal exchange of negative behaviors (e.g., Renick, Blumberg, & Markman, 1992). Although these authors view their program as empirically based rather than founded on exchange theory, the basic interpretive notion of behavioral exchanges remains true to the exchange perspective.

Another area of application for the theory is in the area of family policy. Haveman and Wolfe (1994), following Becker (1981), take a human capital, or rational choice, approach to child welfare and education policy. They view parents, schools, and government as making investments in the human capital of our children. To the extent that we invest unwisely or in a miserly fashion, we reap the failures of succeeding generations and social problems such as crime and economic dependence. Haveman and Wolfe (1994) review the relative costs of geographic moves, parental separation, and several other variables on the eventual success of children. These costs are seen as our inability to invest wisely in the human capital of tomorrow's generation and society. Haveman and Wolfe's *Succeeding Generations* is one of the clearest applications of economic exchange principles to the interpretation of family data and the framing of family policy.

## Critiques and Discussion

Our focus in this section is on the criticisms commonly directed at microexchange theories. We recognize that each of the criticisms discussed is more applicable to some microsocial variants than others. Our central target must be the general notions presented above and principally derived from Nye (1979). One caveat should be mentioned: No social theory solves all the problems we raise in our critiques. Our criticism is not aimed at convincing the theorist or the student that one theory is better than another. Rather, these critiques are intended to illuminate the choices we make in adopting a theoretical stance and to point out the areas that are in need of more creative thinking by the next generation of scholars.

As we mentioned at the beginning, microsocial exchange theories are usually based on *methodological individualism,* the assumption that the individual is the appropriate unit to study to gain an understanding of the family. As far as we know, there has never been a definition of the family as simply an aggregation of individuals. Yet, when we take the individual's ratio of rewards and costs as the basis of our theory about families, we are assuming that the aggregation of individual members is the family. Theoretically, this would make the family no different from any other collection of actors. Yet the family has characteristics that seem unlike other social groups. For most of us, our families are lifelong social groups that we enter by birth and leave by death. Our families have roles that are unlike work group roles, such as filial obligations toward the parents. And our families have biological and social relations (blood and marriage) that are unlike those in any other social group. Thus, to assume that individual actors are interchangeable and that families as social groups can be explained by the motivation of individuals seems problematic.

Explaining social order poses a problem for all the forms of utilitarianism. If we view explanation as emanating from individual motivation, then it is usually difficult to demonstrate how we developed social norms and social institutions. Although most microsocial theorists include a discussion of the norm of reciprocity (you should help those that help you), it is much less clear how this norm is derived from individual self-interest. In addition, in analyzing costs and rewards, theorists readily accept the given nature of social norms and institutions without indicating how these are explained by the theory. For instance, in weighing the rewards and costs of not wearing clothing on a hot summer day, you automatically take into account formal norms (laws) and informal norms. Most of you recognize that no matter how rewarding you might find going without clothing, there are strong formal and informal norms that constrain your behavior. The major answer utilitarians have given this question regarding social order is known as the *social contract*. There are many variants of this idea, but basically it involves the assumption that individuals band together and form a social order so as to have security of person and property. This social contract implies that some individual freedom is relinquished so that order may be maintained. But this view, although admitting the importance and power of social institutions, largely begs the question of how these social institutions evolve and change. Clearly, most of you have no recollection of relinquishing some of your freedoms in exchange for order. Rather, you were socialized by institutions to be on time, to behave in certain ways, and to expect formal and informal sanctions if you transgressed the social order.

Another problematic area for microsocial exchange theory is altruistic behavior. Many times we see (and praise) behaviors that seem to be characterized by the individual giving up rewards and suffering costs so that others may prosper. Some simple examples are a soldier giving up his or her life in combat or a mother running into a burning house to save her child. Exchange theorists would point out that this is a problem of attribution or inference. All we have really observed is the behavior (and not the motive), and we incorrectly attribute an other-directedness to an act that was actually calculated to yield profit. Thus, the mother is acting in the least costly way if she regards the death of her child as more costly than the personal risk she incurs by her attempt to save the child. The soldier who refuses to fight faces court martial, humiliation, and shame. On the other hand, critics might argue that these people are not acting rationally at all, but emotionally.

The assumption of a rational actor provides further difficulties, especially in the study of the family. The family is often considered a social group characterized by intense loyalty and emotions. Most police officers will tell you that domestic quarrels are often emotional and potentially explosive situations because of their irrational nature. Furthermore, the institution of marriage has long been viewed as till death do us part, which flies in the face of the exchange view until profitability declines. And, of course, children do not choose their parents, nor is the family they enter representative of the voluntaristic ideal of unfettered choice needed for the optimization of profit. Thus, it seems natural to question whether the assumption of rational actors calculating their most profitable choice makes sense in the context of the family.

One of the most basic questions in the study of the family is "Why do people have children?" Exchange theory should treat this choice as bearing profit for the parents. But as most economists and parents will attest, children are expensive. Although there are many ways to estimate the costs of raising one child (to age 17, without advanced education, etc.), inflation-adjusted estimates for raising a middle-class child today are usually above a quarter of a million dollars. Furthermore, the decline in the norms regarding filial care of the aged, coupled with social security and institutional care, make returns to the parents in old age unlikely. Nye (1979) attempts to answer this question by saying there is a form of intergenerational norm of reciprocity. You feel an obligation to pass on what your parent did for you to the succeeding generation. But people who are childless by choice can pocket the quarter of a million dollars and seemingly feel little remorse in not passing on the favor. It may be that having children is not a rational decision.

There is a problem of weighing costs and rewards. We have previously mentioned that the salience, or importance, of rewards and costs must be examined to understand a choice. Of course, theorists would like to believe that some costs and rewards have roughly similar value across actors. If this were not so, then it would be unlikely that we could develop successful microeconomics. Even the symbols and meaning associated with economic units may be unstable, however. In our society, there are symbols of wealth and success. Increasingly, both the wealthy and the indebted may attain these symbols. These symbols may vary across cohorts and periods. We know of a very wealthy man who insisted on driving himself in a 10-year-old vehicle. His offspring all had fancier new cars with chauffeurs. And the meaning of rewards and costs changes more drastically once we move our comparisons to other cultures. In Tikopeia, a man's wealth was based on the number of wives he had. But number of wives did not just reflect material well-being. Daughters could be traded for wives, and therefore daughters were a means to wealth and status.

Turner (1991) argues that exchange theory can be accused of tautological reasoning. In essence, a *tautology* exists when terms are all defined by one another and there is no possibility of disproving the statements. Turner argues that reward is defined as that which is valued by the person. The choice that a person makes is the maximization of profit. Thus, all actions are rewarding and the reason we undertake an action is that it brings rewards. For example, we may ask, "Why did Tiffany get married?" Some exchange theorists would answer that Tiffany got married because it was a more profitable choice than remaining single. But we may ask, "How do the exchange theorists know that this maximized Tiffany's profits over remaining single?" If the exchange theorists responded that we know because people always choose those behaviors that maximize their profits, then we have just completed a tautological circle. Turner believes that this circular logic is often found in deductive theories. We do not disagree that deductive systems can be self-referential and closed systems of definitions, but we do disagree that deductive scientific theories are ever like this. Indeed, the hallmark of a scientific theory (as opposed to a theory in general) is that some of its concepts are tied to empirical measures. We may define force ($f$) as $f{:}ma$, but we have standard empirical measures for mass ($m$) and acceleration ($a$). A problem with utilitarian theories is that they often seem to lack this mooring to the concrete empirical measurement system.

## Conclusion

Despite the criticisms, utilitarian, or exchange, theory is one of the most popular social science theories applied to the family. One reason for this popularity is that exchange theories typically have great scope and breadth. The notions of reward, cost, and profit are sufficiently abstract and content free that the researcher may fill in the content from any number of contexts. The assumptions of rational actors calculating profit provides some problems, as does the inadequacy of the theory for explaining how and why institutional and normative constraints operate on choices.

## Suggested Readings

Haveman, R., & Wolfe, B. (1994). *Succeeding generations*. New York: Russell Sage.
*This is a sophisticated but very readable application of microexchange economics to an extremely important area of discourse.*

Sabatelli, R. M., & Shehan, C. L. (1993). Exchange and resource theories. In P. Boss, W. Doherty, R. LaRossa, W. Schumm, & S. Steinmetz (Eds.), *Sourcebook of family theories and methods: A contextual approach* (pp. 385–411). New York: Plenum.
*This is a good general introduction. The authors introduce the macro–micro distinction as "collectivism–individualism" and do not demarcate the theories quite as sharply as we do in this regard.*

# 3

# The Symbolic Interaction Framework

Nicole, Michael, and their teenage son, James, have agreed to participate in a social survey about family life. Survey officials requested that all three of them participate in answering questions. The doorbell rings, and they meet the interviewer, a young woman named Kim. Kim asks that each of the family members fill out a section of the questionnaire independently of the others. James takes his questionnaire to his room, Michael fills his out in the kitchen, and Nicole completes hers in the living room, where Kim is waiting. After all three family members have completed their questionnaires, Kim briefly examines them. She pauses and then says, "Gosh, all three of you answered the question about how traditional or nontraditional your family is in very different ways. Would you folks mind discussing this with me for just a moment? We are supposed to discuss differences of opinion as part of the survey, and if you don't mind, I'll take notes occasionally." The family agrees.

It turns out that James believes that his family is fairly traditional. Nicole believes the family is very traditional. And her husband, Michael, thinks the family is extremely nontraditional. Nicole says that she thinks the family is traditional because she feels she has to do all of the cleaning up after the "guys." Michael says he thinks they are nontraditional because his mother never worked outside the home. He points out that his wife earns more money than he does. James believes they are fairly traditional because he has a mother and father who aren't divorced. Finally, Michael asks Kim, the researcher, what the survey means by "traditional." After the family is told the meaning, Kim asks if that information would change their answers. All three family members say that it would and that the survey meaning is not very close to what they think of as traditional.

Contemporary social science applied to the study of groups such as families is for the most part concerned with people's behavior.

Many of the media through which we communicate are taken for granted. For example, a researcher usually assumes that questions on a questionnaire hold the same meaning and will be interpreted in the same way by all respondents. The variation in answers to questions is supposed to reflect differences in behavior, not in the interpretation of a question. If we ask a husband and wife how many times they quarreled during the past week, we assume that they label the same events as quarrels. Yet even between husbands and wives who must both have been present for a "quarrel" to take place, we find differences in responses. We must conclude that differences in counting quarrels may be a difference of interpretation in what constitutes a quarrel, a difference of memory, or both. In an even broader perspective on diversity of meanings, we know some of the persons responding to our questions may have another mother tongue, the families in which they are raised are different, and they have diverse education levels and abilities. How then can we assume that they will interpret and understand our questions in the same way? Maybe their responses are based not on different reactions to the question but on very different interpretations. Symbolic interactionism, more than any other of the family theories, calls for paying attention to how events and things are interpreted by social actors.

Some social scientists have divided the subject matter of human behavior into disciplines studying personality (psychology), culture (linguistics and anthropology), and social behavior (sociology, economics, and political science). At the base of these distinctions is the assumption that a culture is composed of commonly shared signs and symbols from which actors construct the meanings found in the culture. Many social scientists approach the meaning of symbols and signs in a culture as being relatively uniform, and therefore the words on the questionnaire are viewed as commonly and uniformly understood. But some social scientists have argued that we cannot understand a behavioral response (including answering a questionnaire) unless we know what meaning the situation and the stimulus has for an actor. In broader terms, these social scientists believe that to understand social behavior, the researcher must understand the meanings actors assign to the situation and action. This uniting of the study of cultural meanings with social behavior is the prime focus of theories of symbolic interaction.

## Intellectual Traditions

The symbolic interaction approach has a rich and complex history. Today, the term *symbolic interactionism* represents a diverse set of family theories, and it can be difficult to detect what many of these variants now have in common that unites them under a single banner. The common threads that exist are perhaps best highlighted by understanding the common progenitors from which the current variants developed.

Without a doubt, the greatest single influence on social science thinking in the 20th century came from Charles Darwin. Darwin (1880) provided a concrete and biologically rooted approach that was in stark contrast to the more abstract *idealism* (e.g., Hegel) that was in philosophical favor in Europe at the time. To intellectuals in North America, the more concrete biological approach emphasizing the "adaptation" of organisms to their environment was much more attractive. Three North American scholars were particularly influential in generating ideas that would become incorporated in symbolic interactionism. Charles S. Peirce developed a theory of signs and symbols, William James (1975) developed a notion of self in relation to environment, and John Dewey (1930) developed the concept of mind. As Charles Morris points out in his preface to Mead's (1934) *Mind, Self, and Society*, pragmatists saw no sharp distinction or conflict between science and philosophy. Together, these scholars represent the foundation of the philosophical school called *pragmatism,* from which symbolic interactionism sprang.

The philosophical foundation for symbolic interactionism is complemented by advances in social science thinking occurring in the first two decades of the 20th century. Charles Horton Cooley (1902, 1909) expanded William James's idea of the self into the more elaborate social science concept of the *looking glass self.* The importance of Cooley's (1909) notion is that it conceptualized part of the self as capable of reflection on its own behavior. This later became incorporated in Mead's (1934) conception of the self. W. I. Thomas and D. S. Thomas (1928) expanded on the pragmatic premise formulated by Peirce (1905) that the conception of an object is wholly given by the conception of all possible effects. Thomas and Thomas (1928) reinterpreted the pragmatic maxim as the important social–psychological principle: *What humans define as real has real consequences* (p. 572). This has become known as the *definition of the situation* and provides a linkage between how we perceive our environment and how we act in it. Both of these notions guided the early formulations of symbolic interactionism.

Despite these important earlier influences, it is really the work of George Herbert Mead that most scholars identify as the start of symbolic interactionism. Mead's thinking is, for the most part, only accessible through the lecture notes of his students, compiled and edited by the linguist Charles Morris (e.g., *Mind, Self and Society*, 1934). Indeed, Morris (1934) points out that although Mead's students took notes, Mead never even used lecture notes, and his thinking was constantly evolving. Yet Mead's influence and contribution have been sufficiently strong to establish him as the paternal figurehead of symbolic interactionism.

Central to Mead's approach is the idea that by sharing common symbols, humans can adapt to and survive in their environment. He was especially interested in the process by which the flexibly adaptive infant came to share the conventional understandings in any society. His work incorporated the idea of stages of interactional learning through play and games, an especially important perspective for the study of socialization in the family.

Although Mead is an important starting point, numerous scholars have contributed to symbolic interactionism and it would be misleading to portray its development as monotonic and united. In fact, scholars have quarreled bitterly about the relative emphases and interpretation of ideas. Most secondary sources record an original bifurcation of symbolic interactionism into the Chicago school (Blumer, 1962, 1969) and the Iowa school (Kuhn, 1964), but we see more variants than just these two. We discuss many of these in the variants section below. We believe it is also important for the student to gain some notion of the unifying elements in this theoretical perspective.

It is easy to say that symbolic interaction theories focus on meaning but quite a different and more difficult task to explain what that "means." To understand this complex issue, we must return to the seminal work of Peirce and later Morris. Humans have the ability to mentally form invariant associations. For example, when Event A is associated with Event B, we could say that A is a *sign* for B. Where there is smoke, there is fire. Smoke is thus a sign for fire. An octagonal traffic sign is a sign to stop. A sign is the necessary ingredient for the development of a *symbol*. A symbol is any sign that is agreed on by convention. Now, although there are several important aspects to these distinctions, the question symbolic interactionism poses is, "How do we agree on (convention) the sign?" Let's apply this to language. We have words such as "dad" that stand as a sign for a particular person in our lives. Not only do you have a "dad," but others understand the referent of that utterance. In addition, if you think about this issue for very long, you will note that many words (both written and spoken) refer not to things but to other clusters of symbols. The complexity of human symbolism and meaning as we now know it escapes any simple notion that every sign has a referent, because words can stand for other symbols as well as things.

To understand the term *meaning* in a social context, symbolic interactionists focus on the idea of how these complex symbol systems are shared. Indeed, for communication to take place, symbols must be shared or commonly agreed on. Thus, the focus for Mead and many other interactionists is on the process by which the infant comes to acquire the symbol system of the society.

The symbolic content of any culture is constantly changing. Words such as *limn* leave our system through disuse and abuse, and new words such as *groovy* come into use. Even though the symbol system must be relatively stable for the achievement of agreement and convention, it nonetheless changes. But it changes within the rules of the system. As Chomsky (1965) and other linguists point out, a key ingredient to understanding a symbol system and therefore meaning is that users of the system adopt rules that allow the generation of new and meaningful utterances based on these rules, or *syntax*. This insight is responsible for a second focus for interactionists. That focus is on the process by which meanings are constructed through interaction with both the environment and other people. In fact, most human symbol systems are so complex as to allow the generation of meanings for specific contexts and environments.

The general focus of symbolic interactionism can be summed up to be on the acquisition and generation of meaning. It should not be forgotten that in the study of the family and other social groups, we are assuming that actors think about and act according to the meanings they attribute to their actions and context. For example, a 3-year-old child may show no interest in a particular toy doll. But when an older sibling plays with the doll, it suddenly takes on new interactional and situational meaning. Now the doll is desired. The meaning of the toy is constructed by the situational interaction of the two siblings. Symbolic interactionism is not simply a motivational theory (as exchange); it is much broader. Certainly, symbolic interaction posits that humans are motivated to create meanings to help them make sense of their world. In addition, it encompasses actors' motives as constructed from the meanings available to the actor and relevant to the situation in which the actor is located.

Another example is contained in the following story. A 5-year-old girl abruptly asked her mother, "How do babies get born?" Nervous as to what she should say about sex and reproduction, the mother paused and then responded, "Do you mean where babies come from?" The young girl briskly replied, "No, are they born with clothes on or clothes off?"

Meaning emerges through the course of social interaction. Words have no communicative meaning at all unless they are mutually understood by conversing actors. Of course, as the above episode illustrates, we all may have private understandings that are not identical, so we must construct through an exchange of already meaningful symbols a common understanding of other words and expressions. When misunderstandings occur, we attempt to overcome them.

As focal points for intense interaction, families are crucial sites of meaning creation and verification. When children are young, the meanings of things are usually simply acquired and taken for granted, based on exposure to usage by parents, other family members, and others in society (including Big Bird on *Sesame Street*). Parents, in turn, acquired many meanings from elders when they were younger, so that at least some of our linguistic heritage is passed on from generation to generation. Still, in any specific encounter between humans, there must be a meeting of minds, with some assurance that a shared sensibility either preexists or is capable of being created through a new communicative process. Thus, effective relationships, both in and outside of families, are dependent on nurturing a culture of shared meanings.

## Focus and Scope Assumptions

*Human behavior must be understood by the meanings of the actor.* The most basic assumption in symbolic interactionism is that the explanation of human behavior is impossible without knowing the meaning such behavior holds for the actor. Interactionists believe that to be human is to use symbols. Indeed, they would say we live in a largely symbolic world. Our language structures the way we perceive and the way we think. Material objects, such as jeans and cars, not only perform functions (utility) but have symbolic significance aesthetically, religiously, and socially. Humans live in a symbolic world, and our actions have both physical and symbolic import. If we were to attempt to understand behavior simply from the physical side of the equation, we would miss the mark of understanding. For example, if we were to describe to you a man in the woods cutting down a tree, you would not understand that behavior unless we discovered the actor's meaning (e.g., he is employed as a lumberjack, he is getting a Christmas tree, or he is a vandal). To understand behavior, we must understand the meaning that an action has for the actor.

*Actors define the meaning of context and situation.* The assumption that actors define the meaning of the contexts and situations in which they find themselves is in some ways an extension of the previous assumption. If humans live in a symbolic world, then the context in which humans find themselves will be both physical and symbolic. This assumption is only fully understood, however, by returning to Thomas and Thomas's (1928) maxim that what humans define as real has real consequences. Imagine that a terribly inebriated person hallucinates a herd of pink elephants charging down the street toward where he or she is standing. In response to the hallucinated charging elephants, the person begins to run down the street. Regardless of the fact that no elephants exist, the fact that the person defines the situation as dangerous is important in understanding why the person runs down the street. How we define the situation in which we find ourselves explains what problems we define and what actions and solutions we undertake. The fact that some definitions may be entirely mental rather than physical constructions makes our understanding of the actors' definitions of the situation even more important.

*Individuals have minds.* Another basic assumption of symbolic inter-actionism is that humans have minds. This may seem a trivial assumption unless we examine it more closely. All of us recognize that we have an organ of the body that sends and receives electrochemical impulses. But the idea of an individual mind presupposes an individual self that perceives, reasons, senses, and imagines. The notion of mind includes memory and willing actions as retrospective and prospective operations. Whether there is one organ or a system of interconnected organs that give rise to these complex operations is not totally resolved, even in the neurosciences. In addition, the recent discovery by Nobel laureate (2000) Eric Kandel that synapses are modified by experience further complicates issues in that the organ of the brain may be changed and modified throughout our lives by experi-ence. Indeed, it is the assumption in symbolic interactionism that the human mind acquires, integrates, and processes information. At the same time, the mind is capable of reflecting on its own processes so that the individual can develop a self as both actor (I) and object (me).

*Society precedes the individual.* When symbolic interactionists assume that humans live in a symbolic world and use their minds to mani-pulate and interpret these symbols, it is tempting to ask, "When did this all begin?" At some point in evolutionary time, we as a subhuman species lacked these talents. The problem with asking when we gained the abilities is that it was such a gradual process that there was no single point in time. Indeed, it might be considered a moot question whether symbols, social organization, or mind came first, because they are so strongly interdependent. But because we cannot conceptu-alize without symbols, and symbols are shared, society in rudimentary form must precede the individual mind and self. The single most important point to understand about Mead's conception of mind is that individual minds are results of the society and not vice versa. As Morris (1934) says,

> Instead of beginning with individual minds and working out to society, Mead starts with an objective social process and works inward through the importation of the social process of communication into the individual by the medium of the vocal gesture. The individual has taken the social act into himself. Mind remains social. (p. xxii)

Probably the best known empirical cases illustrating Morris's point would be the two cases of infant isolation documented by Kingsley Davis (1947). In both cases, children lacked socialization and failed to develop language and social skills. The assumption that society precedes individuals leads interactionists to focus on the process of socialization.

## Concepts

### SELF AND MIND

The notion of self is pivotal in symbolic interactionism. But our understanding of this concept is not well served by translating Mead's (1934) concept of self as that which we commonly understand as our identity. For Mead, self, mind, and symbol developed concurrently. Our notion of self is founded on symbols and consciousness. The essence of symbolic interaction is that the self is a symbolic representation of that which did an act (I) and that which was acted on (me). In other words, we may represent ourselves as both subject and object. This means that humans can look at their own behavior as an object (me) and as such take "the role of the other." The concept of taking the role of the other is directly analogous to what Cooley (1902) called "the looking glass self." Mead (1934) extended this concept from looking at our actions as a specific other (How would my father see my action?) to looking at our actions as a "generalized other" (How would others in society look at my act?). The self, then, is constructed by our consciousness from the two perspectives of I and me. The self as object contains the perspective of specific others when we take on the role of particular persons to see ourselves as they might, and it is constructed from the perspective of generalization of roles, or generalized other.

## SOCIALIZATION

Socialization is the process by which we acquire the symbols, beliefs, and attitudes of our culture. Although the notion of socialization is central in symbolic interaction, Mead (1934) did not use it as a concept. Rather, Mead talked about this process as the "importation" of social symbols into the mind as part of the development of the generalized other: "Mind is nothing but the importation of this external process into the conduct of the individual so as to meet the problems that arise" (p. 188). For the child, the process of socialization is marked by two stages. First is the *play stage,* in which the child plays at being something like a police officer or mother. The play stage incorporates Mead's notion of taking the role of the other. Second is the *game stage,* in which the child must be able to incorporate his or her self in an organized activity through the generalized other. As Mead says,

> If we contrast play with the situation in an organized game, we note the essential difference that the child who plays in a game must be ready to take the attitude of everyone else involved in that game, and that these different roles must have a definite relationship to each other. (p. 151)

Thus, the play stage assists in the learning and practice of *role taking,* whereas the game stage assists in the more complex task of learning the rules governing all social actors in the game. It is the game stage that is most similar to the complex social game we play as adults with our ability to "play a role" in society.

## ROLE

Although the concept of role does not originate with symbolic interactionism, it is without a doubt one of the most basic concepts in symbolic interactionism. It is also the concept that has proved most problematic, because Mead (1934) uses the term throughout his work but seemingly takes its definition as self-evident. Probably the closest passage to a definition comes in a footnote in which Mead identifies social intelligence as depending on "the given individual's ability to take the roles of, or 'put himself in the place of,' the other individuals implicated with him in given social situations; and upon his consequent sensitivity to their attitudes toward himself and toward one another" (p. 141n). From this, we can clearly see that a role must be the "place of an actor." Mead also dealt with roles as rules to be learned in the game stage of a child's development. *Role taking* then is to put oneself in the place of the actor, and it includes the rules that the actor is expected to follow. The sketchiness of these references and lack of a clear definition has fueled bitter debates among later symbolic interactionists.

There are several dimensions of the concept of role that are significant in explaining family phenomena. If we assume that roles have the two characteristics alluded to above—rules of behavior for positions—then we can see how these rules also provide others with expectations for what someone in that position is to do. For example, the general norm, or rule, for a person who is "it" in the game of hide-and-seek is to close one's eyes and count to 10 while others hide. If the person who is "it" does not do this, he or she has not performed the role as others expected. Note that the others' behavior is predicated on the expectation of how "it" would behave. Thus, one important dimension of roles is the *expectation* that both the actor and others have about the performance of the role.

The *clarity* of the role expectations or rules of the role is another important dimension. Without clear expectations shared by both the actor and others, it is impossible for the actor to perform the role or for others to know how their behavior articulates with that of the actor. Returning to the game of hide-and-seek, if "it" only counts to five but others expect "it" to count to a higher number, their behavior cannot be successfully meshed nor the game carried on.

*Role strain* is an important dimension of roles. Role strain is where the actor does not have sufficient resources to enact a role or roles. When there are multiple roles, the overload of expectations may be so great as to create role overload or strain. A corollary to role strain is the special case in which the expectations of one role contradict or conflict with the expectations of another role. This role conflict usually produces role strain because the actor cannot enact the contrary roles simultaneously.

DEFINITION OF THE SITUATION

The concept of the definition of the situation originated with W. I. Thomas (Thomas & Thomas, 1928) but is also implicit in Mead's (1934) work in his emphasis on the social situation and taking the role of the other and the generalized other. The definition of the situation refers to the dictum that what we define as real will have real consequences. The definition of the situation sensitizes symbolic interactionists to the role of perception in forming our behavior. Mead, however, seemed wary about an approach that was too perceptually oriented and lacked focus on humans as problem solvers interacting with their environment. He stated,

This process of thinking, which is the elaboration of our responses to the stimulus, is a process which also necessarily goes on in the organism. Yet it is a mistake to assume that all that we call thought can be located in the organism or can be put inside the head. The goodness or badness of the investments is in the investment, and the valuable or dangerous character of food is in the food, not in our heads. (p. 115)

Thus, Mead, in a manner consistent with Thomas and Thomas's (1928) dictum and Dewey's (1930) pragmatism, focuses us once again on the problem-solving interaction with the environment rather than on isolated internal mental processes.

## Propositions

Although numerous authors have employed a symbolic interaction approach in the empirical study of the family (e.g., LaRossa & LaRossa, 1981), none of the contributions to date have equaled the theoretical presentation by Burr and his colleagues (Burr, 1973; Burr, Leigh, Day, & Constantine, 1979). They focus on the general propositions that are directly relevant to understanding families and, in our opinion, provide the most elegant and systematic statement of symbolic interactionism applied to families. For this reason, much of the clarity and power of the theory to explain family behavior and processes originates in the propositional inventory provided by Burr, Leigh, et al. (1979). Here we discuss a few of the propositions that we regard as among the most useful for understanding families.

*The quality of ego's role enactment in a relationship positively affects ego's satisfaction with the relationship.* (Burr, Leigh, et al., 1979, p. 70)

Although most of us assume that our satisfaction in a relationship such as marriage is "made" by the other person, this proposition states a person (ego) is more satisfied in a relationship when he or she is doing a good job of enacting the role in that relationship. For example, a wife would feel more satisfied about her marriage when she feels that she is doing a good job in the role of wife. Burr and colleagues also offer a proposition regarding the role performance of the other, but that would be more expected. The proposition regarding ego's role enactment is a little like the homilies, "You like what you're good at" or "The more you put into something, the more you get out of it."

*The greater the perceived clarity of role expectations, the higher the quality of role enactment.* (Burr, Leigh, et al., 1979, p. 74)

A role is defined as the normative expectations attached to a specific position in a social structure. For example, the role of mother is defined by the social norms or expectations of nurturance and protection of her young. The more clearly defined these are to any person occupying the position of biological motherhood, the easier it is for that person to perform the role in a socially acceptable way. Obviously, a lack of clarity could result when biological mothers receive unclear or no anticipatory socialization as to the expectations of motherhood, or if the society lacks clear expectations and this lack of clarity is passed on through socialization to mothers. In either instance, the result would be decrements in the role enactment of the young mother. For example, years ago breast-feeding of infants was not as socially expected as it is today. Today, the normative expectations for breast-feeding are gaining increased force and clarity as role expectations for mothers.

> *The more individuals perceive consensus in the expectations about a role they occupy, the less their role strain.* (Burr, Leigh, et al., 1979, p. 79)

As Rossi and Berk (1985) point out, one critical aspect of a role is that expectations are shared or consensual. Indeed, Mead (1934) argued that all social symbols are the result of consensus. If a person perceives that there is a social consensus on a norm or expectation, then the role as an instruction for behavior is clearer. As we have seen with the second of our propositions, the clarity of such prescriptions facilitates enactment of the behaviors. Thus, if a young mother believes that there exists a broad social consensus that mothers should breast-feed their infants, she is less likely to feel that expectation is vague or ambiguous. Vague and ambiguous role prescriptions cause people to feel uncertain about what the prescriptions are and whether they can meet those expectations. This is the experience of role strain. Burr, Leigh, et al. (1979) defined role strain as the felt stress generated when a person has difficulty complying with the expectations of a role (see p. 57). The mother who is uncertain as to the socially approved pattern of infant feeding would undergo role strain.

> *The greater the diversification of a person's roles, the less consensus the person will perceive in the expectations about those roles.* (Burr, Leigh, et al., 1979, p. 80)

When a person plays multiple roles, there are multiple expectations. At the very minimum, the multitude of expectations may become murky, and, at worst, contradictory expectations may lead to conflict between the expectations of roles. In both situations, it is difficult for the person to perceive clearly that there is a consensus about the expected behavior. For example, a working mother with an infant may feel that, among nonworking mothers and health care professionals, there is a consensus preferring breast milk for infants. Among fellow workers, she may feel that there is a consensus that expressing milk in the office situation is unprofessional and shows a lack of commitment to work. Among working mothers, there may be no consensus, some siding with fellow workers and some with health care professionals. Clearly, the stay-at-home mothers (without role diversification) perceive greater consensus.

> *The greater the perceived role strain that results from performing a role, the less the ease in making a transition into the role and the greater the ease in making a transition out of the role.* (Burr, Leigh, et al., 1979, p. 86)

Naturally, most of us try to avoid feeling stressed, and it seems reasonable that roles that are perceived as producing stress are regarded as requiring a more difficult adjustment than roles perceived as carrying little stress. For example, the perceived role strain of motherhood suggests that although becoming a mother is a biological function, it is not an easy transition. As a result, we have developed elaborate rituals and forms of anticipatory socialization in attempts to clarify the role expectations and ease the transition. Prenatal classes for expectant parents are one example of such anticipatory socialization.

The systematic propositions above are only a few examples of the many proposed by Burr, Leigh, and colleagues (1979). These authors presented these propositions as part of a deductive formalization of symbolic interactionism. As you may recall from the introductory chapter of this book, one of the strengths of a deductive theory is that propositions can be chained together to produce new and informative propositions. If we assume that the propositions are conceptually equivalent and transitive, we can put them into deductive chains. For example,

> *The greater the diversification of a person's roles, the less consensus the person will perceive in the expectations about those roles.* (Burr, Leigh, et al., 1979, p. 80)

and

> *The more individuals perceive consensus in the expectations about a role they occupy, the less their role strain.* (Burr, Leigh, et al., 1979, p. 79)

lead to the deduction that

*The greater the diversification of roles, the greater the role strain.*

This deduction provides an illustration of how the propositions developed in symbolic interaction theory may be used to produce theoretically derived propositions important in guiding empirical research on families. Let's now turn to some of the variants of symbolic interaction theory.

### Variations

After Mead's death in 1931, two major schools of thought within symbolic interactionism emerged. One of these is known as the Iowa school and is associated with the work of Manfred Kuhn (1964). The other is known as the Chicago school and is identified with the position of Herbert Blumer (1962, 1969). Briefly, Kuhn's Iowa school is more positivistic and based on more structural and normative determinism and less interactional creativity than Blumer's Chicago school. Although many authors, such as Turner (1991), continue to focus on the disagreements and intellectual battles between the two schools of thought, we see this as a useless emphasis. Indeed, although the warriors may still be fighting on the battlefield, the castle has quietly been occupied by noncombatants from elsewhere. Many contemporary family scholars spend no time on the metaphysical questions raised by Kuhn (1964) and Blumer (1962, 1969), such as the nature of causality, the truthfulness of observational versus quantitative methods, and the nature of sociological theory. Many of today's family scholars have returned to the pragmatic roots of symbolic interactionism and use whatever methods are most appropriate to the research question they are asking.

The debate between Kuhn and Blumer served to focus interpretations of symbolic interaction on one or the other of these two, with the unfortunate consequence of de-emphasizing the important and considerable contributions of predecessors such as Dewey and Peirce. It must be recalled that pragmatists, including Mead, formulated symbolic interactionism. Yet this has all but been lost in the continuing interest in the two warring factions that still battle over problems, many of which were resolved by Dewey, Peirce, and James. The focus on these two schools has often forced new scholars to take sides, even though the debate is no longer particularly relevant or sophisticated. Many times, it would be far more helpful to examine advances in *semiotics* (a study founded by Peirce) or *structural linguistics* (such as the work of Noam Chomsky) to see how these might further basic concepts in symbolic interaction such as gesture, sign, and symbol and their relationship to social behavior. But such influences and advances have been neglected because of scholars' narrow focus on the two schools.

A central issue that divides most symbolic interactionists is whether interactions between people are (a) a product of the expectations residing in the social structure or (b) created and negotiated by the actors in each interaction. We use this issue as a theme in exploring the unique contributions of four variants of symbolic interactionism. In the study of the family, four relatively recent major variants of symbolic interaction theory have evolved. We identify these four as the *structural* approach, the *interactional* approach, the *microinteractional* approach, and the *phenomenological* approach. Although each could be related to the schools of thought represented by Kuhn and Blumer, we believe these variants are sufficiently well formulated to deserve to be considered on their own merits and that little clarity is gained by forcing them into the restrictive categories of belonging to either the Chicago or Iowa school.

STRUCTURAL APPROACH

We begin by examining the structural approach. Although many family scholars align themselves with this approach, it is probably most identified with the work of Sheldon Stryker (1964, 1980). Others who have made significant contributions include Nye (1976) and Burr, Leigh, et al. (1979). We intend a general characterization that does not focus on any one scholar but on the group of scholars who assume that social roles are learned and then enacted by people when they occupy positions in a social structure. The focus of the structural approach is so much on the concept of role that many scholars call themselves *role theorists* rather than symbolic interactionists.

The three most basic notions in this approach are position (or status), norm, and role. A position, or status, is seen as embedded in a social network of interrelated positions. Each position has associated social norms or expectations. In our society, as in most societies, a woman in the kinship position "mother" is expected to behave nurturantly toward her infant. A social role simply represents the complete cluster of the expectations or norms for any status, or position. A person may occupy several positions and therefore roles at any one time or across the life span. For example, the young mother may also be a teacher. Much of the research emphasis of the structuralists derives from the fact that an individual may play multiple roles at any one time and thus be exposed to role strain and role conflict.

Jonathan Turner (1991) points out that the metaphor for the structuralists is clearly that of "actors on a stage." Indeed, one approach within symbolic interactionism in which this metaphor is emphasized is Goffman's (1974) "dramaturgical approach." In the most general terms, the structuralists think that the scripts for the roles are passed down to the actors from society, which *precedes the individual*. The actors' performance of the roles is largely a matter of how well they have learned their roles through primary and anticipatory socialization. And although the actors' role performances vary somewhat, the actual normative content of the roles changes little from actor to actor. According to this view, despite decades of talk about equal participation by both spouses in household chores, chores remain largely the province of wives rather than husbands because the norms are deeply embedded in the social structure and are not strongly affected by the whims of individual actors.

The structuralist perspective has produced an impressive array of theoretical propositions (Burr, Leigh, et al., 1979) as well as an impressive amount of empirical research on such topics as role strain and identity. Sheldon Stryker, one of the major theorist in this area, has pioneered work in the area of roles and an actor's identity (e.g., Stryker, 1968, 1987, 1989, 1991; Stryker and Serpe, 1994). Indeed the topic of roles and identity has been of great interest to family symbolic interactionist (e.g., Marks & McDermid, 1996) because of the multiple roles (work and family) assumed by most of today's parents.

The structuralist perspective has garnered some rather severe criticisms, especially from the "interactionist" wing of symbolic interactionism. Most significant among these criticisms is the argument that the structural perspective provides a deterministic view of humans being poured into the molds of the social system. This "oversocialized" self has little freedom to adapt to or change the environment. The problem-solving and adaptive nature of humans stressed by both Mead and Dewey seems lost within the structural symbolic interaction perspective. As a result, interactionists accuse the structuralists as viewing social change as, at best, slow and phlegmatic.

INTERACTIONAL APPROACH

The interactional variant of symbolic interaction is most closely associated with the work of Ralph Turner. Turner (1970) focuses on individual families. His work is not concerned with aggregate patterns for families or cultural patterns. Instead, he focuses on the patterned processes within the family as a small group. Turner, unlike the structuralists, believes that many of these patterns are developed through interaction. Rather than seeing social structure as encompassing and monolithic, Turner believes social structure and culture provide a broad, vague, and often ambiguous outline for behavior. The individual's role taking is not simply the enacting of a well-defined role but is "making" the role through interaction with others and the context. Individuals have the freedom to make roles and communicate those roles to others. Thus, Turner emphasizes the creative and problem-solving dimension of roles that is neglected by the structuralist symbolic interactionists. Whereas the structuralists emphasize how humans are constructed by their culture and society, the interactionists emphasize how culture and society are created by interacting actors.

After Ralph Turner's (1970) work *Family Interaction*, he continued to refine and formalize his thinking on role theory. The formal propositions that Turner and his associates (Turner, 1980; Turner & Colomy, 1987) have developed have led them into more and more structural terrain. For example, Jonathan Turner (1991) describes Ralph Turner's recent deductive system as containing some laws: "Functionality is, therefore, one of Turner's 'laws' of social organization, at least among 'roles' as a basic property of all patterns of social organization" (p. 439). Although it would be inaccurate to describe Ralph Turner as straying far from interactionism, his program to develop a nomothetic deductive role theory is bound to lead to more general statements. He increasingly focuses on the explanation of more aggregate phenomena than any one family or situation (e.g., Turner & Colomy, 1987). It probably is not unfair to say that interactionists may have assumed too much power for the individual to "role-make" and they may have failed to adequately consider the constraints of the preexisting social structure and its tenacity in maintaining the status quo.

## MICROINTERACTIONAL APPROACH

The microinteractional perspective is not so much a coherent school of thought as an extension of interactionism focused mainly on the individual and self. Certainly, the influence of the early work by Ralph Turner resides within this approach, but if we were forced to identify one major progenitor for this approach, it would be Erving Goffman. In his first major work, *Presentation of Self in Everyday Life*, Goffman (1959) elaborated the *dramaturgical* metaphor as central to his approach. This metaphor returns to the notion of role as it is found in stage productions. In contrast to the type of influence Goffman's work has exerted on structuralists, a different dimension of Goffman's work has affected the microinteractionists. Microinteractionists emphasize the fluidity and contingency of roles. Actors play roles with scripts and props; there is a backstage reality and an onstage reality. Roles are contingent on the interactions with other actors and thus are organized by systems of rules, such as rules about talk and rules of relevance. The self is relatively fluid and defined by the interactional context and the way in which the person frames or schematically understands the context and the rules. Microinteractionists view Goffman's work as focused exclusively on microinteraction and make no attempt to extend their explanations to a macroscopic level.

Although Goffman did not directly apply his work to the family, his influence is nonetheless present among family scholars studying family microprocesses, for example, LaRossa and LaRossa (1981), in their study on the transition to parenthood and the ways in which parents formulate "accounts" of their parenting contributions. New fathers were found to have a greater number of socially available accounts to justify noninvolvement in child-care duties than mothers had. LaRossa and LaRossa's work relies heavily on an analytic strategy centered on the way people frame their behavior. This strategy is closely aligned to the microinteractional approach with an emphasis on roles being contingent on other interactions and the context and the frame that the actor is using.

PHENOMENOLOGY OF THE FAMILY

Of the many "postpositivist" schools, phenomenology has received the greatest attention and application in the work of family scholars. Although phenomenology originated in Europe, it has found a North American home within the broad framework of symbolic interaction. The term *phenomenology,* which means the "study of phenomenon," had circulated in philosophy for centuries (e.g., Kant, Hegel) before the French philosopher Edmond Husserl (1859–1938) applied the name to an entire philosophy. Husserl's work was applied to the social sciences by his student Alfred Schutz, who along with the ideas immigrated to the United States in 1939. Schutz's ideas and the more general paradigm of phenomenology landed on fertile ground among the microinteractionists and symbolic interactionists of North America. As Turner (1991) notes, however, Husserl's ideas, then, have been selectively borrowed and used in ways that he would not condone to develop modern phenomenology and various forms of interactionist thought (p. 383). This statement is certainly true of the way in which phenomenology has been developed and applied to the study of the family. Even the most accurate applications of Husserl's project, such as by McLain and Weigert (1979), also include other diverse sources of influences, such as the psychoanalytic theory of

R. D. Laing and the work of ethnomethodologists such as Garfinkel. It seems doubtful that this work can be conceived of as part of Husserl's original project to discover the underlying essences of consciousness by a radical stripping away of associations (phenomenological reduction) that are unnecessary to the way something appears in our consciousness. Rather than pursue Husserl's philosophical phenomenology with its technique of phenomenological reduction, most North Americans and many Europeans (e.g., Schutz, Habermas) have pursued a sociological phenomenology focused on the *taken-for-granted everyday lifeworld* and the ways in which these taken-for-granted meanings are created and maintained.

The major thrust in sociological phenomenology of the family is to identify the assumptions and *typifications* that enter into the construction of the everyday life of families (McLain & Weigert, 1979). For example, phenomenologists insist that families are different from the general taken-for-granted everyday world even though they are part of it. Families share in the "public" dimension of the common everyday world, but they also generate their own "private" understandings. The larger everyday public world acknowledges the family as a relatively private sphere in which many things happen (sexual intercourse, wife assault, intense emotions) that do not routinely occur outside of the family. The private understandings constructed by family members are based on their shared history, perspective, and interpretation of events. Dating and marriage are viewed as a process by which separate individuals "fuse" into a common living arrangement and worldview. On the other hand, children gradually separate from their parents' world (fission) and eventually construct their own families (Berger & Kellner, 1964). The focus in phenomenology of the family is to find out how, at any point in history, the "public" typifies families and how, for any family, family members typify and understand their family activities.

Each individual's report of subjective experience must necessarily contain *intersubjective* components that are shared with and communicable to others. These intersubjective meanings are the foundation of the social world. It is these intersubjective components that are the "data" for most social analyses by ethnomethodologists and phenomenologists.

Intersubjective meanings are shared in a set of actors, whether it be a subpopulation such as convicts, an ethnic group, or the more general society. These meanings compose the commonly held and understood meanings of our everyday life, or lifeworld (e.g., McLain & Weigert, 1979; Schutz, 1967). Sectors of these commonly held meanings in our common lifeworld represent frames of reference, *provinces of meaning*, in which we operate in a more restricted sense.

Within each frame of reference, or province of meaning, such as art, science, and family, there are more restricted shared assumptions and meaning constructions that guide and form our experience. For example, the family domain contains a sense of shared history and future and a sense of "biography." When we marry, we enter a process of "biographical fusion" in which we not only share experiences but increasingly share a common way of typifying and explaining those experiences (Berger & Kellner, 1964).

The way actors explain or *typify* (e.g., Schutz, 1967) their experience, both in the lifeworld and in the more restricted frames of reference, is the subject matter for the social analysis of meaning. These typifications allow us to understand (*verstehen*) the way meanings are constructed and explained to others in the shared lifeworld.

The principal method of contextual understanding is not positivistic measurement but *hermeneutics*. Technically, hermeneutics refers to the interpretation of textual materials. The technique is currently applied to the contextualized actor's language reports and activities. But hermeneutics is not just a technique of analysis. In addition, it is a way the researcher can, to some degree, experience what the actor experiences:

> *Hermeneutics* is both a form of experience and grammatical analysis at the same time. . . . The quasi-inductive course of the hermeneutic sciences is based on the specific capacity of ordinary language, which makes it possible for the function of general categories to be communicated indirectly in a concrete life context. On this foundation the language of the hermeneutic interpreter adapts itself in the course of interpretation to the life experience concentrated around individual meaning. (Habermas, 1970, pp. 162–163)

Thus, hermeneutics offers an openness, sensitivity, and adaptability to the meanings in ordinary language and context of the actor as opposed to the rigidity of a priori techniques such as used in positivism.

Because the focus is clearly on the ways in which actors typify and construct meanings for their family activities, quantitative, statistical data are viewed as largely useless. Quantitative approaches involve use of previously established categories and counting of frequencies within ranges of those categories (strongly agree, agree somewhat, etc.). The result is only mildly interesting to the phenomenologists, to the degree that those categories are indeed the constructs or typifications used by actors. For the "public" everyday world, it is the role of the sociological phenomenologists to discover the typifications used by actors so that they may then be investigated by sociologists. In the more "private" realm of the family, more open and sensitive approaches must be used to discover the typifications and understandings employed by the family members.

In the past 20 years, it appears that phenomenology of the family has increasingly merged with the microinteractionist approach to the family (e.g., Gubrium & Holstein, 1993). Sociological phenomenologists, ethnomethodologists, and interactionists view theory not as a deductive tool but as an open and sensitizing set of concepts that initially guide the researcher but that are constantly altered as interactional research proceeds.

## Empirical Applications

We examine two areas of study in which symbolic interactionists have contributed to an explanation. The first area entails research on the proposition we earlier derived that "The greater the diversification of roles, the greater the role strain." We examine this proposition as it applies to working mothers' role strain. The second area of application is the study of aggression in dating.

### ROLE STRAIN AND WORKING MOTHERS

As a research question, our derived proposition is of some interest. Indeed, it provides one of the two major perspectives on the role strain experienced by working mothers. In the study of working mothers, two relatively simple conceptual hypotheses have been developed. One perspective is sometimes referred to as *enhancement theory* (Marks, 1977). The enhancement hypothesis is based on the assumption that multiple roles lead to an enhancement of role performance in any given role and to lower role strain. The logic behind this claim is that multiple roles allow the person to gain more skills, experience, and coping strategies. These greater skills can be transferred by a person from one role to another so that the ability to competently perform any role is enhanced. As people gain increased competency in their roles, role strain is decreased. The other conceptual hypothesis is derived from the symbolic interaction proposition that states that "role diversification is positively related to role strain" commonly called *role overload*. This theory is based on the assumption that the more roles one has, the greater the strain. Clearly our deduction fits better with the role overload perspective.

Research on role strain among working mothers provides a less-than-clear resolution between the competing perspectives of enhancement and role overload. The dominant finding seems to be that whether a mother perceives work strain or not is related to her reported feelings of well-being and the reports of other family members (Crouter, Bumpus, Maguire, & McHale, 1999). Research reviewed by Menaghan and Parcel (1990) fails to resolve the conflicting hypotheses but does show us that there are more variables relevant to the question than is suggested in our initial derivation. Some of the most salient of these are whether the mother desires to enter the labor force, whether her husband supports her work and family intentions, and the amount of spousal support in household and family tasks. These variables are called *moderating* because they change the effect of maternal employment on role strain.

In addition to learning that more variables than simply the number of roles are necessary to explain role strain, researchers have created some valuable theoretical insights to add to our theory. Voydanoff (1987) proposed that a more processual and dynamic approach is useful for examining the relationship between employment and mother roles. She argues that there are various paths by which families may articulate the relationship between work and family roles and that these change over time. For example, the demands of small children may be so great as to create role strain with most types of employment. As the children become more self-sufficient, maternal employment may have a salutary effect. Thus, Voydanoff argues that the time dimension should be incorporated. Menaghan (1989) correctly cautions that not all roles are equally demanding and that motherhood is especially demanding. Role diversification is affected by the differing strengths and extent of role demands. White (1999) showed that the balance between family and work roles is strongly related to satisfaction with the division of household labor, which further implicates concepts such as role performance and the literature on division of labor (e.g., Voydanoff & Donnelly, 1999). Other researchers caution us that both minitheories may apply. Tiedje et al. (1990) propose that every set of roles probably has some areas of enhancement and some areas of strain and overload.

It also is worth remembering that fathers can experience strain between work and fathering roles, especially when being a good father means more than bringing home a paycheck. Alleviating strain for one family member may simply shift it to another family member. No wonder the question is commonly asked, "If both parents feel like they have to work full-time, who will take care of young children?" You can begin to imagine all sorts of answers, some of which may reduce the total role strain in a family more than others.

The dynamic interchange between empirical research and symbolic interaction theory leads us to some wariness regarding our derivation,

yet we are far from obtaining a definitive resolution to its truth or
falsity at this time. This area of application provides a clear and
important example of how theory guides research and research clari-
fies and extends theory. This interchange between theory and empirical research provides us with an illustration of the very heart of the
process of rational–empirical social science.


DATING AGGRESSION

The study of aggression in dating is one that is particularly salient
for university and college students. It is easy to assume that such acts
occur in groups less privileged than university students, but, as recent
research has shown, this would be an incorrect assumption. In addition, the notion of a hurtful act deliberately aimed at a dating partner,
a person that is supposedly liked, seems almost a contradiction. How
can we explain why such acts occur among university student couples?

Jan Stets (1992) attempts to explain dating aggression in university couples using concepts and propositions from symbolic interaction theory. Stets proposes that interactional rather than demographic
variables can explain date aggression. She argues that taking the role
of the other entails putting yourself in that person's place and feeling
and understanding the other's emotions and actions. She states that
role taking has been previously related to relationship satisfaction and
to the use of less abrasive styles in interaction. It appears that as
role taking increases by both partners in a relationship, the chances of
conflict leading to aggressive acts would decline. Following this logic,
Stets predicts that when at least one person is low in role-taking
ability, there is a higher probability for aggressive acts in dating
relationships.

The findings in Stets's study offer considerable support for this
theoretical perspective. First, interactional variables explain more of
the variance in dating aggression than do demographic variables. This
leads Stets to conclude cautiously that interaction is probably more
important in explaining and producing date aggression than background variables such as age, race, gender, and socioeconomic status.
Role taking is related not only to aggression in dating but also to the
seriousness of the aggression. The less the role-taking ability of one
partner, the greater the seriousness of aggression when it occurs.
Although complete prediction of dating aggression would require
additional variables, this research supports the contention that
symbolic interaction propositions and concepts must be part of any
such explanation.

## Implications for Intervention

Although symbolic interaction theory has been used in many intervention contexts (e.g., Boss, 1993, 1999), one of the major uses of symbolic interaction theory currently is in the area of family life education. Family life education is a professional field in which our knowledge about families is used to better educate family members. It is the belief of family life educators that by establishing more realistic expectations and enhancing the skills needed in family life, families will become more stable and healthy (e.g., Arcus, Schvaneveldt, & Moss, 1993). This perspective fits well with the basic notions of symbolic interaction.

Most of the developed world has relatively high divorce and remarriage rates. For many, remarriage is not as simple as a first marriage. Although one can divorce one's spouse, parental and kin roles and responsibilities are not so easily sundered. Indeed, many remarriages incorporate parental roles from previous families in addition to any children born into the remarriage. These stepfamilies have obstacles and stresses unlike those encountered in first marriages. One focus of family life education has been to better prepare people for the strains encountered in remarriage.

Kaplan and Hennon (1992) developed the Personal Reflections Program to assist in preparing people for remarriage. The program is intended to assist those entering a second marriage in identifying unrealistic or potentially stress-producing expectations by means of self-reflection. The theoretical orientation of Kaplan and Hennon is symbolic interaction: "Grounded in symbolic interactionism, the program includes exercises that emphasize bringing into awareness and sharing self and partner's expectations for playing roles within the structure of a remarriage and/or stepfamily" (p. 127). Thus, concepts such as self, role stress, and role enactment are central in developing this intervention program.

## Critiques and Discussion

Although symbolic interactionism enjoys great popularity among family scholars, it is not without its detractors and critics. Most interesting in this regard is that some of the more vicious attacks on parts of the theory have come from those whose work is included under the same theoretical umbrella. The critiques of structural interactionists offered by microinteractionists and vice versa contain some of the most devastating criticisms. We regard some of these as red herrings and begin this section by identifying those criticisms we believe are relatively baseless.

The branching of symbolic interactionism into the structural and interactional perspectives derived from profound differences, but with time and academic progress, we believe that at least some of the differences between these schools no longer represent valid criticisms. First, is social behavior mainly created by social structural norms or by interactional role making? To a large extent, the contemporary interactional theorists (e.g., Turner & Colomy, 1987) have moved to increasingly include macrostructural elements in their theories, and the macrotheorists have witnessed the interactional emergence of relatively new social structures, such as cohabitation. We think it is now clear to most scholars that there are some norms and roles in every society that are clear and strictly sanctioned and as a result provide little room for role making. There are many other roles and norms that are less clearly defined and are sanctionless (e.g., grandparental roles, mother-in-law role), providing room for individuals to make roles. Thus, we see both perspectives as valid and necessarily complementary for a truly useful analysis of social behavior. The two major critiques associated with this debate have been that the structuralists put forth an oversocialized conception of humans and that the interactionists overestimate the actor's influence in creating roles and downplay structural constraints. In our view, for any given social role, there are degrees of truth to each of these criticisms based on the clarity and strength of the norms for the role.

Although symbolic interactionists agree that perceived clarity of and consensus about roles have important consequences, they do not agree about how common clarity and consensus are. The structuralists believe that social meanings and behavioral expectations are clearer and more widely shared than do adherents to the other varieties of the theory. Perhaps people in relationships usually do have a pretty good idea about reciprocal roles and do not struggle to define situations. Other symbolic interactionists, however, place relatively more emphasis on the necessity of people to create meaning and order as situations and relationships unfold. And, the enactment of roles may depend more on the coming together of unique personalities than on a single generalized formula or script for all actors.

For example, suppose that you marry a spouse who has adolescent or young adult children from a previous marriage. To what extent would you feel like you know in advance how to play the stepparent role with these new children, in terms of power, emotion, or communication? How sure would they be about how to interact with you? It may very well be that some family circumstances are not clearly defined, and that actors must therefore improvise. Therefore, one way to resolve this dispute among symbolic interactionists is to seek and specify the conditions under which each is correct.

The ongoing construction or reconstruction of meaning may be most important in times of rapid social change. When relationships of a particular kind are fairly new and uncommon in the collective historical experience of a population (or in the biographical experience of the actors themselves), the search for meaning and order is likely to be a process with some duration. One way that you might judge which aspects of family life are ill defined is to visit a major bookstore and explore titles in the family or relationships section. If there are a variety of self-help or "how-to" books on a particular topic, this suggests that social norms and meanings are somewhat ambiguous. After all, if almost everybody already knows how to act when the topic becomes relevant in their lives, there would be a small market for books that provide advice.

A second area of disagreement between these two perspectives that we believe fails as a valid criticism of either is the argument about qualitative versus quantitative methods of data collection. Again, we see this dispute as being resolved by the earlier pragmatists, such as William James (1975). Indeed, this argument is only unresolvable when it becomes a metaphysical argument about which method is "true," similar to asking how many angels fit on the head of a pin. Most researchers now agree that there are research questions that are best addressed by qualitative methods and those that are best addressed by quantitative methods. If we are interested in how people in specific situations feel, perceive, and experience, then qualitative methods are appropriate; if we ask questions about how many people behave in a certain way or what most people do, then quantitative methods are appropriate. If we want to know why young people find cohabitation appealing as an added step toward marriage, we would start with in-depth observation and talk. But if we want to know what proportion of young people who finish university then cohabit, we would use quantitative methods. Many times both methods can fruitfully be used in a multimethod approach to answer a research question. Thus, we see no critique of substance for either school of thought.

One of the principal criticisms of symbolic interactionism as a whole is that the concepts it offers are vague and poorly defined. Although this may be a problem in some cases, researchers such as Burr, Leigh, et al. (1979) are careful to define and elaborate their terms. Still others, such as Turner (e.g., 1970), have argued that some terms such as *role* should not be defined at the outset, but rather one should allow definitions to arise from how the terms are used.

Certainly, such a strategy has a long history in mathematics, in which certain terms are considered "primitive" or are defined as tautologies, such as "equals" and "identity."

Symbolic interactionists in the family field no doubt sometimes offer vague and ill-defined concepts. But the root of this criticism probably lies in the fact that symbolic interactionism is so fecund. It has given birth to many variants. Critics would say that some of this richness is supplied by vagueness and ambiguity in the original concepts. There is some truth to that claim, but today's symbolic interactionists seem to be on the way to rectifying this shortcoming. Indeed, it may be that every theory starts out containing ambiguity and vagueness, and it is the task of future theorists to refine the efforts of the forebears. We must also remember that symbolic interactionism emphasizes the processes by which meaning is constructed. Groups of family scientists are meaning makers just as families are. Both sets of actors can be vague and ambiguous while the process unfolds. Ultimately, of course, what scientists say about families should bear some connection to what family members say about them.

Another major question about symbolic interaction theory is whether a symbol-specific theory can ever be nomothetic, or cross-culturally relevant. The interpretation of behavior in symbolic inter-actionism relies in large part on the meaning of symbols and context to the actors. Not only does the actor's interpretation depend on his or her culture and situation, it is also subjective. If our explanations are always subjective and context and symbol specific, can symbolic interactionism ever amount to more than low-level interpretations constrained by the culture and time in which they occur? Another way of posing this question is to ask if symbolic interactionism can generate statements such as the general laws associated with scientific theory. This criticism is a fairly easy one for symbolic interactionists to answer, because the propositions provided by scholars such as Turner (e.g., Turner & Colomy, 1987) and Burr (e.g., Burr, Leigh, et al., 1979) are clearly not culture or period specific. In addition, social psychology has a long history of scientific (and objective) study of the uniformities in subjective interpretations, such as attitudes and attributions.

The problems surrounding the concepts of mind and self are more serious. The concept of mind incorporates aspects of neurophysiology that are not rooted in the organ of the brain. Indeed, even Mead (1934) was aware of the reflex arc (muscle memory) and the problems it provided his concept. The fact is that the mind, like our notions of group and society, turns out not to be a "thing" or "organ" but a complex system for which we have a name. Most social scientists have not had to confront this conceptual problem, but when they do they will find that it provides the same problems inherent in the question "Are families just a collection of individual members or are families something more than just the individual members?" This is a very old question in philosophy and social science. The early pragmatists, especially William James, paid a great deal of attention to this question. We do not pretend that others or even that we have resolved this question to the satisfaction of those who believe that a function must be attached to an organ that performs that function.

The problems with the concept of mind carry over to the concept of self as a construction of the reflexive activity of the mind. Just because humans act (I) and are able to see themselves as actors (me) does not necessarily imply the existence of self. Because the mind is unidentified and self is a construct of mind, self raises the same problems as our concept of mind. Particularly when you add in the notion of developmental change and maturation, the notions of self and identity become difficult to pin down. At least one symbolic interactionist, Turner (1970), does not use the concept of self but prefers the concept of "self-conception," for it appears more fluid and less of an immutable structure than does the concept of the self.

LaRossa and Reitzes (1993) mention the criticism that symbolic interaction theory has failed to deal effectively with emotions. The absence of emotions, feelings, and affect as major concepts has in some ways limited the theory's conceptual utility. Symbolic interactionists invariably discuss an actor's feeling as part of the definition of the situation but leave the details of conceptualizing the type and degree of the actor's emotional experience to psychologists and psychotherapists. LaRossa and Reitzes expressed some optimism that this oversight is being addressed, but we do not share their opinion. None of the major contemporary theorists, such as Turner (1970), seem inclined to tackle this question. Furthermore, it may be that dealing with the subject of emotion would move symbolic interactionism into a more subjectivist position. Nevertheless, it is possible to clearly theorize about emotions and their symbolic significance. Family members certainly look for cues about how other family members are feeling, and they communicate with each other as if those feelings matter. Indeed, mixed emotions may be common in families. What parent or adolescent has not worried about his or her feelings concerning independence, trust, and loss when the adolescent first leaves for college? Is this occasion ever 100% cheerful? Perhaps we will see in the future more family theories about ambivalent emotions and attitudes between spouses, across generations, and among siblings (e.g., Lüscher & Pillemer, 1998).

Some critics of symbolic interactionism see the theory as too focused on the individual and "self as agent," ignoring the causal efficacy of social institutions and social structure. Although some of these criticisms can be dismissed as more feuding between the structuralists and interactionists, some of the critiques apply to both schools of thought. For example, the notion of norms is central to both the structuralists and interactionists, but neither examine the development and change of institutional norms. The structuralists take institutional norms for granted with the axiom that "Society preceded the individual." Interactionists see norms as emerging from interaction but fail to explain how it is that social institutions exist with relative permanence.

Additionally, we could accuse symbolic interactionists of losing their way. The early pragmatists and Mead (1934) took the interpretation of sign and gesture as central to their study of human behavior. Among today's symbolic interactionists, we seldom hear theoretical discussions about the nature of signs and gestures. Today, in discussions of interpretation and meaning it might be needed to incorporate "schematic processing" from psychology into the concept of "framing" as well as the work of linguists and contemporary semiotics.

Lastly, some have voiced concern about the continual emphasis by symbolic interactionists on the person's construction of meaning even in quantitative measures such as marital satisfaction. These critics worry that the *behavioral* sciences are forgetting that the observation of behavior may be significantly different than phenomenological reports by actors. Indeed, Gottman and Notarius (2000) voice such a concern in relation to the study of marriage: "Observational measures will always be [the] most informative data source we will ever get about process, which will be the richest source we will ever have for describing and building theory" (p. 942).

## Conclusion

There can be little doubt that symbolic interactionism has had an influence on how we study families. Both role theorists and interactionists have contributed greatly to our understanding of families. Thus far, however, although interactionists' claims about the symbolic nature of human interaction have sensitized researchers, they have not tackled many critical questions, such as how patterns evolve as lasting rather than momentary and idiosyncratic. Within symbolic interactionism, role theory undoubtedly offers the most formal theoretical propositions and conceptual definitions. All four variants that we have discussed offer promise as we move away from dogmatic divisions toward a more systematic and thorough investigation of which and what type of family interactions lead to and sustain longer-term social patterns of behavior within the family.

## Suggested Readings

Burr, W., Leigh, G., Day, R., & Constantine, J. (1979). Symbolic interaction and the family. In W. Burr, R. Hill, I. Nye, & I. Reiss (Eds.), *Contemporary theories about the family* (Vol. 2, pp. 42–111). New York: Free Press.

*This is an excellent propositional approach to symbolic interactionism. The diagrams within this chapter should assist anyone in thinking about role variables.*

LaRossa, R., & Reitzes, D. C. (1993). Symbolic interactionism and family studies. In P. Boss, W. Doherty, R. LaRossa, W. Schumm, & S. Steinmetz (Eds.), *Sourcebook of family theories and methods: A contextual approach* (pp. 135–163). New York: Plenum.

*This more recent chapter on symbolic interactionism is especially good on the microinteractional variants.*

# 4

# The Family Life Course Development
# Framework

Tim and Rebecca are expecting their first child. They have just attended their first prenatal class and are driving home in their car discussing what they learned. At one point in the class, the instructor divided the class by gender and asked the prospective fathers and mothers to write down three things that they thought about on hearing that they were to become parents. Tim says to Rebecca, "You know, I was surprised that every one of the guys had thought of taking out life insurance or getting more life insurance!" He continued, "Some of those guys are barely shaving and a few must be around 50 years old. Yet they all said life insurance." Rebecca replied, "I guess a really important part of being a father is still being a 'provider.'" "Yeah," said Tim, "but what I was astounded by was that these guys are all different ages, races, and backgrounds, yet they all had similar ideas as to what becoming a father means."

Tim has discovered an important element in what family development and life course scholars study as the "transition to parenthood." For years, scholars thought variables such as "taking out life insurance" were predicted by the age of a person. What Tim (and family and life course developmental theorists) noticed is that it is not the age of the person that matters but where the person is in his or her family's development. Young children are dependent and require lots of parental time. The loss of one spouse's income would represent a severe burden for most families. But the impact of this loss of income is dramatically different at each stage of family development. For families with infants, the loss might mean reliance on day care and less parental attention from the remaining parent. For families with adolescent children, it might mean restrictions in teenage recreation and the necessity for after-school work to help the family. In other words, it is the family stage that is important, not the chronological age of the family members.

Family life course development theory focuses on the systematic and patterned changes experienced by families as they move through stages and events of their family life course. Family development is not to be confused with theories about individual development, such as those offered by psychologists (e.g., Erikson, Freud, Piaget). Although family development theorists acknowledge the importance of individual development, the development of the family as a "group" of interacting individuals and organized by social norms is their major focus.

Of all the theories you will find in this book, family development theory is the only one that emerged out of a specific interest in families. All the other theories have broader applications to other social groups and social structures. For example, both exchange theory and conflict theory can be applied to competition between labor and management as well as to relations between husbands and wives. Family development theory, on the other hand, has focused exclusively on the family.

As a theory, family development has several other unique dimensions that characterize its focus. Family development/life course theory incorporates time and history as major components. Although other theories may include time in the measurement of change, they do not involve discussion of the theoretical nuances of the conceptualization and measurement of time. Family development theorists have discussed time as measured by clocks, social processes, and event histories (Rodgers, 1973). A second unique dimension of family development theory is the focus on forms of family change. Family development deals with the changing content of social roles in the family as well as macroscopic changes in the membership structure of the family. Of all the current theories about the family, family development theory is unique in emphasizing the dimensions of time and change.

Although some scholars might argue that family development and life course are two unique frameworks, we argue that they represent slight variations on a singular theme of the groups' change and development over time. Life course theory has had only one major statement in regard to the family (Bengtson & Allen, 1993). On the other hand, family development theory has a long and well-established history as a theory of the family. However, the two statements in the 1993 *Sourcebook on Family Theories and Methods* were written independently from one another but reached a startling convergence of similar and complementary ideas (e.g., Bengtson & Allen, 1993; Rodgers & White, 1993). We therefore treat them as representing a common framework.

## Intellectual Traditions

Family development theory has gone through three distinct phases of maturation. The first phase was characterized by the rise of the idea of the family life cycle. Researchers viewed families as having a *life course,* or what in biological studies was commonly referred to as a "life cycle." Similar to a biological organism, the family group went through analogous processes of birth, growth, maintenance, shrinkage, and eventually death. We do not know the exact origins of the family life cycle concept, but we do know it has a long history. Mattessich and Hill (1987) supply a genealogy that traces the rudiments of the notion back to 1777. The idea of the family life cycle appears in the work of rural sociologists such as Lively (1932) and Loomis (1936) during the Great Depression. Through the work of Paul Glick (1947), the notion of family life cycle entered social demography as a descriptive tool. This first phase was the *descriptive phase* of the theory's maturation.

The second phase of the theory's maturation was characterized by the *conscious formulation* of the contemporary theory. This phase began after World War II with work on family stress by Hill (1949) and a textbook by Duvall (1957). But it was the chapter by Hill and Rodgers (1964) that truly provided the first systematic statement of the approach. In their statement, the family is composed of social roles and relationships that change with each stage of the family. Hill and Rodgers also identified three levels of analysis for the study of families over time: the individual–psychological, the interactional–associational, and the societal–institutional. The approach first systematized by Hill and Rodgers received further expansion in Rodgers' (1973) book. He suggested abandoning the family life cycle concept in favor of a concept oriented toward the life course, the family career. Aldous (1978, 1996) further developed the notion of the family career. She conceptualized the family career as containing subcareers such as the sibling career, the marital career, and the parental career, all influenced by careers external to the family such as the educational and occupational careers. This middle phase could be characterized as the phase in which the theory was first systematized and the family career concept emerged as preferable to the family life cycle concept.

The third and most recent phase of theoretical development may be viewed as a reaction to new techniques for data analysis and some strong critiques of the theory. In 1979, several scholars launched critiques of the family life cycle concept (Nock, 1979; Schram, 1979; Spanier, Sauer, & Larzelere, 1979). Note that Rodgers (1973) and

Aldous (1978) had already abandoned the family life cycle concept in favor of the life course oriented family career concept. Klein and Aldous (1979) represent the lone response to these critiques. In 1980, Holman and Burr relegated family development theory to the status of one of the "minor" theoretical approaches in the study of the family. Holman and Burr (1980) argued that what little theoretical formulation had been achieved in family development theory in the 1960s had been largely subsumed under the aegis of life course analysis in the 1970s (p. 733).

Despite the epitaph by Holman and Burr (1980) and the critiques by Nock (1979), Schram (1979), and Spanier et al. (1979), Mattessich and Hill maintained the notion of family development unfolding through invariant and universal stages linked to some inherent family dynamic. Although the conception of development proposed by Mattessich and Hill (1987) has met with great criticism (Bengtson & Allen, 1993; Rodgers & White, 1993; White, 1991), it nonetheless provided some basis for Aldous (1990) to argue that family development theory and life course analysis could not be considered to be the same. Aldous (1990) analyzes differences between the life course and family development approaches and argues that the major difference is that the life course approach is focused on the individual whereas the family development approach is focused on the family level of analysis. According to Aldous, neither approach deserves to be called a scientific theory.

Contrary to Aldous (1990), White (1991) argues that family development is a scientific theory containing definitions and general propositions implying a formal model of the process of development. He couples methodological distinctions in *event history analysis* (Allison, 1984; Tuma & Hannan, 1984) with an expanded conception of levels of analysis in his formalization of the theory. More recently, Rodgers and White (1993) argue that the "old" perspective of families moving through deterministic, invariant stages is moribund. They revise and simplify the concepts in the theory and produce formal propositions. In this latest phase of theoretical development, family development scholars have attempted to revise and reconstruct the theory so as to answer the relevant comments of critics as well as incorporate new methodological techniques. This latest phase can be characterized as the *formal* phase of the family development theory's maturation.

Life course analysis evolved from a sociological concern about the contingent events experienced by individuals over the life course. For example, Hogan (1978) demonstrated that the sequential pattern of events such as starting the first job and finishing one's education are related to later life course events such as divorce. Life course analysis received a major boost with the popularization of "event history analysis" (e.g., Allison, 1984). Aldous (1990) discussed the major difference between the family development and life course perspectives as being that family development focused on the "family group" level of analysis, whereas life course focused on the "individual." This distinction certainly did not stand up in the work by Cowan and Cowan (1992) on the transition to parenthood. Furthermore, the first formal theoretical statement related to the family features multiple levels of analysis, including both the individual level and family group level. Rodgers and White (1993) supported the notion that family development theory is also a multileveled approach. Many of the propositions developed by both teams were extremely similar. As a result, these approaches seem to be merging into a single, stronger, and more comprehensive framework.

In summary, the major behavioral focus of family life course development theory is on the patterned changes in the family group over time. Family development theory has gone through three phases of maturation: a descriptive phase in which stages of the family life cycle were used to study families; a systematizing phase in which the theory received its first conscious statement as a theory; and an ongoing, formal phase in which, as a response to criticisms and new methodologies, the theory has been formally stated as propositions and formal models. This last "formal" phase has also allowed for the unification of life course and family development theory. This more complete theoretical framework continues to seek to explain family change over time.

## Focus and Scope Assumptions

Many theories require basic assumptions about the nature of individual motivation (exchange theory) or about human nature (conflict theory). Family development theory relies on basic assumptions about the family. These assumptions are not restricted to the family group but extend to the broader fabric of the social institution of the family. Here, we enumerate the basic assumptions that provide the foundation for family development theory. These are the assumptions of multiple levels of analysis, the definition of the family group as a semipermeable unit, and a multidimensional view of time.

*Developmental processes are inevitable and important in understanding families.* This assumes that individual family members, the interaction between family members, the structure of the family, and the norms composing expectations about family roles all change with the passage of time. Individuals age, relationships have duration, family stages are traversed, and family structure changes. The changing roles and expectations for different stages of family are viewed as essential to an understanding of the family.

Family developmentalists, from the first systematic statements (Aldous, 1978; Hill & Rodgers, 1964; Rodgers, 1973), have suggested that families be analyzed on different levels of analysis (e.g., individual family member, group, institution). Most theorists start with the family as a *social group*. Below the family as a social group are subgroup *relationships* such as the husband–wife relationship and the sibling relationship. And below the relationship level is the *individual* family member, who experiences his or her family and the relationships in it. If we move up a level from the family group, we find relatively homogeneous *aggregate clusters* of families and social norms that are structured by social class and ethnicity. And moving up levels once again, we find that each social system maintains general *institutional* norms and conventions about the family. Some of these norms are codified as legal expectations, such as those found in child neglect or child abuse laws, but more often the norms are less formal. These general social norms represent the level of analysis of the family as a *social institution*. The institutional level of analysis is generally the one we refer to when we talk about "the family" and is the level on which we often conduct cross-cultural comparisons (the United States family compared with the Japanese family).

A second major assumption that family development scholars make is that the *family group is affected by all the levels of analysis,* including the social norms of the larger society and the social norms of clusters such as social class. For example, the norms about techniques of child discipline are related to social class as well as to the codifications of the larger social system. Component lower levels, such as the nature of a sibling relationship or an individual disability, also affect the family group.

*The family is a semiclosed or semipermeable group.* The intermingling and integration of effects on the family group have led family development scholars to adopt a definition of the family as semiclosed and semipermeable. Although the family group sets up distinctive boundaries usually demarcated spatially by household or domicile, the effects of the larger society permeate these boundaries. This semipermeable nature of the family group is directly cited in some definitions of the family (Aldous, 1978; Rodgers, 1973) and is referred to indirectly by others who incorporate social norms both external and internal to the family group. For example, Rodgers and White (1993) and White (1991) defined the family as a social group that contains at least one parent–child (intergenerational) relationship and is organized and governed by social norms, many of which are based on expectations by people and groups external to families.

All family life course developmental theorists assume that *time is multidimensional.* To understand this assumption, we need to examine our notion of time. Time is a monotonic process—once a moment in time is gone, it doesn't come back. Time is measured by the *periodicity* of some recurring event. In ancient Greece, time was measured by a sundial. During the Renaissance, time was measured by the dripping water in water clocks. During the industrial revolution, time was measured by gears turning in mechanical clocks. Today, time is measured by the entropy, or decay of an element, in an "atomic" clock. All of these ways of measuring time are attempts to make sure that there is an equal interval of time between each event on the clock. For example, the gears in your wristwatch are the same distance apart. The problem is that there is absolutely no guarantee that the experience of time is so orderly (Daly, 1996). Furthermore, because all our methods of measuring time rely on recurring discrete events, there is no guarantee that time is continuous. Even the assumption that time moves at a uniform rate, as measured by gears in your wristwatch, is counter to much of our experience. Most of you have experienced an hour spent in an enjoyable pursuit as "flying by" or an hour spent in a dull and boring pursuit as "dragging on." In other words, your experience of time is perhaps not as regimented as your wristwatch would lead you to believe. Not only does your experience of time deny the orderliness of your wristwatch, but most of us use our family experiences as a separate way to divide up time. Thus, we might discuss with our family what we did in 1990 and 1991. More likely, we might abandon the calendar notion of time in favor of listing events, such as "when we first married," "before your sister was born," or "just after your father died." Interestingly, these events lack periodicity for any one family (you only expect your sister to be born once), but these experiences are commonly understood "markers" on the family life course calendar because they happen to most families over time.

This alternative conception of time is called *social process time* (Rodgers, 1973). Social, or family, process time is an important dimension of our conception of time for family scholars because social norms are tied more closely to this social process dimension of time than to calendar or wristwatch time. For instance, "when you get married" is tied to "finishing school" more closely than to any given calendar date. Other social and biological dimensions of time are age and historical period. Fortunately, because we conceptualize time as monotonic and only flowing in one direction, all of the different ways of conceptualizing time can be organized into temporal maps of our life course and that of our family. A socially important stage can be identified by the events such as "after our father's death" but "before our sister got married." Because family members usually recall the calendar dates of such major events, we can trace the multiple time lines of calendar and family process time. For family development theory, the family process dimension of time is critical to understanding and explaining family change.

It is interesting to note that of all the family theories, family development theory makes few if any basic assumptions about the individual. Rather, family development theory is true to its focus on the family group. Individuals are viewed as subcomponents of the family group, which is not merely the aggregate of individual members. The family group is affected by institutional norms that, along with the characteristics of individual family members and their relationships, determine the social organization of the family group.

## Concepts

### FAMILY CHANGE AND DEVELOPMENT

Early family developmentalists were not clear about the distinction between change and development. Indeed, some seem to have used the two terms interchangeably. But with the rise of child development theory in the 1940s and 1950s came a new concern among family developmentalists that development meant more than all of family change. Child developmentalists such as Piaget brought the notion of *ontogenetic* change to the forefront of their discipline and likewise raised the issue for family development scholars. Although the exact nature of family development has been a long-standing issue, recently the notion of developmental change has received significant scholarly attention (e.g., Baltes & Nesselroade, 1984; Dannefer, 1984; Dannefer & Perlmutter, 1991; Featherman & Lerner, 1985; Mattessich & Hill, 1987). The outcome of all this attention is that two distinct versions of development have emerged. Child development focuses on "ontogenetic development," which is founded on the genetic capacity of the species to progressively learn language and thought. A second, sociological meaning of development is focused on the traversing of normatively expected family events. Although there have been some attempts to unite these two versions, such as the definition of development proposed by Mattessich and Hill (1987), most developmental scholars shy away from the teleological and moralistic overtones inherent in an ontogenetic view of family development.

Both White (1991) and Rodgers and White (1993) argued for the sociological view of development. Although Bengtson and Allen (1993) clearly acknowledge ontogenetic development of the individual (rather than group) in their propositions, the great bulk of their propositions are either interactional (ontogenetic development combined with social–environmental factors) or sociological. White and Rodgers (1993) incorporate the proposal by Featherman (1985) that development is linked to the stage of the family and the duration of time the family has been in a certain family stage. White (1991) defines development similarly, arguing that family transitions are dependent on the stage a family is in and the duration of time they have been in that stage. According to the sociological approach, family development is a process following age- and stage-graded social norms. Unlike the rigid stage sequencing of ontogeneticists such as Piaget, family developmental stages may be sequenced in a variety of ways, however, and family developmental change is only one type of many possible changes a family may experience. Of course, family development theorists believe that developmental change is an important form of family change.

## POSITIONS, NORMS, AND ROLES

We cannot forget that our families are embedded in kinship structures. Indeed, it is the positions in the kinship structure that supply our relatives. A *position* in the kinship structure is defined by gender, marriage or blood relations, and generational relations. The basic positions within the family are husband, wife, father, mother, son, daughter, brother, and sister. From these basic positions other society-specific positions can be defined. For example, the North American term *uncle* usually refers to brothers of either your father or mother (father's brother, mother's brother).

*Norms* are social rules that govern group and individual behavior. For example, the incest taboo is a strong and pervasive social rule forbidding mating between certain family members. Norms may be rules about the way something is to be accomplished at various stages of the family and at various ages for an individual. Thus, many norms are age and stage graded. For instance, you do not apply the same rules to a toddler that you do to a teenager.

A family *role* is defined as "all the norms attached to one of the kinship positions." In most societies, the role of mother, for example, entails the norm of nurturance of the young. Because positions are defined structurally, however, the content of a role (the norms) may change from society to society or ethnic subculture to ethnic subculture. And like the norms that compose them, social roles may be *age and stage graded*. For example, the nurturant role for a mother with an infant is quite different from that for a mother with adolescent children. The use of role concepts in family development theories is virtually the same as it is in symbolic interactionism, and, as we will see later in this chapter, developmental theorists differ among themselves in their emphasis on structural versus interactional views of roles just as symbolic interactionists differ among themselves on this point.

FAMILY STAGE

A *family stage* is an interval of time in which the structure and interactions of role relationships in the family are noticeably and qualitatively distinct from other periods of time (Aldous, 1996). A stage at the group level represents a pattern of role interaction between family members distinct from those stages that precede and follow it. The stage is usually inferred from events that indicate a change in the membership of the family or the way in which members are spatially and interactionally organized. For example, launching a child into adulthood does not mean the end of the parental role but a change based on the spatial and interactional organization of members.

TRANSITIONS

Transitions are shifts from one family stage to another. A family's career is composed of many such transitions between stages. Magrabi and Marshall (1965) were the first to conceptualize family transitions as a branching process; others such as Klein, Borne, Jache, and Sederberg (1979) have further developed the notion. The concept that has emerged is that family transitions viewed over time consist of paths taken and not taken. For example, at any one time a married couple may stay married or get divorced, one of the spouses may die, or they might have a child. Each of the possible events would move the family to a new series of possible alternative transitions. The process charted over time would look like a tree with many branches; the path that any one family takes would be one series of branches.

Transitions from one family stage to another are indicated by the events between stages. Family stages and events are experienced as "on time" or "off time" with the expected timing for these events. For instance, giving birth to a child when your postadolescent children are leaving home would be "off time." In general, the age- and stage-graded social norms supply timing expectations. Not only might events be "off time," but sequences of events and stages might be "disorganized." For example, the sequence of getting married before the birth of your first child is normatively organized, whereas a premarital birth would be departure from the normative expectations for sequencing marriage and births.

## DEVELOPMENTAL TASKS

Early developmentalists thought transitions were linked to developmental tasks that arise in the life course of individuals and families. The successful achievement of these tasks was thought to lead to happiness and success with later tasks (Havighurst, 1948). The notion of developmental tasks was an attempt to integrate age- and stage-graded social norms with the ontogenetic maturation of individual family members. However well intentioned the concept, it has fallen into a myriad of difficulties. The notion of developmental tasks has been criticized as making nonscientific value judgments about what constitutes "success." In addition, the notion of developmental tasks is tied to a preformational, ontogenetic view of child development that has largely been rejected by those studying the social group of the family. As a result, researchers early on redefined the concept as a set of norms (role expectations) arising at a particular stage of the family career (Hill & Rodgers, 1964; Rodgers, 1973, p. 51). Rodgers and White (1993) posited that the task concept is redundant with the age- and stage-graded notions of norm and role and no longer include it among the core concepts of the theory; the concept also is not central in the work of Bengtson and Allen (1993).

## FAMILY LIFE COURSE (FAMILY CAREER, FAMILY LIFE CYCLE)

For most developmentalists, the concept of the *family life course* has replaced the earlier concept of *family life cycle*. Some theorists (Aldous, 1996; Rodgers, 1973) have attempted to replace the notion of life cycle of the family with the concept of *family career*. This "replacement" has so far failed to become popular with scholars and students. The original concept of family life cycle contained the connotation that family life somehow "cycled." This was not the meaning life course theorists meant to convey. Rather, development as a process is viewed more like a career, in which current stages are affected by the past, but there is no teleological end to the process that would bring it full circle. The family's life course is composed of all the events and periods of time (stages) between events traversed by a family. For families in any one society, such as North America, we find that stage-graded norms are indicated by the sequence of events followed by most families (White, 1987, 1998). For example, the great majority of people get married before having a child, and for most people a premarital birth is considered out of the normative sequence. Every culture and society has a range of both variations and deviations from the normative expectations.

NORMATIVE VARIATIONS AND DEVIATIONS

The extent of accepted *variations* in the family life course indicates the strength of the norms within any given birth cohort and historical period. The stronger and more rigid the norms regarding how families are to live their life course, the less accepted are variations. For example, the Chinese government's one child policy represents an official institutional norm regulating how many children families may have and is buttressed by strong negative sanctions. The difference between variation and deviation at the aggregate level of analysis is that variation about a measure of central tendency (mode or median) is random, whereas deviation is nonrandom and systematic. *Deviation* by large numbers of families from a normative career sequence is viewed as a source of social change. Clearly, people only deviate from the normative path when they perceive that there are rewards for doing so. Once an individual or family is out of sequence and off time with the expectations in a society, it is often difficult to resume a normative course. Sometimes, such situations arise from individual mistakes; these would be random. Other times, large numbers of families seem to deviate from social norms, such as at present with the popularity of premarital cohabitation. If such deviation becomes systematic (it is one as opposed to many forms of alternatives to marriage) and larger and larger numbers of people follow this "new" path, at some point the social norms shift so that it becomes deviant *not* to live together before marriage as part of mate selection.

One of the reasons such deviance comes about is to align family timing and sequencing norms with those of other institutions such as education and work. In the past few decades, there has been increased pressure from the labor force for higher skills and more education. This pressure to get more education coupled with the sequencing norm of "finish your education before you get married" has resulted in the delay of marriage for younger people. But with the delay in marriage, another problem arises. A dominant norm in mate selection is that women seek mates who are the same age or older, and men seek mates the same age or younger. As a result, older men have a higher probability of marriage and, as they marry, there are fewer of them available for younger women. If women delay relationship formation until 27 or later, then there are fewer available men their same age or older. Cohabitation becomes a way to establish a residential intimate relationship without entering marriage. Indeed, as both genders delay marriage to finish school and start careers, cohabitation represents a way to enter an intimate relationship with a potential spouse but without the constricting roles of husband and wife and without pressure to have children. Indeed, the norms would suggest that before people would ask, "When are you two going to have a child?" they would ask, "When are you two going to get married?" Thus, social change comes about because individuals seek to align their sequencing of family stages with the sequencing and timing norms of nonfamily institutions (such as education and occupation). These cross-institutional norms, such as "finish your education before you get married," encourage systematic deviation in family careers and ultimately social change.

## Propositions

Rodgers and White (1993) caution that propositions that might be reasonable for one level of analysis might not be as accurate for other levels of analysis. For example, we can reasonably talk about an individual's "motivation," but it might be unreasonable to assume that groups or social institutions are "motivated" in the same way as individuals. It is usually more appropriate to move propositions from higher to lower levels of analysis than the reverse. Thus, we focus our examples of propositions from family development theory on the more general institutional and group levels of analysis.

> Family development is a group process regulated by societal timing and sequencing norms.

This proposition asserts that family development is a process defined by social norms. Because norms are different from culture to culture, the process of family development may be different from culture to culture. We have used the North American norm regarding premarital births as an illustration of a sequencing norm. In many cultures, such as the Polynesian culture, a premarital birth was expected before marriage and considered a necessary step in mate selection. How could a prospective husband discern the reproductive capacity of a woman if she had not demonstrated her fertility? This proposition also asserts that because family development is regulated by social norms, the central focus for understanding this process must be on the institution of the family. The institution of the family is composed of all those norms that regulate and define family life within a culture or social system. The assertion that the process is governed by social norms involves the assumption that family development is not a form of biological preformationism or ontogenesis. Rather, social systems are viewed as defining the norms of family development, and like all social norms, those regulating the process of family development change over historical time.

Although timing and sequencing norms are interrelated, research suggests that the sequence (order) of stages or events is more strongly regulated than the timing of stages or events (Hogan, 1978; Modell, 1980; White, 1987). People appear more likely to attempt to maintain the order of events, such as "first comes love, then comes marriage, then comes Suzy with the baby carriage," than they are to maintain a set number of years between these events. What this suggests is that the family career as a sequence of stages or events is probably more important in explaining family behavior than is the timing. Indeed, military men returning after World War II were conscious of needing to compress the timing of family events but did not change the order of events or subtract events. Those pursuing advanced education, such as a medical degree, may also delay family events and then compress the time between events without changing the order.

*If a family or individual is "out of sequence" with the normative ordering of family events, the probability of later life disruptions is increased.*

Like it or not, every society must be organized. A significant part of social organization is the age and stage grading of various institutions. An often-overlooked dimension of the social fabric is that timing and sequencing norms, such as those regarding education, must be synchronized with norms in other institutions, such as work and family. If a person or family gets out of sequence within one institution, the result is that they are more likely to be thrown out of synchrony with other institutions. Most of the research in this area has suggested negative consequences for families and individuals, such as higher rates for marital disruption. There is, however, the argument that when the norms are changing, successive cohorts pursuing what is originally deviant behavior and suffering the consequences of being out of sequence or off time gradually come to represent the new dominant norm (normative succession). This new dominant norm gradually synchronizes with other institutions as they realign. A useful example of this process of normative succession is premarital cohabitation. During the 1980s, researchers invariably demonstrated negative effects for premarital cohabitation on later marital stability (e.g., Teachman & Polonko, 1990). Gwartney-Gibbs (1986) suggested that premarital cohabitation was on its way to becoming a normative stage in family development. By 1992, evidence surfaced that the most recent cohorts of cohabitants seemed to have less probability for marital disruption than their noncohabiting counterparts (Schoen, 1992).

The concept of normative succession does not preclude the widening or narrowing of acceptable life choices. For example, there has never been a specific number of children that any couple should have in America, so we cannot speak of one best number replacing another best number. Because social norms often allow a range of acceptable behaviors, we cannot say in this example that the childbearing stage has a definite acceptable duration. In some cultures, the norm is that you should have as many children as you can afford to raise, and affordability is situationally variable.

*Within the family group, family members create internal family norms.*

Within the family group, each family creates social rules such as bedtimes, rules about how much television can be watched, and rules about staying out late. The institution of the family provides the broad parameters within which families can interactively create their internal rules. For example, in North America, few parents would suggest to their children that they have multiple premarital births. The internal family norms or rules are further circumscribed by the institution of the family in that internal rules must not overly threaten institutional functions of the family. For example, parents who do not want to educate their children would probably find their children declared wards of the state. Although many of the internal family norms are not developmental in the sense of timing and sequencing norms, some clearly are. For instance, when a parent says to a child, "You can go in the canoe when you can swim," the parent is stating a sequencing rule. Or, more relevant to family relations, "You can baby-sit your brother after you demonstrate that you can responsibly stay at home by yourself." Many such norms in the family rest on the stage of individual development of the members, such as, "When you can accomplish this" or "Your grandmother can't do that for herself anymore." Thus, some of these internal norms are developmental. There are, of course, a great number of internal family norms that are not developmental and many of these could be said to be universal because they are neither age or stage graded, such as "Always tell your parents the truth."

*Interactions within the family group are regulated by the social norms constructing family roles.*

Family interactions are predictable and uniform across families because of the institutional norms and expectations regarding family roles. As we indicated previously, these norms provide the parameters within which family members can create rules unique to their family. The parameters for roles such as mother and father of young children are especially restrictive because the society at large has a tremendous stake in the reproduction and socialization of new members of society. Indeed, when mothers and fathers fail to meet these roles, emissaries of the state step in to supervise or seize the children from the parents. For example, mothers are expected to be nurturant of the young. Failure in this regard can show up in behavior disorders in the children and more seriously in an infant's failure to thrive. Less codified norms exist about parental disciplinary techniques, such as spanking and control of the children. Even the method of infant feeding—"breast or bottle"—has become the focus for normative pressures and informal sanctions from health care professionals and resource groups. In addition to the regulation of parent–child relationships, there are general social expectations regarding other family relationships, such as the sibling relationship. Siblings are expected to care for and watch out for each other. The norms constructing this sibling relationship extend into old age, when siblings rely on each other for support.

*Transitions from one family stage to another are predicted by the current stage and the duration of time spent in that stage.*

Although families move through their life course making what seem to be individual decisions about when to get married, have a child, and so on, there is a high degree of predictability for families in general. This is not surprising, because this process is largely formed by social timing and sequencing norms. Couples who are recently married have a high probability of having a child, whereas the longer the couple stays in the childless stage, the less the probability that they will have a child. These patterns of family development vary from culture to culture. Even within one culture, there may be variation. The variation within one culture demonstrates the strength of family timing and sequencing norms. For example, in at least one totalitarian state, the government has attempted rather successfully to control family size. The norms are formal and enforced with strict sanctions. In North America, our norms are less formal, and people respond more strongly to the need to be articulated with the timing and sequencing of educational and work careers.

It is useful to keep in mind that the effect of duration in a stage depends on the topic and on the stages involved. For example, it is rather obvious that the longer you have been in the child-rearing stage, the more likely you are to begin launching children into adulthood. In contrast, after the third wedding anniversary, the longer you are married, the less likely you are to divorce. So, the direction of the effect of duration in a stage on entering another stage may be positive, negative, or curvilinear.

Beyond the proposition here about one stage influencing another, developmentalists often argue that stage placement, duration in a stage, and the transition to another stage help predict or explain other things about families, such as how they function or the likelihood of problems. The empirical applications later in this chapter deal with such propositions.

*Individuals and families systematically deviate from institutional family norms to adjust their behavior to other institutional norms, such as work and education.*

The timing and sequencing norms for family transitions do not stand in isolation from other major social institutions. Indeed, in the past, religious institutions reinforced and strongly sanctioned norms about family life, and religious organizations organized their own normative content to be in conjunction with family norms. Today, the family is less buttressed by institutional religious norms but strongly forced to articulate family sequencing with sequencing in work and education. Indeed, the conjunction of timing and sequencing norms from various institutions constructs the normative life course for individuals and families. For example, an educational norm such as "Get more education" in conjunction with a cross-institutional sequencing norm such as "Finish your education before you get married" and "Get a job before you get married," all conjoin to form the normative life sequence of "Finish your education, then get a job, then get married." Although there are no formal sanctions for not following this sequence, there are informal ones. The informal sanctions are subtle; they derive from the fact that all social institutions are age and stage graded. In work, as in family, there are stages of development, such as "formative" and "consolidation" stages of career development (e.g., Voydanoff, 1987). If an individual or family becomes off time or out of sequence within one institution, its members find it increasingly difficult to meet the timing and sequencing expectations in other institutions. For example, a premarital birth does not just put one out of sequence in family life but also has distinct ramifications for meeting the timing and sequencing norms in education and work. The resulting modifications in the family, work, and educational careers make for difficulties and hardships associated with being out of synchrony with the social fabric of society and its reward systems. Of course, deviance is necessary as part of social change and adaptation to a changing society. As with premarital cohabitation, however, those in the vanguard of such adaptive deviance suffer to bring in the new normative order.

## Variations

There are three major variants of family development theory, each on a specific level of analysis. The structural perspective represented in the work of White (1991) and Rodgers and White (1993) is focused on the institutional and cross-institutional processes affecting family development. The interactional perspective represented in the work of Aldous (1978, 1990, 1996) is focused on the relationships within the group and the construction of unique family norms and roles. The third variant of family development theory is life course analysis, represented in the work of Elder (1974) and Bengtson and Allen (1993). The life course approach is focused on the individual rather than the family group. It is especially concerned with the life course from the individual's perspective rather than an institutional family perspective. Thus, the three variants represent the institutional and group levels of analysis (structural), the group and relationship levels of analysis (interactional), and the individual and institutional levels of analysis (life course).

### STRUCTURAL PERSPECTIVE

In the structural approach, commonly shared social timing and sequencing norms in a social system are emphasized. Although the structuralists admit that norms internal to the family can emerge through the interaction of family members, they emphasize the societal timing and sequencing norms that constrain any idiosyncratic emergent norms or roles. They argue that what family social scientists should be concerned with are the aggregate patterns and variations of family development within societies. Furthermore, the structuralists argue that a focus on the aggregate patterns also provides a way of addressing social change within the institution of the family as well as other institutions. The principal concept structuralists use to explain social change is cross-institutional adaptation of the timing and sequencing norms of one institution with the norms of other institutions. In their view, the institution of the family is continually adapting to align and synchronize with other institutions. Deviance from the timing and sequencing norms of one institution (often to conform to the norms in another institution) is the mechanism by which social change occurs.

As you might expect, theorists following the structural perspective of family development are also concerned with stating theoretical propositions and definitions that are cross-culturally applicable. They argue that family development is social in nature and thus varies between societies. The aggregate patterns of family development from each society provide a window on the society-specific timing and sequencing norms for each society (e.g., Kumagai, 1984). The degree of random variation in each society indicates the relative strength of the norms; the degree of systematic deviance demonstrates the direction and intensity of normative social change in each social system.

The structural perspective tends to be formal in its approach to family development theory, as is evident in the propositional statement of the theory by Rodgers and White (1993) and the use of formal models by White (1991) to model the transitions from one family stage to another. The structural school provides a readily accessible theory for demographers and cross-cultural researchers in part because the formal and abstract nature of presentation is relatively free of the cultural contents of any one society. This great strength is also a weakness in that scholars as well as students of the family typically find more immediate relevance from theories constructed about and within their own culture.

INTERACTIONAL PERSPECTIVE

The interactional approach to family development theory is identified with symbolic interaction, especially the approach proposed by Turner (1970). Essentially, those adopting the interactional perspective maintain that the norms constructing social roles in the family can in large part be created by the individual family members and their interactions. Contrary to the structuralists, interactionists maintain that emergent norms and roles are not just idiosyncrasies of one family within the constraints of the larger society's timing and sequencing norms. The interactionists argue that family members can construct social roles (role making) and thereby set the course for social change. For example, there are many ways in which a mother may nurture children. Some mothers may take their infants to work, other mothers may stay home, and still others may judiciously select a warm and nurturant caregiver. The interactionists argue that all of these behaviors fit within the broad framework of being a "nurturant mother," but there is sufficient scope for the individual to construct her own norms and rules about "mothering." Furthermore, the interactionists argue that such role making and norm making is how social change comes about. First, the individual family constructs its norms and roles to adapt to the social and economic situation. As larger numbers of people join in similar adaptations, the norms and roles become more common and acceptable until these norms eventually become the new norm.

In the interactional perspective, the internal dynamics of the family are emphasized. The consensus family members reach on norms and roles provides an understanding of family behavior and possible directions of normative change. The interactionists view family development as a process governed by the interactions of family members. Family developmental stage is defined similarly to the structuralists' definition, but the emphasis is somewhat different. The interactionists argue that each stage of family development represents a qualitatively distinct pattern of interaction between family members. Whereas the structuralists define stages mainly by the more cross-culturally relevant dimension of group membership, the interactionists use more qualitative assessments of interaction. For example, in North America, the age of the oldest child's entry into school has been used to demarcate a change in family interaction because the child is now away from home for extended periods of time and integrated into the community (e.g., Aldous, 1978; Rodgers, 1973). Structuralists would point out that incorporating such society-specific content in the theory makes it less cross-culturally applicable. On the other hand, interactionists would argue that the qualitative interaction patterns need to be studied in each society without imposing a predetermined definition of stage on these diverse families.

The interactionists' perspective on family development remains a vital part of family development theory. Not only does the interactionist perspective support research more sensitive to the definitions and processes used within each family (Klein et al., 1979), but the interactionists have throughout the history of family development theory provided the most popular North American formulations of the theory (e.g., Aldous, 1978; Duvall, 1957).

INDIVIDUAL LIFE COURSE ANALYSIS

The past three decades have witnessed the emergence of a type of analysis of individual event histories referred to as "life course analysis." Although this form of analysis has largely been developed independent of family development theory, much of life course analysis is focused on family events. Family development theory has both contributed to these formulations and received impetus from this approach to expand developmental theory by incorporating some of the methods used in life course analysis. Indeed, Mattessich and Hill (1987) criticized family development theorists for not incorporating the effects of the timing of nonfamily life events on family development. Rodgers and White (1993) and White (1991) expanded family development theory to incorporate these other institutional events (e.g., education and work) in the developmental paradigm as "cross-institutional" timing and sequencing norms. Bengtson and Allen (1993) argue that life course analysis is a theory in its own right. They endeavor to produce a set of propositions unique to life course analysis. It is our opinion that many of their propositions are long-standing in family development theory, and thus the differences between life course analysis and family development seem largely a matter of emphases rather than content.

Life course analysis, like family development, incorporates the historical dimensions of change: period, age, and birth cohort. Besides the recognition that timing and sequencing norms are affected by and change with historical period, the age of the individual experiencing events, and the norms carried by the birth cohort, life course analysis appears to rely mainly on methodological innovations in studying the sequencing and timing of events (e.g., Allison, 1984). Similar historical dimensions and event history methods also show up in the work of family developmentalists as early as Glick (1947) and as recently as White (1991). White treats event sequences such as the event ordering of marriage, first job, and first child as independent variables predicting marital disruption. Before Mattessich and Hill's (1987) call for developmental theorists to incorporate these cross-institutional events in developmental theory, there was perhaps more reason to consider life course analysis as an independent school of thought. The current situation seems to evidence that this type of analysis is now within the scope of family developmental theory.

A contrary view is proposed by Aldous (1990). She argues that because family development theory is focused on the family group and life course analysis is focused on the individual, the two approaches are not the same. But more recent contributions, such as Rodgers and White (1993), suggest that because in both variants explanations rest on institutional and cross-institutional timing and sequencing norms, the variants are the same. What little difference there is can be attributed to the emphasis on individual units of analysis rather than on the family group. As we have seen, that emphasis is a matter of the level of analysis selected by the researcher rather than a substantive theoretical difference.

One example of the approach used in life course studies is provided in the collection of chapters, edited by Glen Elder, John Modell, and Ross Parke (1993), titled *Children in Time and Place*. These authors and their colleagues from the social sciences undertook an ambitious project to unify historical, psychological, and sociological approaches to the study of the life course. For example, using two longitudinal cohort studies, successive authors demonstrated age; age and cohort; and age, cohort, and period effects on such diverse topics as children's aptitudes and anorexia nervosa in girls and young women. In the end, the ontogenetic explanations of the life course seem difficult to incorporate into social explanations, much as they had provided difficulties for the concept of developmental task discussed earlier. Life course analysis often remains moored to the notions of age, cohort, and period also important in family development (e.g., Rodgers, 1973; White, 1991).

## Empirical Applications

There exists such a myriad of applications of family life course development theory that is difficult to select only a couple of examples to demonstrate the great strength and richness of this framework. This theoretical perspective continues to inform family historians and demographers (e.g., Elman, 1998) and guide researchers into new areas of study (Price, McKenry, & Murphy, 2000; Watt & White, 1999), and the sequencing of events continues as a major focus in marital dyads (Marks & Lambert, 1998). We have, however, selected two areas with a long history of study within the family life course framework. These are the areas of family stress and the transition to parenthood.

### STRESS IN FAMILIES

One of the major empirical applications of family development theory has been in the area of stress. One of the early architects of family development theory, Reuben Hill (1971), was responsible for the original theoretical formulation in this area. Boss (1988) argues that although individuals experience stress as a felt inability to cope with change, families are organized units that also demonstrate group symptoms of stress. She defines family stress as a disturbance in the organization and process of family life. Although individuals perceive and react to stresses, it may be the resources of the family that explain the successful management of stress. Furthermore, individuals' perceptions of what a stressor is are guided by their understanding of timing and sequencing norms for family development. For example,

> The event of pregnancy is viewed more positively by the families of a couple in their thirties than by the families of a couple still in their teens. The different levels of family stress caused by the same event (in this case pregnancy) can be explained by developmental context. (Boss, 1988, p. 32)

Accordingly, family stress and individual stress must be explained by using multiple levels of analysis focusing on both the individual and family resources and coping skills. Furthermore, family life course researchers are examining the effects of sequencing family stages along with work stages. For example, White (1999) following Voydanoff (1987) showed that simultaneous sequencing of certain combined "formative" stages of work and family resulted in increases in stress.

The study of stress and recent therapeutic applications of family development theory (e.g., Carter & McGoldrick, 1988; Falicov, 1988; Klein & Aldous, 1988) have emphasized significant events and "pileup" of events in the individual and family history. For example, we all appreciate that a recent event such as a divorce places family members under significant stress by requiring emotionally intense adjustments. In recent analyses, researchers have examined not just such events but where the event falls in the family's event history. A family may have moved to a new house, then experienced a prolonged illness of a family member, and then undergone a separation and finally a divorce. Clearly, each event alone would be considered stressful, but the compression of the events in a brief time span also must be considered in an analysis of stress on individuals and family members.

TRANSITION TO PARENTHOOD

Family life course development scholars have also turned their attention to the stress attached to particular transitions in the family life course. Hill and Rodgers (1964) argued that particular transitions from one family stage to another might be stressful. Menaghan (1983) examined the stress associated with the transition to parenthood. She argued that the stress on individuals of assuming the roles and norms of parenthood was mitigated by anticipatory socialization and coping skills. Belsky and Rovine (1990) documented that many families suffered declines in marital role relationships during the transition to parenthood. The transition to parenthood continues to occupy developmental researchers as they incorporate events such as prenatal preparation, infant feeding practices, and the timing of work-related events in their analyses. For example, Bulcroft, Forste, and White (1993) argued that the decision to breast-feed an infant must be studied as part of the transition to parenthood because the choice of infant feeding technique is linked to strains on the marital relationship that are elevated by breast-feeding. An important part of the strain put on the marital relationship by the entry of the first child is due to changes in the content of the roles. Cowan and Cowan (1992) observed that they become much more traditional and gender based. Levy-Schiff (1994) found that when fathers are involved in caregiving, there is a positive effect on marital satisfaction for both husbands and wives. Demo and Cox (2000) suggest that there is general agreement that the degree of stress experienced in the transition to parenthood is related to the level of marital adjustment before the birth of the child (e.g., Cox, Paley, Burchinal, & Payne, 1999).

Although we do not as yet know whether all family transitions are stressful for family members, we do have an indication that the birth of the first child and transition to parenthood is fraught with potential strains for individuals and relationships in the family. As family life course researchers study the factors in this family transition, we find not just the details of how and why couples experience such stress but also how intervention strategies may assist families with such a transition. For example, Cowan and Cowan's (1992) study titled *When Partners Become Parents: The Big Life Change for Couples* demonstrates the stress that couples feel during this transition and also developed an effective intervention strategy to reduce the stress couples experience.

## Implications for Intervention

Family development theory is rich with implications for interventions and policy. The notion of the family career and its stages alerts policymakers to the fact that there is not "a" or "the" family but myriad family patterns and paths. Indeed, family development as a perspective sensitizes policymakers as to some of the more salient dimensions of these patterns, such as age and membership structure. For example,

Aldous (1994) recently discussed how developmental insights shed light on the issue of family caregiving:

> In the formation and child-rearing stages, families are the most hard pressed with respect to caregiving resources. Trying to maintain marriages, starting parenthood, divorcing, remarrying, and preparing youths to leave home in the economic context of stagnant or falling wages and troublesome unemployment rates make these family stages careseeking rather than caregiving periods. (p. 61)

Policymakers must take into consideration not only what is happening in any one stage but also the dynamic process as families move from stage to stage. Such general insights are not simply restricted to policy made in one culture but may be used to address policy questions in cultures other than North American.

The concepts of normative and nonnormative timing and sequencing of family career events and the synchronization of these family events with work and educational careers have proven useful in family and individual therapy. Carter and McGoldrick (1988) argue that the family career is a useful framework for family therapy. They and others have pointed out that the family context of stress and coping change throughout the family's stages. Falicov (1988) focuses more on the concepts of off time and out of sequence as important constructs for the therapist. Finally, Russell (1993) notes that the stage formulation presented by Rodgers and White (1993) has already been used by therapists as a form of *genogram analysis* that includes the household. Russell (1993) notes that the move away from developmental tasks to a more probabilistic approach to family development (Rodgers & White, 1993) will help both family practitioners and their clients accept "a realistic level of unpredictability in family life" (p. 257), and this in turn assists in addressing both long- and short-term problem solving for families.

## Critiques and Discussion

One of the outstanding debates for developmentalists is the conflict between the interactional and structural perspectives within family development theory. The interactionists assume that individuals and families have great efficacy in constructing their own family norms. The structuralists assume that institutional timing and sequencing norms so constrain family members that there is limited room for such constructions. This conflict between these two perspectives is an old one. Both are probably correct but not as correct as each would prefer. Indeed, this is probably similar to whether "the cup is half full or half empty." Every role has some prescriptions, or it would not be a "role." On the other hand, no role is completely prescribed, and therefore there will always be some opportunity to "make" or "construct" the role.

Another problem area for family developmental theory is the identification of the process of development. Mattessich and Hill (1987) offered a definition of family development that was influenced by the thinking of scholars in child development. As a result, their definition contained elements such as "progressive structural differentiation." The more "ontogentic" versions of life course theory have a similar problem in regard to the invariant stage conceptions in some "ontogenetic" developmental perspectives. But family groups are more social and less biological in their development than are individuals. For individuals, developmental scholars argue that there are ontogenetic, or biologically based, stages of development. But for the family, the argument about a biological basis doesn't stand up. The only established biological parameters are fertility and mortality, and with the onslaught of fertilization technology, fertility may not last as long as a parameter of family life.

White (1991) suggested that family development theory should explain the transition from one family stage to another. As a result of this emphasis, White's definition of development is that it is a process in which the probabilities of a transition change according to the family's current stage and how long it has been in that stage. For example, usually newlyweds allow themselves a period of adjustment before having a first child. The probability for a first child peaks during the early years of marriage; after 5 years, the probability of a birth rapidly declines. The developmental process is where a transition to a family stage, such as parenthood, is dependent on the current stage (childless marriage) and the duration of time in that stage (less than or greater than 5 years). This view of family development relies on the behavior of individuals and families as being guided by social norms rather than ontogenetic causes.

The ontogenetic–sociogenetic argument will continue to plague family development theory until there is a clear theoretical link with ontogenetic child development theories. There can be little doubt that the maturation of children makes for large changes in interaction in families, but family developmentalists have not studied these interactions longitudinally to discover which norms and patterns change and which do not. On the other hand, child developmentalists have largely ignored the family context of ontogenetic development, and we have little idea of the interactions between a child's development and family norms and patterns. The only conclusion we can reach is that the goal of a theoretical linkage between individual and family development remains elusive.

A substantial problem for the family life course framework is using behavior to infer norms. Marini (1984) argues that norms cannot be inferred from behavior. She states that norms always carry sanctions and are part of a group. The aggregate patterns of family development cannot be used to infer social norms because there is no demonstration that these norms are carried by group members and have sanctions. White's (1991, 1998) response to Marini's (1984) argument is that she fails to incorporate the many levels of analysis appropriate for analyzing norms. He states that Marini's definition is suitable only for the group level of analysis, not for the institutional level of analysis. Marini's argument, however, raises important questions about the conditions under which scholars may validly infer norms from patterns of family behavior. Claiming that there are institutional norms does not relieve us of the duty to provide independent empirical evidence for their existence. If institutional norms cause behaviors, we do not want to infer institutional norms from behaviors. No cause can be inferred from its presumed effect.

A long-standing critique of the stage concept is that it cannot incorporate the myriad family forms and is not cross-culturally relevant. Today, we must wonder whether there is so much diversity of family forms that the stage concept cannot work. We believe that although this criticism might have been appropriate for earlier versions of the theory in which stages were given culture-specific content, it is no longer appropriate for the recent versions of the theory in which stages are based on either possible membership structure or patterns of families. Indeed, family development stages are appropriate as long as there are patterns of family life.

A more serious criticism of the theory is that many of the changes viewed in family development theory as discrete jumps associated with changing family stages are more realistically conceptualized as gradual, continuous changes. For example, critics would argue that the preparation for a first child is more continuous than discrete. Even among family developmentalists, there is the view that transitions are not a point in time but a process (e.g., Aldous, 1978; Bohannan, 1970; Klein et al., 1979). A possible rebuttal is that no matter what the preparation, if the relatively discrete event of the birth of the first child does not take place, then we cannot say that a transition has taken place. This rebuttal relies on the fact that transitions are usually tied to a relatively discrete event and that such events are turning points for the family. Contrary instances can be noted, however. For example, when does an American child become an adult, such that we can identify when families enter and exit the launching stage? Given how often young adults leave home and return again for periods of partial dependency on parents, it seems clear that the transition to adulthood is now a rather complicated and extended process (Goldscheider & Goldscheider, 1999). And it could occur repeatedly for one or more children in the family.

Another problem we see for family development theory is its scope. Family development theorists attempt to explain the uniform and patterned ways in which families develop not only within a society but also from society to society. Much of family development theory, however, has been focused on family development during the decade of the 1960s within middle-class U.S. families. Although older versions of the theory appear to lack cross-cultural applicability, there is some cause for optimism with the newer theoretical versions. For example, research by both Kumagai (1984) and Rodgers and Witney (1981) demonstrated the utility of family life course development in cross-cultural comparisons. The generality of the newer theoretical propositions and the specification of events hold greater promise for cross-cultural researchers than did the older culture-specific stages.

The single most important contribution of developmental perspectives on the family is that they alert us to the importance of changes over the course of a family's existence. So, whenever it is asserted that families with a particular characteristic have a certain outcome, we are alerted to ask when the characteristic emerged in the family and when the outcome changed. And we want to find out the reason why the change happens when it does, rather than assuming that changes are random in families.

## Conclusion

Family life course development theory provides a broad theory to explain the patterns of family formation and dissolution (e.g., Bengtson & Allen, 1993; Rodgers & White, 1993). Family development theory grew and matured throughout the second half of the 20th century. In this chapter, we have conjoined family development and life course analysis as a single framework. We have no doubt that some scholars will criticize our approach, but we feel it is justified on the basis of the great similarities these approaches have and the ways in which they may complement each other. We have little doubt that a conjoined theory of family life course development will provide both students and scholars insight into the ways families grow and change over time.

# Suggested Readings

Bengtson, V. L., & Allen, K. R. (1993). The life course perspective applied to families over time. In P. Boss, W. Doherty, R. LaRossa, W. Schumm, & S. Steinmetz (Eds.), *Sourcebook of family theories and methods: A contextual approach* (pp. 469–499). New York: Plenum.
*This chapter provides the first systematic statement of life course analysis as a theory. Before this, few had claimed that life course analysis was much more than a methodology.*

Cowan, P. A., & Cowan, C. P. (1992). *When partners become parents: The big life change for couples.* New York: Basic Books.
*This book provides a wonderful introduction to family life course analysis that focuses exclusively on the transition to parenthood. It is rich in examples that illustrate concepts and processes.*

Rodgers, R. H., & White, J. M. (1993). Family development theory. In P. Boss, W. Doherty, R. LaRossa, W. Schumm, & S. Steinmetz (Eds.), *Sourcebook of family theories and methods: A contextual approach* (pp. 225–254). New York: Plenum.
*This chapter provides a thorough sketch of the newer, structural version of the family development theory, laying the foundation for a move to family life course development as a framework.*

# 5

# The Systems Framework

Today is Jack and Jan's 10th wedding anniversary. For the past 10 years, Jack has always presented Jan with a dozen yellow roses. When he gives her the roses this year, Jan makes a funny face. She says thanks and puts the roses aside while she finishes reading a newspaper article. Jack is disappointed that Jan did not respond more positively to his gift. He asks Jan what is wrong. She informs him that she has an allergy to roses. Jack says that he remembered her liking them even before they were married. She says she has always been allergic but received them enthusiastically because of the "thought." Jack responds that the thought is still there. Jan counters that after 10 years of marriage she had hoped that his knowledge about her would grow deeper. Jan said that she has sent a number of messages that not only does she not like roses but some variety would show more thought on Jack's part. Instead, all she receives is the message that their marriage has sunk into thoughtless routine. After all, says Jan, variety is the spice of life.

Let's take a closer look at this example, for it illustrates some general principles about a communications system. First, Jack inferred from Jan's premarital behavior that she liked roses. He has incorporated this into his understanding of his wife for the past 10 years. Jan is disappointed that Jack does not know her better, but unless Jack asked Jan about her flower preferences or had occasion to observe Jan being disappointed previously, he would have no reason to doubt the validity of his premarital inference. Indeed, the only reason Jack would change his inference would be if he received new information. Jan, on the other hand, thinks Jack's perceptions are shallow. She thinks he should have been sensitive to her subtle cues that she liked the thought but not the flowers without her having to say it. She feels she provided sufficient nonverbal cues to alert her husband and that he is simply insensitive to the information she sends (e.g., Gottman & Porterfield, 1981).

In general, then, we can see both spouses as being linked in a system in which one person's behavior becomes the other person's information. In turn, this person's information provides the beliefs and basis on which future actions are taken. Those actions become evidence that the other spouse doesn't understand him or her and has not received the more subtle messages. Jan is thus disappointed in what she believes is her husband's insensitivity to her behavioral cues. In a distilled sense, this interactional spiral, composed of behaviors between the spouses and each one's perception and reception of the information carried by those behaviors, captures the notion of a marital interaction system.

In this chapter, we address the question, "What is a system?" rather than examine marital communication. Through defining and discussing the properties of a system, we become more adept at analyzing cases such as that of Jack and Jan. Indeed, the study of marital and family interaction has been an important component in the recent development of systems theory in the social sciences. What we now call *general systems theory* does not have a simple pedigree or lineage, however. Originally, systems theory evolved from a set of diverse influences, such as biology, robotics, and mathematics. Of all the theories we consider in this book, systems theory is among the most recent, following only family development theory. Most if not all of its evolution has taken place within the 20th century.

## Intellectual Traditions

Before the beginning of the 20th century, there were two major influences that were to prove foundational for systems theory. One of these was the *organic* and *evolutionary* perspective on society launched by Herbert Spencer (1880). Spencer's belief that the same basic processes operated throughout the universe led him to assume a set of principles that would apply within biology, psychology, and sociology. He viewed the universe as a continual process that forms and dissipates structures. Spencer's work is one of the major contemporary sources for the idea of *emergence* and the notion that aggregations may come together to form "more than the sum of their parts." Of course, this notion was voiced by the ancient Greek philosopher Democritus (460–360 B.C.) and after the turn of the 20th century was tied up with the notion of *vitalism* in biology and the process cosmology of Alfred North Whitehead (1929). Spencer's work also rekindled the age-old quest for unity among the sciences. This quest for universal principles common to all domains of study reached an apex during the 1950s and 1960s as evidenced by the publication of the *International Encyclopedia of Unified Science* with such illustrious contributors as Charles Morris (see Chapter 2), Rudolph Carnap, Niels Bohr, and Carl Hempel (see Chapter 1).

The second major influence came from the emerging science of information and automata. Along with the invention of the telegraph and telephone, new ways of conceptualizing and measuring the flow of information developed. This was the start of communications theory. The digital codes that could be sent on telegraphs were the subject of early research that culminated in the invention of digital computers. At the same time that the study of these message systems was evolving, new technologies for control and guidance were being developed. For example, the servomechanism used on ships' rudders incorporated the ideas of error detection and feedback. But the greatest single impetus for the growth of information theory came from technological demands during World War II. For example, with the increase in the ability of aircraft to fly faster came a need for antiaircraft guns to anticipate the position of such fast-moving targets. Probably one of the more familiar examples is that of the early rockets developed by Germany. The first V1 rockets were notorious for having a guidance system as rudimentary as a skyrocket's "point and ignite." Although these rockets were aimed at London, they probably terrorized more cows in rural Britain than Londoners. The subsequent version of the rocket, the V2, incorporated an error detection and trajectory correction feedback loop that increased the accuracy. Fortunately, these advances occurred only as the war was coming to a close.

The technological developments during the war created a need for theory to unite areas such as guidance systems and information flows. This need culminated in a series of academic developments. Soon after the war, Norbert Wiener (1948) published what became acknowledged as the seminal work on cybernetics and control systems. At about the same time, C. E. Shannon, a research scientist with Bell Laboratories, developed a mathematical theory of information and coding that he subsequently published with W. Weaver as *The Mathematical Theory of Communication* (1949). This theory consolidated the measurement of information (bits and bytes) in a way that we still use and offered several propositions regarding coding and error detection. From Shannon and Weaver's (1949) work, we find that the amount of information carried on a channel is inversely related to the amount of redundancy used for error detection. Another important postwar development was the founding of the Society for General Systems Research in 1954 by such notable social scientists as

James Miller and Margaret Mead. It was at this point that systems theory started to gain a particular focus among those using it to study families.

The way in which systems theory evolved in the study of the family is especially interesting because its application to families preceded its entry into more established domains such as sociology (Buckley, 1967). This was principally due to the influence of a small group of researchers in San Francisco. Gregory Bateson, an anthropologist, had explored both psychiatry and systems theory during his postwar years at Harvard University. Don Jackson was a psychiatrist who, along with Bateson, forged the early entry of systems theory into the study of the family. These scholars founded the Mental Research Institute (MRI) in 1958 after Bateson, Jackson, Haley, and Weakland (1956) published their influential paper *Toward a Theory of Schizophrenia.*

In this and subsequent papers, Bateson and his colleagues argued that the family represents a communications system in which, if double binds occur, one member may show signs of schizophrenia. The notion that the schizophrenic individual is a symptom of a family system pathology rather than an individual pathology gave rise to terms such as *dysfunctional family.* This view is seductive to many even though decades of research have failed to produce any substantial empirical support for the double-bind hypothesis (e.g., Mishler & Waxler, 1968; Olson, 1972; Schuham, 1967). The view of the family as a system, however, continues to operate as a strong metaphor within family therapy circles. For example, Kantor and Lehr's (1975) book *Inside the Family: Toward a Theory of Family Process* typified the family as being a self-regulating system in which members control each other's access to meaning, power, and affect. The applications of systems-type thinking in the realm of family therapy has become identified as one of the major variants of general systems theory and is commonly known as "family process theory" (see Broderick, 1993).

The initial entry of systems theory into the subject area of family through practitioners and therapists was closely followed by more formal statements from disciplinary scholars. The impact of von Bertalanffy (1968) in biology and Buckley (1967) in sociology was complemented in the social sciences by the more traditional "functionalist" approach used in anthropology, biology, and sociology. In all three of these disciplines, researchers had made arguments that when we observe an existent structure, it must exist because either currently or at one time it performed functions for the organism or society. Thus, when we examine what seem to be nonfunctional organs in the human body, such as the appendix, we argue that the structure (the appendix) must have served some function at a previous time or it wouldn't exist. These *structural–functional* arguments reached a theoretical zenith in the work of Talcott Parsons (1951). Although Parsons used the systems metaphor and even incorporated many systems notions such as "hierarchy of control," most scholars would not classify him as a general systems theorist.

General systems theory is sufficiently abstract and general to be applied to both animate and inanimate objects. We can speak coherently about "planetary systems" and "family systems" even though the two subject matters differ dramatically in many regards. Indeed, this great generality is one of the compelling points of the theory and is tied to the unification of science movement. Yet several systems theorists (e.g., Buckley, 1967) have noted that although nonliving systems tend to follow the second law of thermodynamics and exhibit increased states of randomness (*entropy*), living systems tend to increase in order and differentiation (*negentropy*). Because all physical matter emits radiation, it loses energy used to organize its structure. This loss of energy creates the dissipative process of entropy. But as Toffler pointed out in his foreword to Prigogine and Stenger's (1984) book, biological systems do not seem to follow the same pattern as physical systems:

> Evolution proceeds from the simple to complex, from "lower" to "higher" forms of life, from undifferentiated to differentiated structures. And, from a human point of view, all this is quite optimistic. The universe gets "better" organized as it ages, continually advancing to a higher level as time sweeps by. (p. xx)

The diametrical opposition of these processes gave rise to the suggestion that the processes of living systems must be studied separately from nonliving systems. This view is most thoroughly explored by James G. Miller (1978) in his book *Living Systems*. Miller provides a classificatory view of living systems based on subsystems functions, such as "reproduction," that are necessary for living structures. Each subsystem function is examined at various levels of analysis. For example, the subsystem function of "reproducer" at the cellular level is performed by the chromosome and at the group level by the "mating dyad." The taxonomic approach used by Miller bears some resemblance to functionalist theory in sociology and has led at least one scholar (Turner, 1991) to discuss systems theory as "general systems functionalism." Regardless of Miller's (1978) similarities to Parsons and other functionalists, one critical dissimilarity is that he presents some general theoretical propositions that go beyond mere class inclusion. Also, Miller represents the currently dominant view that living, as opposed to nonliving, systems are driven by different *negentropic* and organizing processes.

This dominant view of living systems—one of which would be the family—as characterized by processes atypical of nonliving things has recently been challenged within biology. Researchers in the natural science of biology assume some continuity with other physical sciences, such as chemistry and physics, and this has perhaps made the disjunction with the physical science perspective more sharply felt. The idea that there are two distinct processes at work, one for living and another for nonliving systems, threatens the continuity of science as well as the unification of science envisioned by Spencer and others. More recently, two biologists, Brooks and Wiley (1986), argued that the contradiction between nonliving systems being entropic and living systems being negentropic can be resolved by sorting out the level of analysis. Brooks and Wiley proposed that the problem is largely resolved by clarifying levels of analysis. Their argument is too complex to present here in full, but the essence is that what might seem "organizational" at an aggregate level of analysis may be entropic at a microlevel of analysis. The importance of their claim for us is that we are cautioned that the division in systems theory between living and nonliving systems may not be as clear and obviously acceptable as many authors in the social sciences have claimed. This caution leads us to present the concepts and propositions of general systems theory rather than only those deemed appropriate for living systems.

## Focus and Scope Assumptions

*All parts of the system are interconnected.* Although the assumption of interconnectedness in a system seems obvious, it is far from trivial. Burr, Leigh, et al. (1979) stated, "The discovery by the family process group that changes in one part of a system influence all other parts of the system should be greeted with as much enthusiasm as the observation that people talk and think" (p. 98). We would agree with this comment if this assumption were to be treated as a claim to knowledge rather than as a basic orienting assumption. But this assumption is a basic *epistemological* statement announcing that systems theory is not concerned with isolating Cause A and Effect B from the environment in which they occur. In this sense, the assumption is a statement about the ecological validity and inclusivity of systems theory.

*Understanding is only possible by viewing the whole.* The assumption that one must consider a system in its entirety serves a similar epistemological function to our first assumption. This assumption in systems theory largely resulted from the "vitalism" tied to the discovery that when some animals, such as the paramecium, were sliced in two, they would grow a new half. Clearly, these animals were "greater than the sum of their parts" because when you divided them, they would replicate. This assumption was immediately relevant to sociology and family studies. Indeed, the argument that social groups such as families were "real" and greater than just a collection of individuals has raged in these fields for a considerable time (White, 1984).

*A systems' behavior affects its environment, and in turn the environment affects the system.* Some of the output of a system becomes input of the system (*feedback*). The notion of feedback is twofold: It is both a concept and an epistemological assumption. The most simple of systems may not incorporate direct feedback loops, but this assumption serves to sensitize us to the fact that even the most simple systems affect and are, in turn, affected by their environment. In this sense, all systems have some form of feedback. This is the epistemological assumption, and it coheres nicely with the previous two assumptions of wholeness and connectedness. In the study of the family, we are usually concerned with the type of feedback whereby some of the output of a system becomes input to the system. In this sense, feedback represents a particular type of system operation that can be specified and measured. This second meaning of feedback does not refer to the assumption but to the concept.

*"Systems" are heuristics, not real things.* Systems theory is not reality but a way of knowing. This fourth and last major assumption is one that has only recently been formally recognized in systems theory. The assumption is that defining an object as a system composed of subsystems, inputs, and outputs is just one among many possible ways we might study the object. The systems perspective offers no special claim to veracity. But most of all, to say something behaves like a system is a model or metaphor, not the thing itself. Ernst von Glasersfeld (1987) summed up this "constructivist" perspective as the "view that knowledge must not be taken to be a picture of objective reality but rather as a particular way of organizing experience" (p. 10). It follows from this perspective that we should not consider the "model" to be the "thing." Indeed, the systems model becomes a heuristic for understanding our world. If we attribute reality to a family system rather than see it as a heuristic device, we make the mistake commonly called *reification,* or what the philosopher Alfred North Whitehead (1929, p. 11) called *the fallacy of misplaced concreteness.*

In summary, there are four basic assumptions underlying the systems perspective: (a) system elements are interconnected, (b) systems can only be understood as wholes, (c) all systems affect themselves through environmental feedback, and (d) systems are not reality. These four assumptions are necessarily broad but represent the foundation on which the architecture of concepts and propositions rest.

## Concepts

### SYSTEM

Hall and Fagan (1956) defined a system as a set of objects and relations between these objects and their attributes. This definition is useful for those who understand the formal set theory behind the definition, but for many students this definition doesn't seem to say much. For this reason, we characterize systems in a more familiar and, we hope, approachable manner. At minimum, *a system is a unit that can be distinguished from and that affects its environment.* We regard this as a "minimalist" definition, and usually we would say additional things, such as that a system has exchanges with its environment and has internal elements. But the major characteristic needed to identify something as a system is that it is separable from its environment and has an effect on its environment. That effect may only be that the system requires energy as input from the environment, such as a black hole, or it may only be that the system has output that affects the environment, such as a perpetual motion machine. In both cases, the system is a system because it affects its environment and can be distinguished from its environment.

### BOUNDARIES

All systems have some form of *boundaries*. A boundary is a border between the system and its environment that affects the flow of information and energy between the environment and the system. Boundaries can be measured on the dimension of permeability to the environment as running from "closed" boundaries, through which nothing goes in or out, to completely "open" boundaries, in which there is no impediment to energy and information transfers of any kind. Clearly, a completely closed system can only be imagined (as in mathematics), and a completely open system would lose most of its identity as a system because it would be difficult to separate from its environment. Fortunately, most systems occupy a position between these two ideal types. This means that the great majority of systems can be categorized by their "degree of permeability." So families usually live in households on plots of land, with fences, doors, walls, and so forth. Still, families differ in their openness to outsiders and in their ability to maintain privacy.

RULES OF TRANSFORMATION

All systems have internal *rules of transformation*. A rule of transformation represents a relationship between two elements of the system. For example, a husband and wife are both elements of the marital system. A rule of transformation for the marital system would be the quid pro quo rule that whenever the husband is nasty to the wife, the wife is nasty in return. One of the major functions of a rule of transformation is to transform inputs to the system from the environment into outputs from the system. For example, if a family's house is on fire and the smoke alarm goes off late at night, this information is transformed by the family into output as behavior that may doom or save them. If the family has a "rule" that upon hearing the smoke alarm they are to exit the house according to a "fire plan," then they might be saved. On the other hand, if the family's "rule" is a less organized response—some members want to "shut the damn thing up" and others pull their pillows over their heads—they might be in considerable danger.

FEEDBACK

We previously developed the idea of *feedback* as an epistemological assumption. Now we turn to feedback as a concept in systems theory. Feedback refers to the circular loop that brings some of the system's output back to the system as input. Feedback can be of two types. On the one hand, it may be *positive*, or *deviation amplifying*. Do not confuse positive feedback with the concept of positive reinforcement from psychology; the two are very different. Positive reinforcement makes the goal behavior more likely, whereas positive feedback (deviation amplifying) may make reaching the goal less likely. On the other hand, *negative feedback* is *deviation dampening*. To make this categorization of feedback, we must rely on the identification of either the past output or the goals of the system. With higher-order systems that monitor error from their goals, feedback is invaluable in error correction, as when you get a poor grade on an exam. In lower-level systems that lack error correction or monitoring, feedback can either increase the amplitude of output or decrease the amplitude. In families, we are mainly concerned with goal-oriented systems.

## VARIETY

All systems have degrees of *variety*. Variety in a system refers to the extent to which the system has the resources to meet new environmental demands or adapt to changes. A system that has a large array of diverse resources would have more options (variety) available to meet the diverse adaptations required by a dynamically changing environment. Some systems may lack the requisite variety to adapt to changes. For example, a family with rigid rules may lack the flexibility to adapt to changes such as a daughter wanting to marry someone from another religion or race. The lack of variety in such a rigid family might result in a rupture to the family system because it is unable to adapt to this change.

## EQUILIBRIUM

*Equilibrium* refers to a balance of inputs and outputs. For example, most families require a balance of income and expenditures. A family system can also be described as *homeostatic*. A homeostatic system dynamically maintains equilibrium by feedback and control. A physical example of a homeostatic device is a thermostat; an organic example is the dynamic maintenance of your body temperature within fairly limited parameters. A family may maintain its dynamic equilibrium by using its resources to maintain its rules. For example, a family that goes camping in Alaska might purchase sleeping shades so it can maintain the rule that everyone is to go to sleep by 8:30 p.m. even in the land of the midnight sun. As you can see, homeostasis is neither inherently good nor bad but describes the manner in which equilibrium is maintained over time.

## SYSTEM LEVELS

Systems have *levels*. A first-order system is simply composed of environmental input filtered through the system's rules of transformation and exiting as output into the environment. There is no method of control or error correction. A second order system (and all higher order systems) has a *comparator* that monitors the output and compares the output to the goals of the system. If the comparator computes an error, it then corrects the first-order (level) rules of transformation. A simple example of a comparator is a thermostat. A thermostat set at 70°F that senses that the ambient air temperature is 60°F should attempt to correct by turning on the furnace. We will provide another example of these second-order control systems shortly.

SUBSYSTEMS

Not only do systems have various levels but they may also contain subsystems. For example, one way of viewing the family system is that it contains sibling subsystems, marital subsystems, and parent–child subsystems. Each of these subsystems could be further analyzed in terms of subsystems. In general, a subsystem is a part of a system that is analyzed separately as to its exchanges with the system and other subsystems. Some system characteristics, such as the "control" system discussed earlier, can only emerge with a system that has two subsystems, one containing rules of transformation and the other comparing output with the goal of the system. For example, a thermostatic system can be broken into one subsystem that performs heating, including elements such as the furnace and ducts, and another subsystem that senses the air temperature and turns the heater on if the temperature is not within the goal parameters. In a family system, we might see the parental subsystem as the control subsystem. It must be kept in mind, however, that subsystems, like systems, are intellectual ways of understanding and analyzing our world. There are many ways to conceptualize subsystems and systems in families, and some serve one purpose better than others, but none are "true." They have heuristic value but no "ontological" reality.

## Propositions

Systems theorists such as Mesarovic (1970) and Miller (1978) have offered general propositions regarding the behavior of systems. These propositions, because of their necessary abstractness and generality, are less immediately applicable to the study of the family than are several applications of systems theory to the family, such as Kantor and Lehr (1975); Wilkinson (1977); Burr, Day, and Bahr (1993) and Broderick (1993). In this section, we incorporate some of the more abstract propositions but especially concentrate on examples of propositions that are directly applicable to the study of the family.

As far as we know, all family systems theorists conceptualize the family as a goal-oriented system with a control subsystem (comparator). Broderick and Smith (1979) talked about this as a Level 2, or cybernetic, system. Most scholars conceptualize the family as having many more levels of control than just one. Perhaps an example will make this more clear.

Jack and Jan now have a 3-year-old who is in the process of developmentally "dropping" her afternoon nap. This has made the family rule of a 7 o'clock bedtime even more important for both Jack and Jan. Jack is putting his overtired and cranky daughter to bed when she rebels and begins to throw a screaming tantrum about not going to bed. Jack first tries to manage the rule breaking by increasing the level of threats and punishments, threatening to close the door if she doesn't settle down. The tantrum continues until Jack realizes that by continuing to "follow the rule" he is escalating the conflict. He is getting further from the important goal of making sure his daughter gets some sleep. He takes his daughter out of bed. Holding his daughter in his arms, he rocks and sings to her, and the exhausted little girl is asleep in a few seconds.

This example illustrates several important concepts in systems theory such as the notion of variety, goals, and control. The initial rule of the system was set by the first-order goal of "7 o'clock bedtime." But this first-order goal was actually deduced from a higher-order goal of "ensuring their daughter gets sufficient rest." Likewise, "ensuring the daughter gets sufficient rest" is deduced from a much higher-order goal of "being good parents." What happened in the example is that Jack attempted to correct the negative feedback (error from the initial 7 o'clock bedtime), but his correction by enforcing the rules produced positive feedback (amplified the deviation from the goal) and more error. As a result, Jack changed control levels to "check" what was wrong. What was wrong was that with an overly tired child, tantrums are positive feedback loops, and the way to break those loops is less enforcement of the Level 1 rule. In other words, the way you achieve the goal of rest for the child is by not enforcing the Level 1 goal of the 7 o'clock bedtime. This example also shows that if Jack lacked the requisite variety to change behaviors in midstream, he would have been trapped in his daughter's positive feedback loop.

What theoretical propositions does systems theory supply to help us understand our example? Miller (1978) suggested that the greater the number of channels for processing information in a structurally differentiated living system, the less the strains and tensions among subsystems. Miller's proposition would seem to illustrate just one advantage to variety in a system, however. Wilkinson (1977) stated a similar proposition using the concept of variety:

> The adaptability and therefore viability of a (family) system (as contrasted to rigidity and vulnerability) is positively related to the amount of variety in the system.

and

*The adaptability and therefore viability of a (family) system (as contrasted to rigidity and vulnerability) is related negatively to conflict and tension in the system.*

These two general propositions help us identify that in Jack's family system, variety is related to the dampening of tension. This general proposition does not, however, entirely capture the process in our example whereby Jack reassessed and corrected his behavior by reference to higher-order goals. Both Mesarovic (1970) for general systems and Broderick (1993) for family systems clarified this point, and Broderick added a further proposition that is useful in this regard. Broderick proposed that family goals are organized into hierarchies:

*Higher level goals define the priorities among lower level goals and are intrinsically less likely to be revised and abandoned.* (p. 43)

According to this proposition, the variety of a system is positively related to the number of levels of the system. This explains why Jack was guided by one set of goals over another and suggests how he could reassess the utility of lower-level goals by comparing them and the output to the higher-level system goal of sleep for his daughter.

It would be somewhat misleading to portray most of the explanatory work by systems theorists as being incorporated in theoretical propositions such as the ones we have identified above. Much of the "explanation" provided by systems theorists is by means of flow charts or diagrams. Despite the often-heard claim that systems theory provides an approach that is nonlinear, most of the diagrams and the solutions to systems equations are by means of either linear algebra or linear programming.

Figure 5.1 represents a simplified comparator, or control, system. In this figure, information is expressed as signal quantities, and these signals are transformed by transformation functions (in boxes). We could also express what is going on in this system as a series of functional transformations of the initial signal entering the system from the environment. When the environmental signal ($I_{e1}$) enters the system, it is transformed by the receiver (r). After the receiver function, the signal becomes system input ($I_s$) rather than environmental input ($I_{e1}$). The system input enters the rules of transformation and then becomes system output ($O_s$) until it is transformed by the sender function (s) to be sent into the environment ($O_{e1}$). The system output is also sent to the comparator for monitoring against the goals (g) of the system. The comparator compares the goals against the output. This output would be Jack's escalation of his punishments and thus

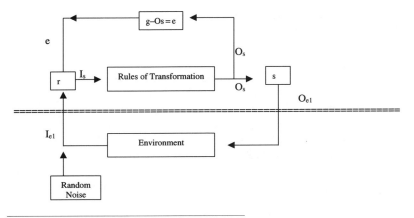

**Figure 5.1**    A Level 2 Comparator System

keeping his daughter awake by trying to put her to bed. This is then subtracted from the goal signal (g) of a good rest for the child. A positive or negative result from the comparator is error (e). The error message is then used to change or modify the input into the system or to modify the rules of transformation. The resulting message is then transformed by the sender function (S) for certain channels and enters the environment as output $(O_{e1})$ from the system. At this point, Jack decided to enforce the bedtime by threats and punishments. The environment transforms the output $(O_{e1})$ so that it is changed to another quantity $(I_{e2})$, and the sequence is reiterated. The child, already in an irrational state, saw Jack's behavior as further reason to be upset. The environmentally transformed output of the system is joined with other systematic signals from the environment and random noise to compose the totality of the environmental input back into the system $(I_{e2})$. The example of Jack and his daughter did not contain a lot of other systematic signals (such as visitors in the house), and other sorts of random interferences were not a question. Most of the environmental input $(I_{e2})$ was the daughter's tantrum.

To use a diagram such as in Figure 5.1 to explain higher-order goals, we would have to add a linkage where the error signal (e) becomes input to an even higher-level comparator containing a higher-order goal that is not included in the simplified version in Figure 5.1. In our example, the higher-order goal was getting sufficient rest for the child. The level one rule of transformation was a 7 o'clock bedtime. When a higher-level comparator compares the error with its goal, it may send an error message to change the lower-order rule of transformation or even a lower-order goal. This is commonly called recalibration. Every time you turn the heat up on the thermostat in your house, you (a higher-order goal system) recalibrate the goal in the lower-order thermostat in a way similar to what Jack did.

The model in Figure 5.1 seems very appealing. We can follow a sequence of events and paths and feel we "understand" what is happening. Furthermore, if we could identify all of the mathematical functions indicated by the boxes, we could know exactly how any message or signal (indicated by the lines) would be produced. Indeed, any system could be represented by a group of linear or dynamic equations. This approach, first suggested by Rapoport (1960, as cited in Broderick and Smith, 1979), has been used to investigate marital interaction (Cook et al., 1995).

There are differences in the type of explanation afforded by using systems diagrams rather than systems propositions. Although much of the thinking and analysis are similar, the two provide very different explanations because the questions each addresses are distinctively different. The systems diagrams address the question of *how* the process works, whereas the system theory propositions address *why* the system works as it does. In general, this is the distinction between *modeling*, which supplies an analog of how things operate, and *theory*, which explains why things work in this way. Systems diagrams have proven popular because they allow us to visualize and simplify complex processes. According to one theory of knowledge (*epistemology*), the operations (or *how*) question is all we need to know, and the *why* question represents a very limited "billiard ball" understanding of causation. As we shall see, von Glasersfeld's (1987) catholic, "constructivist" view of knowledge as multiple models fits this operationalist epistemology. This basic distinction, however, gives rise to some significant variation among systems theorists as to the type and form of the explanation. Furthermore, as we will find later, this constructivist epistemology is a prime target for critics of systems theory who say that systems theory is not a theory at all but simply a general model.

## Variations

This section covers three of the major variants in family systems theory. There are many variants of systems theory, but we limit our discussion to what we regard as the three dominant approaches. The first of these is a general systems approach to the family. This approach tends to include use of the full arsenal of systems concepts and tools. Second, we examine family communications theory. And last, we examine family process theory, in which unique constructs for extending and modifying the systems approach have been developed, particularly for the use of family therapists. Although there are many other ways to cluster the theoretical variants in family systems, such as those using mechanical, organic, or cybernetic analogs, we feel that these other approaches would less accurately represent the true nature of the variation in family systems theory.

GENERAL SYSTEMS THEORY

Broderick and Smith (1979) provided a sound introduction to the ways that systems thinking might be applied to the study of the family. Their presentation can be characterized as "cautiously optimistic." These authors suggested that family systems are minimally cybernetic, or control, systems with at least two levels. For example, they provide an introductory analysis of family systems as a four-level system in which the first level has an environmental feedback loop, the second level (cybernetic) has a comparator for error detection and correction, the third level (morphogenesis) has a higher-level comparator allowing for control of lower levels, and the fourth level (conversion) is the highest-level goal system—if goals are changed at this level, all lower-level systems are changed. More detailed models might have six or seven levels, as William Powers (1974) found necessary in his application of systems theory to individual psychological systems. Broderick and Smith (1979) were cautious to make limited claims for the application of general systems theory. They call it an "approach" rather than a "theory," responding to the perception that it largely offers models rather than theoretical propositions. They viewed attempts to produce propositions from systems theory, such as by Wilkinson (1977), as "premature." In part, their caution and judgment are due to the point in time at which they authored their contribution, but subsequent developments have not provided much more than was available in 1979 (e.g., Miller, 1978; Wilkinson, 1977). Moreover, Broderick and Smith (1979) seemed to approach systems theory with the positivistic, axiomatic notion of theory rather than the operationalist view currently touted by most systems theorists. This undoubtedly adds to their caution in regard to the promise of systems theory. Yet to date, Broderick and Smith's (1979) statement remains one of the better outlines for the application of general systems theory to the family.

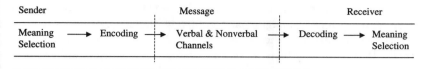

| Sender | | Message | | Receiver |
|---|---|---|---|---|
| Meaning Selection | → Encoding →| Verbal & Nonverbal Channels | → Decoding →| Meaning Selection |

**Figure 5.2**    Sender–Receiver Communications Model

## COMMUNICATIONS THEORY

Communications theory originates with the work by Shannon and Weaver (1949) titled *The Mathematical Theory of Communication.* The mathematical theory of signal communications is complemented and extended by work in the area of automata and cybernetics. The particular path on which this work entered family studies was mainly from the concerns about family communications raised by Bateson, Jackson, and others at the Mental Research Institute (MRI) in Palo Alto, California, during the late 1950s (Bateson et al., 1956). Family process theory, our third variant, shares this common ancestry with family communications. Unlike family process theory, the study of family communications largely became the focus of those in the then-emerging academic field of communications studies.

The field of communications uses a basic sender–receiver model of communications. Although there are many variants of the model, the basic elements are contained in Figure 5.2.

To understand Figure 5.2, let's follow a simple message through the model. Jack wants to tell Jan that he loves her. Of all the possible messages he could send to Jan, the meaning he selects to send is "I love you." The next step is that Jack must select the type of encoding most appropriate for the message. There are two types of codes, *digital* and *analog.* An analog message "bears a resemblance" to that for which it stands. Thus, analog codes have a degree of *isomorphy*, or similarity, to the object, idea, or feeling they represent. For example, in many film or theater productions actors "fool" you by making their behavior similar to a person in love. A "picture of an apple" is an analog code for an actual apple. Digital codes, on the other hand, are "arbitrary assignments" that receive their communications effectiveness by consensus or agreement. For example, children often play games with the arbitrary character of language by getting everyone to agree that no means yes and yes means no and "Now, let's ask Dad for ice cream cones." Arabic numerals provide another example: 2 bears no resemblance to *two* things, nor does the sound have any inherent *twoness* to it.

Returning to our example, if Jack selects a digital code, it will most likely carry accurate, commonly agreed-on information but will probably not carry much of the affect intended in his sentiment of "I love you." Indeed, imagine a completely digital message such as Morse code carrying the message "I love you"—not much affect there! If Jack is an effective communicator, he will select either both types of encoding or the more affectual analog codes.

The selection of the code directly affects Jack's choice of channels. Nonverbal channels are most appropriate for analog codes (Gottman, 1979; Mehrabian, 1972). Verbal and written channels are most appropriate for digital codes. If Jack is going to write Jan a letter saying "I love you," he will most likely embellish it with metaphor and other techniques to carry more affect or rely on Hallmark to come up with the correctly packaged digital communication. On the other hand, if Jack sees Jan face-to-face, he will probably use analog and digital codes carried on nonverbal and verbal channels simultaneously. Not only does this multiple channel carry both affective and cognitive dimensions of a message, but it provides message *redundancy* so that if noise interferes with one channel, the message will get through on another. For example, if Jack is holding Jan's hand, gazing lovingly into her eyes, and smiling, the fact that an airplane flying overhead obliterates the sound of his words "I love you" may not result in loss of the message.

Jan must have the appropriate sense receptors to receive the channels on which the message is sent (Figure 5.2). For example, if Jan hears a noise and is distracted from Jack's nonverbal message and in addition the noise drowns out Jack's verbal message, then much of the message is lost because of poor reception. Once the channels are accurately received, to get the message as Jack sent it, Jan must decode in the same way in which Jack encoded. A far-fetched example of decoding error would be if Jack meant his eye gaze to carry the analog affect of "love" but Jan decoded his "blinking" as something caught in his eye. Once the decoding occurs, then Jan must select from among the repertoire of possible "meanings" of messages she expects from Jack. If Jack and Jan had been married only a short time, the probability of decoding and selecting the message "I love you" might be fairly high. Finally, feedback in this model is simply where Jan becomes the sender and Jack the receiver. Perhaps in response to Jack's message of love, Jan will send Jack the digital message "ditto."

The complexity of the processes in the basic communications diagram is enormous. Most scholars focus on the most directly measurable and observable part of the process, which is the message. Great strides in the study of marital interaction have been made by studying gender differences in decoding verbal and nonverbal messages. For example, Gottman and Porterfield (1981) reported that dissatisfied husbands are poor decoders of their wives' nonverbal messages. Many researchers have also worked on the sequential dependencies between husband and wife messages (Gottman, 1979). The research in this area has reached such magnitude that there are several excellent reviews of the marital interaction literature, such as Noller and Fitzpatrick (1993) and most recently Gottman and Notarius (2000). This area continues to be one of the most active and encouraging areas of scientific research of all the variants of systems theory.

FAMILY PROCESS THEORY

Family process theory, for the most part, can be identified with the more applied practitioners and therapists studying the family. As we have previously noted, scholars such as Bateson and Jackson had very tangible concerns, such as the treatment of schizophrenia (Bateson et al., 1956). The tangible interests giving impetus to such scholars should in no way demean their theoretical contributions, however. After all, before a therapist can effectively treat a psychopathology, he or she must have some idea of the causative factors.

The most recent statement of family process theory is by Broderick (1993), who, like other family process theorists (e.g., Kantor & Lehr, 1975), views the family as a goal-seeking system. Much of the family system, however, is devoted to maintaining social and spatial relationships within the family and between the family and the environment. Within the family, social and spatial relationships between dyads must be managed so that individuals are protected from each other's demands (buffering) and individuals are linked to each other (bonding). The relations between the family and its environment are composed of transactions that bridge and link the family to external systems while maintaining the boundaries of the family system. Broderick's (1993) view of the family system is one of the most ambitious to date because he sought to identify both internal and external relationships.

Another influential process theorist has been Pauline Boss (1999), who explored ambiguity in family system boundaries as a crucial concept. Her work links systems theory to family stress, which we noted in chapter 4 has also been an important idea in developmental theories. In systems theories, stress on a family may be random or situationally induced, whereas in developmental theory the stress is always experienced in connection with culturally based life course expectations.

Because many family process theorists are also immersed in the treatment of psychopathology, in some senses the theories they have constructed are more theories of family therapy than of the family. The emphasis to scientifically test claims may seem less important than if the theory "works" in the therapeutic situation. This has led to family process theory being considered metaphorical. Because so much of family process theory is concerned with applications, much of it strays from the precision we would seek in scientific theory and is more focused on guiding metaphors. For example, Minuchin (1974) developed the notion that boundaries are critical in distinguishing pathologies in families. He pioneered aspects of family process theory linked to distance regulation and closeness and coined the term *enmeshment* to describe these processes. Nowhere, however, did Minuchin provide a systematic definition of his concept of boundaries. Indeed, terms such as *enmeshment, bounding,* and *buffering* offer sensitizing metaphors for the clinician (e.g., Rosenblatt, 1994). These metaphors are similar to the ones offered by psychotherapists such as Carl Rogers, Jung, and Freud. They may prove useful in the formulation of more rigorous scientific and theoretical concepts, but this development will never happen if family process scholars are content to view these collections of metaphors as "theory."

## Empirical Applications

### MARITAL AND FAMILY COMMUNICATIONS

Systems theory has proven to be the major conceptual framework used in the study of marital interaction and family communications. As we have seen, the systems approach first entered family studies through the work of therapists such as Don Jackson who were very concerned with the family system of communications. This impetus later bifurcated into the two variants of communications theory and family process theory. It is in the study of marital and family communications that systems theory research seems to have made the most scientific progress. In this section, we examine only a few of the many contributions made by researchers in this area.

From the outset, systems ideas and ideas from communications theory were fused because a communications system is simply one type of general system. Researchers in the 1960s had been guided by the early work of Bateson et al. (1956). Following in this tradition is the work by the MRI group of Watzlawick, Beavin, and Jackson (1967). This book goes far beyond earlier explorations into systems theory by Jackson (e.g., 1974). Its major contribution is to introduce family scholars to communications theory and to establish a systematic approach to the encoding and decoding of both nonverbal and verbal messages. Many of the suggestions in this work regarding nonverbal communications were simultaneously developed by an independent group of scholars in psychology led by Mehrabian and Wiener (1968).

In 1968, Mishler and Waxler published their now-classic study on family processes, *Interaction in Families*. In their research, they examined patterns of marital and family communications and the possible linkage to schizophrenia. Their empirical work raised significant doubts about the "double-bind" hypothesis (Bateson et al., 1956) but at the same time demonstrated how complex questions about family communications patterns could be scientifically studied. Indeed, their finding that families containing a schizophrenic child showed more orderly patterns of interaction than the chaotic patterns of interruption and lack of rule following demonstrated by "normal" families turned previous suppositions on their head. Mishler and Waxler's conclusions exemplified scientific caution; they pointed out that they could not determine from their research whether the interaction patterns in the families with a schizophrenic child were the cause of the child's problem or the effect of the family's adjustment to the child's problem.

Building on the contributions of Watzlawick and colleagues (1967) as well as Mishler and Waxler (1968), in *Communication, Conflict and Marriage*, Raush, Barry, Hertel, and Swain (1974) developed the sender–receiver model as a system of contingencies. These authors proposed that marital interaction was a system in which the next action of the husband toward the wife was contingent on the previous message the wife sent to the husband. Because messages are behavior, this model could be examined as a time series of spousal behavioral contingencies. A simplistic example of this process is if a husband is nasty to a wife, the "reciprocity" model of contingencies would predict that she would be nasty in return.

Although this notion seems somewhat obvious common sense, it turns out to be largely untrue. It is addressed in a much more sophisticated formulation by Gottman, Markman, and Notarius (1977) and later by Gottman (1979). Their approach was to test the contingencies between spousal verbal and nonverbal messages over time using a series of contingent probabilities (a discrete-state Markov chain). Their findings are important. They found that the emotional affect carried in nonverbal messages is a better discriminator of distressed from nondistressed couples than more traditional verbal measures such as spousal agreement. Second, they found little support for a simple quid pro quo, or spousal reciprocity, hypothesis. The patterns of marital interaction over a series of time points showed that research in this area is both complex and worthwhile. For John Gottman, this has become a programmatic theme in his research, culminating in the identification of specific patterns of interaction that lead to couple disintegration and to the specification of causes for these patterns (e.g., Gottman, 1979, 1993, 1994; Gottman & Krokoff, 1989; Gottman & Levenson, 1992; Gottman et al., 1977; Gottman & Porterfield, 1981; Gottman & Notarius, 2000; Levenson & Gottman, 1983). This program of research has certainly resulted in a much better understanding of the behavioral contingencies between marital partners. Indeed, Gottman claimed that researchers can now predict with great accuracy whether relationships will fail or not (see Gottman & Levenson, 1992; Gottman, Coan, Carrere, & Sawnason, 1998).

Gottman's work remains strongly moored to the measurement of behavior rather than attitudes and beliefs. As a result of this focus, he has largely ignored questions about message reception and perception. Mary Ann Fitzpatrick (1988) in her book *Between Husbands and Wives* studied some of the verbal and nonverbal codes tied to disclosure and intimacy for traditional and nontraditional marriage. Her work, and that of her colleague, Patricia Noller (1984), culminated in a joint project providing a systematic overview of communication in the family (Noller & Fitzpatrick, 1993). Although there remain significant unresolved theoretical problems, there can be little doubt that scholars studying communications systems have provided the clearest example of the force and utility of a systems approach for the scientific study of the family.

## Implications for Intervention

One cannot think of the usefulness of systems theory for intervention without at once thinking of family therapy. Family therapy is not the only area for which there are applications for systems theory. Anderson (1993) suggested several implications for family policy studies. But systems theory has provided several generations of family practitioners and therapists with the basic tools for theorizing about their interventions. This history of application is far from a monotonic, progressive march forward but might be better viewed as a tree with numerous branches. Undoubtedly, some of these branches of family systems therapies may not bear fruit whereas others might.

Broderick (1993) and others see family systems theory and theories of family therapy as united in what he termed *family process theory*. The history of this linkage between systems theory and therapy is usually traced to the work by Bateson, Jackson, and their colleagues (1956) at the MRI in Palo Alto, California. This group of scholars popularized such notions as *homeostatic* family patterns and *dysfunctional* family systems. The legacy of their work is with us today in explanations of various individual psychopathologies (e.g., anorexia nervosa) by family system characteristics, even though empirical support for pathogenesis and family patterns has been weak (e.g., Mishler & Waxler, 1968; Olson, 1972; Schuham, 1967).

The application of systems theory to family therapy is not guided by simply one theory. General systems theory may serve as an overall metaphor, but various scholars have focused on different dimensions of the metaphor. For example, Minuchin (1974) focused on the maintenance of system boundaries, and Bowen (1978) focused on the individual's differentiation of self.

Among the more prominent contributions to systems approaches to the family is that of David Olson (1995). Over the past three decades, Olson has complemented his therapeutic approach with rigorous scientific research. He has developed a systems model called the *circumplex model*, according to which he categorizes families by their degree of adaptability and cohesion. Some families are high in cohesion (enmeshed) and low in adaptability (rigid); other families may be low in cohesion (disengaged) but high in adaptability (chaotic). Olson views normal families as occupying a range in which cohesion and adaptability are balanced rather than at the extreme points of the continuum. His system approach can incorporate the changes in the balance that families experience over time. The therapist addresses imbalances in the system by helping families move to more balanced distributions of cohesion and adaptability. For some families, this might entail learning to regard family rules as less important. In other families, it might entail helping the family to become more organized. Olson's systemic approach has a broad range of applications, from dating to elderly families, including families of orientation as well as procreation. His work stands as one of the most popular of the systems approaches and one of the better examples of the fusion of science with therapy.

## Critiques and Discussion

Without a doubt, the criticism of systems theory that has the potential to be the most damaging is that it is in truth a "model" or "flow chart approach," not a theory. Critics charge that even the concepts in systems theory, such as variety and feedback, are more heuristic than theoretical. These concepts lack any real substantive content, compared with concepts such as "power" and "consensus" in other theories. Critics also argue that systems approaches using mathematical models may seem to provide "prediction," but they do not succeed. The critics make a distinction between "forecasting," which as in weather forecasting is simply based on past records, and "prediction," which is a deduction from a set of substantive theoretical propositions. Even Gottman's work would not be immune from such criticisms because there are few if any theoretical propositions from which to deduce marital outcomes.

Systems advocates argue that the accusation that the systems approach is a model and not a theory is only tenable if one adopts a specific view (epistemology) of how science works. The traditional model of science is called the *hypothetico–deductive* model in that a set of propositions is logically linked to produce a deduction that can then be empirically tested. In this view of science, whichever theory produces the most efficient explanation is the best theory. In this sense, theories are in competition with one another. This hypothetico–deductive perspective is based on a viewpoint (epistemology) that is counterpoised to the *constructivist* position. You may recall that according to the constructivist position, different models may be useful for different purposes. Even models intended to explain the same phenomena may illuminate different aspects, as in the parable about the blind men feeling the elephant in which no one description was an accurate description of the whole elephant, yet all of the descriptions were true. Thus, systems theorists do not see themselves as playing by the same competitive rules as traditional science. This is not to say that systems theory is less scientific in the broad sense, but it does adopt a less competitive view of scientific theory.

A second criticism that has plagued systems theory is that it is too abstract and global to be of much use. The ideas in systems theory are so general as to be almost meaningless. In their quest to unify the sciences, systems theorists have abstracted to a level in which there is little meaning. Critics claim that when systems theory is applied to concrete empirical situations, the generality of its concepts trivializes and glosses over important distinctions. Turner gave the example that notions of "information" do not communicate the properties denoted by more traditional concepts such as norms, values, beliefs, ideology, and so forth (1991, p. 130).

Systems theorists say what most of these critics miss is that it is always easier to apply "general" ideas across diverse contexts then to apply "specific" ideas. For example, the "information processing" of crustaceans provided a basic analog for Gottman's (1979) work on marital communication. Although no one doubts that discipline-specific concepts and theories are important, it is increasingly difficult to see parts of the natural and social world as not being tied together. Naturally, systems theorists would argue that the only way we can move between diverse contexts and species is by using a common set of concepts that will help us see the connections and similarity of processes.

Another criticism is that family systems theorists tend to reify the idea of system. This criticism is perhaps aimed more at the family process variant of systems theory. For example, family therapists who claim they are using systems theory in simply calling a family a system of interrelated parts or interacting personalities are attributing reality to a heuristic model for understanding. Family process theorists, like many other scientists, would like to see their knowledge benefit humankind. But in their attempts to apply systems theory to the family, they seem prone to slip from viewing the family "as" a system to the view that the family "is" a system. This slippage from an epistemology favoring knowledge as possible heuristic models to a way of knowing that clearly makes ontological claims about the nature of family reality is a prime example of reification, or what Whitehead (1929, p. 11) called "the fallacy of misplaced concreteness." In the social sciences, this is always a threat. Hard on the heels of this threat of mistaking knowledge claims for ontological claims are the arguments that what is ontologically given represents the correct moral order. This argument from "what is in reality" to "what should be reality" is typical of 17th-century "natural law" arguments. The following quote provides a vivid example of how clinicians, scholars, and practitioners may get caught in reification and moralism:

> In reviewing this attempt to summarize how family systems *do* operate, I am struck by how clinicians spend a good deal of energy trying to get families to operate as they believe a good family system *should* operate that is by establishing joint goals and monitoring progress toward them, These clinicians work hard to make family members more aware of the dynamics of their previously unmediated escalating cycles so that they can bring these cycles into line with their intentions. In short, such clinicians do all they can in their power to make families more cybernetic, less reflexive, and less opportunistic. (Broderick, 1993, pp. 85–86)

Clinicians and systems theorists might respond that this criticism can be substantiated by an ample number of instances in which scholars make such incautious claims in almost every area of science. Systems theorists might argue that every field contains its proportion of naive participants and outrageous claims. The rejoinder that systems theorists offer is that reification is totally inconsistent with the constructivist epistemology according to which systems models are not models of "reality" so much as heuristics for different purposes. Therefore, systems theorists feel that their area is no more prone to reification than any other theory. Furthermore, systems theorists would argue that the constructivist epistemology militates against such abuses more than is the case in the traditional theoretical approaches.

## Conclusion

Family systems theory has proved useful in two areas of family studies. One of these areas is family therapy. Family process scholars have found systems theory to be a useful metaphor in guiding intervention and interpreting the complex relationships between individuals and their families. The second area in which family systems theory has proved useful is that of marital and family communications and interaction. Communications theory is properly a form of systems theory because it incorporates many of the basic concepts such as feedback and variety (see Shannon & Weaver, 1949). It has proven a most useful approach for the scientific study of the family. The conflict, if any, between these two variants is whether systems theory is both metaphor and science. A clear understanding of the constructivist epistemology behind systems theory allows both interpretations. The same model may be used for different purposes and in different ways.

Is the future of systems theory in the study of the family a bright one? Turner (1991) was pessimistic because he felt the concepts and models in systems theory do not fit well with social phenomena. For example, efforts to adopt decision theory, game theory, information theory, analysis of servomechanisms, and similar bodies of precise concepts have never proven very useful. The experience of family scholars appears to differ with this assessment. Furthermore, Turner's view of what has "proven very useful" may be at odds with the more open perspective assumed by systems theorists. In the final analysis, optimism or pessimism about systems theory may largely depend on how scholars view the noncompetitive epistemology of constructivism. Von Glasersfeld (1987) ended his essay with the warning of a true believer: "Looking at the world today, one must conclude that this way of thinking, rather than fostering competition, may be the only way to maintain human life on this planet" (p. 11).

## Suggested Readings

Broderick, C. (1993). *Understanding family process*. Newbury Park, CA: Sage.
*This is an excellent introduction to family process theory that nicely unifies both scientific and therapeutic contributions to the theory.*

Whitchurch, G., & Constantine, L. (1993). Systems theory. In P. Boss, W. Doherty, R. LaRossa, W. Schumm, & S. Steinmetz (Eds.), *Sourcebook of family theories and methods: A contextual approach* (pp. 325–352). New York: Plenum.
*This chapter provides a good general history and survey of systems theory.*

# 6

# The Conflict Framework

Bill and Mariel have been living together for about a year. They have decided to get married. They both wanted to have a church wedding. The minister they contacted told them that the church requires all those wanting to be married to attend a marriage preparation course offered by the church. Tonight, they are attending the first of the marriage preparation classes. Bill is quite skeptical of the course. He believes that because he and Mariel have lived together for almost a year, they should know a lot about what to expect in marriage. Bill and Mariel complete their answers to an inventory of questions regarding expectations for marriage before they sit down with their counselor. The counselor's first question is, "The two of you have answered the question 'How many arguments and fights do you expect per month?' in very different ways. Mariel expects about four per month and Bill only envisions one per month. Can you each explain to me how you view fights and why you have such different expectations about the number of fights?"

Bill answers that perhaps he and Mariel have a different definition of what a fight is. He defines a fight as not just a disagreement but one person being angry toward the other person. To his surprise, Mariel agrees with his definition. Bill then asks Mariel, "So, if there is no difference between our definitions, why do you think we will fight that much?" Mariel responds that her parents have been happily married for 30 years and that is about how much they fight. Bill says, "Fighting that much isn't healthy for a relationship," but Mariel counters that fighting is normal in a marriage as long as it doesn't get out of hand. The counselor then asks, "If a couple were always harmonious, what would spark them to grow and change?"

Bill and Mariel have encountered some differences in their basic expectations about marriage. Bill appears to believe that happy marriages are harmonious, with few disagreements or fights. Mariel seems to be more accepting of conflict as being "natural" in marriage. The counselor's final question about growth and change would appear to support the view that conflict in marriage might even play an important dynamic role. Bill and Mariel are faced with an important task. They are being asked to identify what they see as the role of conflict in marriage. Are good marriages free of conflict? Is conflict always destructive, or can it be a source of growth and nourishment for a relationship? And how do partners in a marriage keep conflict from getting out of hand?

These questions are part of what we address in this chapter. This chapter is concerned with the way conflict theory explains family behavior. In every theory, there reside assumptions about the nature of humans and the constraints under which humans operate. In addition, we all carry around our own assumptions and expectations, such as assumptions about what our marriage will be like and what is "normal" and "not normal" in marriage. In a sense, then, this chapter on conflict theory will not answer the questions posed above. But perhaps more than any other of the theoretical frameworks in this book, conflict theory allows us to fully discuss and examine these important questions and assumptions about conflict.

## Intellectual Traditions

The central question for conflict theory was first and perhaps most simply stated by the social philosopher Thomas Hobbes (1651/1947) as "How is social order possible?" Without an understanding of the perspective Hobbes and later conflict theorists have about human nature, the question regarding social order might appear naive. Like utilitarian theorists, Hobbes believed that the first law of all organisms is self-preservation and self-assertion. He emphasized that among humans, this law is elevated to a natural right. As a result of the natural right of the human self to survive and assert itself, the first law presents us with a natural order in which people's self-interest collides with the self-interest of others. The basic state of nature then is a "war of all against all." Hobbes acknowledges that such an existence would be short, brutish, and largely intolerable. This leads Hobbes to his second law, according to which humans form a social contract whereby all humans give up some of their rights of self-interest to live in a stable and secure society of laws. Unlike the utilitarian perspective, once a society of laws is established, much of human self-interest is regulated and governed by laws rather than negotiated. Hobbes did not see all rights of self-interest being relinquished to the state, however. Human self-interest continues to provide the impetus for collision and conflict but within the framework of the laws of the state.

It may be helpful to note that both conflict and exchange theorists recognize the importance of human disagreements, disputes, and hostilities. A difference between the two major perspectives, however, is that exchange theorists assume a basic similarity in the resources of social actors, so that there is potential for freely bargained agreements that are fair to all negotiating parties, and with a willingness to renegotiate when the net profits to involved actors become misaligned. Conflict theory, however, becomes especially relevant when resources are decidedly unequal. In such cases, relatively dramatic and temporarily disruptive actions on the part of deprived and powerless persons and groups may be necessary to restore or create a social order that is fair to all participants.

Hobbes and other social contract theorists set the stage for much of the evolution of conflict theory. The assumptions of human self-interest and the need for a social contract are ideas held by most conflict theorists in one form or another. But it was Karl Marx and Friedrich Engels who not only developed a more thorough and sophisticated view of conflict but directly applied their perspective to the family. Marx and Engels developed a theory of history (*historiography*) in which they envisioned social and historical change occurring by means of class conflict. Marx and Engels, like most of their cohort in Europe, were influenced by the German idealist Friedrich Hegel (1770–1831). Hegel viewed history as ruled by a dialectic of ideas (thus the moniker *idealism*). According to Hegel's dialectical logic, each idea (thesis) automatically presupposed its opposite (antithesis), and out of the tension between the idea and its opposite, the mind would seek to unify the opposition, doing so by creatively moving to a more encompassing idea (synthesis). This synthesis would form a new thesis and presuppose another antithesis, followed by an even more encompassing synthesis, and so on.

Marx and Engels vehemently attacked the Hegelian notions (e.g., Marx & Engels, 1845–1846/1965). They argued that history was ruled not by ideas but by material production. Using Hegel's dialectic, they explained that there were, in fact, only two relations to production. People could either control the means of production or labor for those who controlled production. Marx and Engels then proposed a *dialectic material* explanation of history from primitive to modern times. For example, in feudal times the opposition was between the lords who owned the land and the serfs who worked the land. In the industrial era, the opposition was between the new industrialists (*bourgeoisie*) and the factory workers or *proletariat* (e.g., Marx,

1913). Marx and Engels envisioned an end to the dialectic of class opposition only with the development of automation and communal society.

The family occupies a unique niche in the conflict theory of Marx and Engels. They recognized that the family was rooted in biological self-interest (sex and reproduction) and yet is also a form of social organization. Engels (1884/1946), in his book *The Origin of the Family, Private Property and the State*, attributes the move from matrilineage (mistakenly termed "mother right") to patrilineage, patriarchy, and monogamy (father right) as being the result of the first division of labor, based on gender. Out of this biologically rooted division of labor came the first class conflict: The first class opposition that appears in history coincides with the development of the antagonism between man and woman in monogamous marriage, and the first class oppression coincides with that of the female sex by the male (Engels, 1884/1946, p. 58). Although Engels did not see the family as a "causal" influence, he did see it as a microcosm of the conflict in the larger culture: It is the cellular form of civilized society, in which the nature of the oppositions and contradictions fully active in that society can already be studied (p. 58). Thus, for Engels, the family provided a microcosm of the class conflict in the larger society rather than having its own independent microsystem process of conflict. This introduces a basic question in conflict theory, which is, "Does conflict in marriage and the family simply mirror a macrosocial process or is the conflict in the family of a different kind?"

At the core of the conflict theory of Hobbes, Marx, and Engels lies a basic assumption about scarcity of resources. If there were a surplus of resources, then even if humans act out of self-interest, there would be no reason for them to pursue conflict. Indeed, Marx made this scarcity a key to the last phase of his dialectical materialist view of history in switching from resources being distributed "to each according to his work" to "to each according to his need." Later, family conflict theorists (e.g., Scanzoni, 1972; Sprey, 1979) became more conscious of this assumption as being the basic factor underlying the notion of conflict. The ideas of resources and power have become central to what many consider to be the true nature of conflict in the family.

Although some conflict scholars undoubtedly see resources as the key to understanding conflict, others believe that conflict also has a structural dimension. Georg Simmel (1904) viewed conflict as being embedded in the structure of groups. Moreover, he emphasized the positive role of conflict in achieving greater unity for the group. Sprey (1979) has a more concrete perspective on the structural characteristics of the dialectic within families. He envisions "a perpetual confrontation between the quest for autonomy and jointness as characteristic of all groups, but especially small intimate ones, such as marriages and families" (1979, p. 141). Indeed, Sprey sees this form of structural conflict as so endemic that "issues involving individual autonomy and the competition between privacy and jointness cannot be 'solved' except through the termination of the relationship" (p. 147). One of the implications of the structuralist perspective on conflict is that because conflict is endemic in the group the only alternative is to "manage" conflict so that it does not escalate to damaging levels or reduce the group to totally separate individuals.

In the century that has passed since Marx and Engels, conflict theory has developed as one of the theories in the pantheon of social science theories. The writings of Marx and Engels contained both a theory of history and what Turner (1991) calls an emancipatory call to action (e.g., Marx & Engels, 1867/1971). This emancipatory element has led some scholars to view conflict theory as essentially nonscientific:

> Conflict theory tends to be only a step away from *ideology*, which may be defined as the organization of ideas for the promotion of social movements or for the defense of social institutions. An ideology is a system of ideas intended to serve practice rather than to promote the aims of understanding. (Martindale, 1960, p. 151)

On the other side, some proponents of the emancipatory vision of conflict theory argue that all social science theories are ideologies because they all defend one institution or another. Marx and Engels argued that understanding is emancipatory and that knowledge and political action are always tied together (praxis). Without pretending to resolve this argument, we should nonetheless point out that some family conflict theorists view the theory as providing both understanding and political direction.

Summing up, the focus of conflict theory is on both conflict within groups (e.g., family interaction) and conflict between groups (e.g., class conflict). Some conflict theorists of the family view internal family interactions as being part of the larger social process, and others view the conflict in the family as being unique because of the affectual nature of the resources (Scanzoni, 1970). Most conflict theorists accept the assumptions from Hobbes that humans act out of self-interest and that social order needs to be negotiated and ritualized. The existence of social order in the form of the state and laws does not mean that conflict is absent. Rather, conflict continues between interest groups and between self-interested individuals, and these conflicts must be managed to keep the group from the extremes of social breakup on the one hand and war on the other hand.

## Focus and Scope Assumptions

*Humans are motivated principally by self-interest.* Individuals' self-interest is rooted in the will to survive and persevere. By extension, humans generalize this orientation of self-interest from mere survival to a more general mode of operating in the world. Thus, if one desires something owned by another who has more power or force, the solution is to ban together with like-minded persons to gain sufficient force to realize your desires. This is the state of nature. In contrast to utilitarian theories, this self-interest is not necessarily tied to an ability to be rational. This rather unbridled primitive self-interest is the source of Hobbes's "war of all against all."

*Conflict is endemic in social groups.* People who join together to attain a goal of common interest such as having children nonetheless have conflict because of disagreements on other issues and the structural opposition between autonomy and togetherness. Indeed, we can imagine that in those social groups (family) in which we spend the most time and have the greatest expectations for "togetherness," we might also find the greatest conflict.

*Conflict is inevitable between social groups.* We expect to find conflict within small, intimate social groups, but also *between* social groups. Individuals have "interests," but in any society those interests must be pursued by means of group affiliation. All social groups have "interests," even if only for survival. Usually, these interests are far reaching, such as for wealth or land. Because not all groups can simultaneously achieve their goals (resource scarcity), there is conflict. The assumption is that groups and individuals must compete for scarce resources. Indeed, resource scarcity is the necessary condition for competition.

As a result of both structural conflict and competition, we find that *the normal state of society is to be in conflict rather than harmony.* Harmony is an achieved rather than a natural state. This assumption is crucial to our understanding families through the perspective of conflict theory. Accordingly, when you get married you should expect to be entering an arrangement more prone to conflict than to harmony.

*Because conflict is both endemic and inevitable, the primary concern in the study of social groups such as the family is how they manage conflict.* If conflict is the rule, then the Hobbesian question "How is order possible?" makes sense even in the study of such close and intimate groups as the family. Indeed, much of family conflict theory involves examination of the techniques used in marriages and families to keep these groups from either separation or war.

## Concepts

### CONFLICT

Of course, the most basic concept in conflict theory is that of *conflict*. Conflict has been variously defined as disagreement, clashes, and discordance in interests or ideas. The definition that Sprey (1979) offers is exceptional in its clarity. He says that conflict *as a process* "is defined as a confrontation between individuals, or groups, over scarce resources, controversial means, incompatible goals, or combinations of these." (p. 134). Sprey's emphasis that conflict is a process rather than a behavior is consistent with Marx and other theorists who emphasize the dialectical nature of conflict. Thus, behavior might be used to infer this process, but the process itself is not necessarily observable. For example, your parents might want you to visit on the weekend, but this clashes with your plans for a fishing trip. This particular example of parent–child conflict of goals may not be obvious to an external observer and represents a more covert conflict. The same might be true of a clash in ideas. But the conflict between runners at a track meet attempting to be first across the finish line is readily observable and overt.

### STRUCTURE

*Structure* has two meanings in conflict theory: the *structure of the situation* as either competitive or cooperative and the *structure of the group*. Let's examine the cooperative or competitive situational structure first.

*Competition* does not refer to a process but to an observable organization or structure of scarce resources. Competition is the way in which a situation is organized or structured. For example, if we tell students that we will "fit" their grades to a "normal" curve so that only 5% will receive an A, then we are structuring the learning situation in a competitive way. In this case, it makes sense for students not to assist one another because they lessen their own probability of getting an A in the course. If we tell all students what the standard is for attaining an A and that all may get As if they attain these standards, then we structure the learning situation in a noncompetitive way, a way that emphasizes *cooperation*. In this situation, the free exchange of ideas and assistance makes sense. Competition and cooperation, then, are set by the social rules, or norms, that organize an activity or social system. These rules, or norms, structure the situation so that not all parties interested in the goal can achieve it (competition) or so that potentially all parties interested in the goal can achieve it (cooperation).

The second meaning of structure is the *structure of the group,* or social structure. There are several dimensions to the social structure of the group that conflict theorists view as salient. First, and most obvious, is the number of members in the group. Conflict theorists from Simmel (1904) to the present recognize that group size affects the techniques with which the group can manage conflict. For example, a two-person group cannot be democratic; a dyad can only argue and negotiate. Groups of three or more can form power coalitions to get their way (e.g., Caplow, 1968). A second dimension of group structure is the age of the members. Marx and Engels (1867/1971) pointed out in *The Communist Manifesto* that children and women were subjugated to the male bourgeoisie. Later, Caplow (1968) argued that resources and power accrue with the aging of children in the family. He supposed that as children developed social skills and resources, their power in the family increased. Likewise, becoming elderly may involve some loss of resources and power. The third dimension of the structure of the group is gender. Marx and Engels viewed gender as important in the internal dialectic of the family in the first division of labor. Some later theorists concentrate on gender and the family (see Chapter 7 of this volume; see also Firestone, 1970). Thus, most conflict theorists analyze the structure of the group by the number of members, the age structure, the gender structure, or a combination thereof.

RESOURCES

The notion of *resources* is a pivotal concept for conflict theory. Marx and Engels viewed the basic resource as the "control of the means of production." Their focus on the material economy has proved too narrow for most current conflict theorists. The concept of resources is a broader concept, closely aligned to the notion of *power.* There exists considerable scholarly debate over the exact relationship between power, resources, and authority (e.g., Brinkerhoff & Lupri, 1989; Cromwell & Olson, 1975; Szinovacz, 1987). We present what we believe is a coherent picture of the relationship between authority, power, and resources. Resources is the broadest of the three concepts and includes the other two (power and authority) as subsets. Resources include all the knowledge, skills, techniques, and materials that are at the ready disposal of a person or group. Clearly, resources provide a potential base for the exercise of power. Power, according to Sprey (1979), is the ability of an individual or group to exercise effective control over others and things. By this definition, power can only be measured by its outcome, which is control, whereas resources provide the potential for power and control. Authority is a type of resource that is constructed by the normative system of a specific culture (Rodman, 1967). Thus, for example, a woman in Greece might have more resources (potential) than her unemployed husband, but if there is a strong cultural norm for patriarchy, then the husband may have greater control (power) in the family. Under more egalitarian or democratic authority norms, the greater resources of the female would give her greater control (power; Scanzoni, 1972). Thus, the relationship between authority and power is that the normative system (authority) can serve as one among many resources. Resources that are relevant in a situation can be used to exert control or exercise power.

## NEGOTIATION

*Negotiation* is one of the major techniques used in families to manage conflict. Negotiation is restricted, however, to those situations in which each person or group desires a goal that cannot be attained without the assistance of other parties. A simple example of this is playing a board game such as Monopoly. Although winning may be one person's goal, without the cooperation of at least one other family member, that is, his or her willingness to participate, winning is impossible. Another example is when a mother wants to take the family on a picnic, but the father prefers taking the family to the swimming pool. Behind both options is the notion of "doing something with the family," which means that willing cooperation is needed to reach the goal. Negotiation happens when both parties state their goals and then use their resources to induce or coerce the other to move closer to their goal. Argument, bribery, and deceit may all be involved in negotiations.

## CONSENSUS

*Consensus* means agreement. It is the preferable outcome of negotiation. Consensus is achieved when parties to a negotiation agree. For example, many family members enter into temporary coalitions with a sibling or parent to achieve an end. Such coalitions rely on agreement between the coalition partners. Agreement or consensus can also be achieved in mate selection by selecting mates with the same values and orientation and by socialization of mate or children to accept the same view one holds. The opposite of consensus is disagreement. Dissension is discord arising from a disagreement. It is an interesting trademark of close relationships that we spend enormous amounts of time focused on areas of disagreement but seldom feel a need to focus on areas of agreement because these areas have been success- fully managed.

### Propositions

Conflict theorists have often concentrated on macrosystem analysis of society and global confrontations. Some conflict theorists believe that the family is simply a microcosm of these larger processes and that what is said of the larger society is naturally also true for the family. A significant number of family conflict theorists have claimed, however, that the family (and some other small groups) is sufficiently unlike larger social units and that they must be analyzed separately. Sprey (1979), for example, argues that the autonomy–togetherness issue is atypical of macrolevel analyses and yet important in analyzing the family. Caplow (1968) argues that there are distinct and important structural differences between even two- and three-person groups. The propositions we include below principally focus on the family.

Social groups such as the family are structurally disposed to conflict both within and between groups. This supposition implies that variables subsumed under structure of the group (membership, age, gender) and structure of the situation (competition and coopera- tion) are related to the degree of conflict. Even the most homogeneous group (two women of the same age) in the most cooperative norma- tive situation would still be predisposed to conflict, because in a dyad there is the structural issue of autonomy–togetherness, and in dyads all issues can only be resolved by direct negotiation.

*Conflict between groups is based on resource allocation and competitive social structure.*

There exists no known society in which resources are allocated equally to all. This is not to say that resource allocation is unfair. Indeed, even Marx was not egalitarian in this regard but said "to each according to his need" and needs are not distributed equally. Thus, the mere fact that some families have more than others ensures com- petition. Families may participate in larger interest-group clusters such as Children First or other profamily or prochild groups. Regardless of the validity of the perceptions involved, the recent uproar over "family values" attests to the fact that many families see themselves competing for scarce benefits against what they perceive as "non-family" groups such as gays, singles, and even single-parent families. As a corollary to the above,

> *Conflict within the group (e.g., family) is due to the inequity of resources between individuals.*

Resources are differentially allocated in a social system, often by group membership, age, and gender. As a result, resource differentials exist in the family so that some members have more resources than other members. This resource inequity leads to conflict to the degree that the norms internal to the family are competitive rather than cooperative. For example, women generally make less money than men, ensuring that they have fewer resources and, therefore, even in egalitarian authority structures, have on average less power in relation to their husbands.

Conflict within marriages and families is minimally structural. Regardless of gender and age, dyads and larger groups are faced with the conflict of individual members over autonomy versus togetherness. This issue is especially salient for the dyad in two regards. First, togetherness necessarily involves the only other member. A family group offers several levels of togetherness (sibling, mother–child, etc.), but togetherness in the dyad always involves the other person. The second reason the issue of conflict is especially salient for the dyad is that negotiations are always against the same adversary. In families, coalitions can be formed to overpower the resources of any one individual. One implicit strength of family coalitions is that your coalition partners on today's issue might well be your adversaries on tomorrow's issue, and today's enemy might be tomorrow's coalition partner. The dyad lacks this dynamic; today's adversary is also tomorrow's adversary in negotiations (Caplow, 1968).

> *Negotiation, as a form of conflict management, is more likely in egalitarian authority structures.*

and

> *The outcome of negotiation is more likely to favor the person with the greatest resources in the family.*

The authority pattern in the culture sets up the norms or rules as to who has authority based on age and gender. The more unilateral the authority pattern (matriarchy, patriarchy), the less room there is for negotiation. Indeed, negotiation is most likely in democratic or egalitarian families.

*Negotiation involves resources; whoever has the greatest resources can negotiate the greatest rewards in a compromise.*

This proposition is somewhat akin to the old saying, "Them that's got, gets." It must be remembered, however, that there are many forms of resources in addition to money and occupation. Indeed, personal abilities to manipulate, lie, and cajole must be counted among the resources of relevance in negotiations. Negotiations are almost invariably used in egalitarian marriages, whereas once children are present, coalition formation might play a larger role than negotiation.

*Coalition formation is most likely in groups (families) with democratic authority patterns.*

and

*In democratic groups, material resources alone do not necessarily predict family coalitions and outcomes.*

In most North American families, one person does not make all the decisions. Decision making is a complex matter of consultation, coalition formation, and lobbying. Caplow (1968) points out that as children grow and mature, they gain increased interpersonal competence, knowledge, and material resources. The power that they have is not sufficiently great as to countermand the father's residual patriarchal authority and greater material resources, but coupled with the mother and other siblings, children might have significant influence over decision making. Indeed, even before the children are old enough to participate in such coalitions, they are assumed to be coalesced with the mother and constitute a resource for the mother in that she might voice what is best for the children as part of negotiations.

These few propositions represent a small subset of the many that have been developed in conflict theory. These few should be sufficient to demonstrate how conflict theorists deal with the sources of conflict and the management of conflict in families. Most scholars would agree that the family is the central building block of social systems, and we might propose that the techniques of conflict management and authority patterns learned in the family influence the directions to be taken by the entire social system. In this sense, it could easily be argued that Marx's view that the family is a microcosm reflecting processes in the larger society could be turned on its head. It is equally defensible to propose that family structure and conflict resolution techniques are imitated by larger social institutions to maintain balance and resolve disputes.


## Variations

There are many variants of conflict theory. Some variants involve latching on to one dimension of conflict, such as gender, and elevating it as the major explanatory variable of all conflict, much as Marx elevated the "means of material production" to such explanatory status. The four variants we focus on below represent the most conspicuous schools of thought on family conflict and the most productive to date. Although these variants do not exhaust the varieties of conflict theory in general, we feel that they represent the range of work on family conflict theory.


### STRUCTURAL CONFLICT

One of the acknowledged fathers of sociology is Georg Simmel. Simmel's sociology was "formal" and theoretical, following the style of the formal philosophy of nature of the German philosopher Immanuel Kant. Simmel viewed conflict as a constant process of associative and dissociative forces that brought unity and coherence to society. Simmel did not identify one underlying cause of conflict such as Marx's relation to the means of production, nor did he view the processes in the family as simply a microcosm of larger-scale processes. In regard to the family, Simmel focused his attention on the formal properties of small-group structure and interaction. He viewed marriage and family as distinctly different social structures with different social properties. Marriage, because it is a two-person, or dyadic, structure, involves one individual being totally dependent on the other:

> This dependence of the dyad on its two individual members causes the thought of its existence to be accompanied by the thought of its termination much more closely and impressively than in any group, where every member knows that even after his or her retirement or death, the group can continue to exist. (Simmel, 1950, pp. 123–124)

Simmel (1950) argues that marriage is unlike most dyads in one regard: "namely, absence of a super-personal unit" (p. 129). He argues that the institution of marriage seems to transcend the two individuals involved, in part because it is socially regulated. Even though marriage is different from other dyads, it lacks the structural dimensions of three-person and larger groups. Indeed, Simmel says, "a marriage with one child has a character which is completely different from that of a childless marriage" (p. 138). The critical difference for Simmel is that once the group grows beyond the dyad, "parties of interest" may form alliances. Simmel sought to characterize the types of triads that are universal to this social group. The task of fully formalizing and applying the notions of "ties" and "coalitions" to the family fell to later sociologists, however.

Caplow (1968) calls the mother–father–child triad the "primary triad." He acknowledges that there are other significant family triads, such as sibling triads, but views this parent–child triad as most basic. In Caplow's view, family members form coalitions based on each person's relative power. If the father had greater power than either the mother or child, a winning coalition between the child and mother might be possible. Caplow suggested that over the family's life cycle, the relative power of family members changes, and potential coalitions also change. One of the strengths this has for families is that today's coalition partner might be tomorrow's opponent, and today's opponent might be tomorrow's partner. Caplow (1968) suggests that the typical family evolves from a dyad in which the husband (father to be) usually has more power than the wife (mother to be) $(F > M)$. As a child grows, the mother–child coalition tends to equal the individual power of father $(F:M + C)$. This might increasingly force the father into a coalition with mother $(F + M > C)$. Eventually, the mother–child coalition surpasses the relative power of the father $(F < M + C)$. Because the mother would be the dominant member of the mother–child coalition, she would effectively have the greatest power in families with one adolescent child. Of course, Caplow recognizes that coalition strategies become more complex when there is more than one child or a parental member is absent. Caplow's theory is a direct extension of Simmel (1950). It adds the ingredient of the ordinal $(<, >, =)$ computation of individual power and graph theory to the prediction of coalition formation. He acknowledges that social norms of authority and the compatibility of coalition partners play a role in coalition formations, but the initial step in the theory is to outline the logically possible coalitions. In the end, Caplow (1968) provides a systematic and scientifically measurable approach to the resolution of family conflict through coalitions.

Caplow (1968) is sensitive to criticism that he might be ignoring the emotional context of family life. He argues like Simmel (1904),

Coser (1956), and many other conflict theorists that the "function" of conflict is "solidarity." Caplow argues that emotions are tied to coalitions because coalition partners attempt to reinforce and protect one another. Out of this coalition partner interaction come the emotions that we associate with being in a family: "Love is an intense preference for a particular coalition partner. Hate is an intense reaction against an opponent" (Caplow, 1968, p. 78). For Caplow, then, conflict and coalitions are not a sideshow in family life but compose the very essence of being in a family:

> Family life is fraught with the tension of conflicting emotions precisely because it is based on coalitions and every coalition involves an opponent. Begun with a husband–wife coalition, continued by a mother–child coalition, a family is sustained by the interlocking forces of love and hate in somewhat the same way that buildings are held up by opposing forces of tension and compression. (p. 78)

In their structural conflict approach, Simmel (1904) and Caplow (1968) attempt to provide a scholarly and scientific approach to conflict in families in which love, partnership, hate, and solidarity emerge from conflict.

### MICRORESOURCE CONFLICT THEORY

Microresource theory is unique in incorporating the giving and receiving of affection in an accounting of resources. Macroresource theory tends to be focused on larger social structures rather than the interpersonal dimension of "affect" or "expressiveness." As a result of this interpersonal emphasis, microresource is more prone to stress "negotiations" as a technique of conflict management, whereas macroresource theorists are more prone to see the need for more revolutionary forms of conflict to bring about structural social change.

Scanzoni's (1972) microresource theory eclectically draws from a diversity of theories, such as exchange theory, conflict theory, and even functionalist theory. It is somewhat difficult, not to mention risky, to identify Scanzoni's (1972) theory with any one framework. But because the basic focus is on marital conflict and its resolution through negotiations, it appears to us to best fit as a variant of conflict theory.

Although Scanzoni (1972) accepts Simmel's (1904) argument that conflict may lead to solidarity, he also shares with Coser (1956) the suspicion that this glosses over "what tears families apart." Following Coser, Scanzoni (1972) distinguishes two forms of conflict: basic conflict, which brings into question the most basic "rules of the game," and nonbasic conflict, which is played out according to the rules of the game. He provides a tidy analogy. Imagine a game of football. The two teams can conflict and yet build solidarity as long as they follow the rules of the game. But if they lack agreement on these rules, then we have basic conflict. Scanzoni then portrays the basic rules of the family or marital game.

Scanzoni views the rules (norms) of the family as governing the exchange of the husband's instrumental duties for expressive rights and likewise the wife's expressive duties for instrumental rights. The husband's right is the reciprocal of the wife's duty, and the husband's duty is the reciprocal of the wife's right. An instrumental activity is a means to some end, whereas an expressive activity tends to be an end in itself and carries affect or emotion. For example, the father holding a baby while the mother searches for a diaper is instrumental in the sense that a playpen might also do the job. On the other hand, holding, cuddling, and playing with a baby enjoying the simple affectual expression of love is an expressive activity. Scanzoni argues that the traditional rules for family are that the husband has instrumental duties, mainly as a provider, and the wife has mainly expressive duties, such as tension reduction, child care, and sexual services. The wife has the right to expect the husband to adequately provide for the family, and the husband has a right to expect expressive services from the wife. Nonbasic conflict may occur within these marriages over the discipline of children, economic matters, and so on, but such conflict does not bring into question the basic rules of the game. Indeed, Scanzoni, following Simmel (1904), says this nonbasic conflict may enhance the stability of the marriage and the family and bring about change and growth.

Basic conflict, on the other hand, challenges the rules of the game. According to Scanzoni (1972), there are several ways that basic conflict emerges. One is if one partner fails to live up to role expectations such as provider or sexual partner. This is a key to feelings of inequity in the marriage. Other sources are exogenous, or outside of any one marriage, such as the change away from patriarchy and the increased accessibility for women to their own resources such as education and work. As these changes come about and women have greater instrumental resources, they would want to renegotiate the basic rules, because those rules are now a source of inequity for them. Wives now have instrumental resources of their own, devaluing the contribution of husbands' resources. When women have approximately equal instrumental resources to those of the man in a relationship, they may renegotiate the expressive roles they have fulfilled in traditional marriages by demanding more expressive duties from the husband as their right or reducing the expressive duties they perform, because the value of the man's provider role (resources) has been reduced.

Although Scanzoni's (1970, 1972) analysis began over three decades ago, it continues to be refined (Scanzoni & Szinovacz, 1980) and remains one of the more cogent analyses of changing gender roles in the family and the resulting conflict that surrounds such basic redesignation of family roles. Today, we can see that there are a number of forces exogenous to the family that might also be responsible for the decline in male ability to fulfill the provider role. For example, the rate of increase for male earnings relative to female earnings has decreased. Furthermore, the purchasing power of families has been eroded to such a degree that most families require two incomes simply to maintain living standards equivalent to one-earner families in 1970. Female participation rates in education and the labor force have increased dramatically. Women have tended to seek work in the growing service sector (tertiary) of the economy rather than the downsizing production sectors (primary and secondary). As a result, women find themselves increasingly to be the more stable provider in a marriage. Of course, women still do the lion's share of the housework, or "second shift," compared with men. Thus, women have increased their instrumental duties for the family but with no corresponding reduction in their expressive duties. Two decades later, this inequity in the family's rules and roles seems to have become greater and still provides the foundation for the basic conflict predicted by Scanzoni (1972).

DIALECTICAL HISTORIOGRAPHY

There are few attempts in the area of family theory to follow the grand historical mapping and dialectical interpretation of scholars such as Hegel and Marx. Ogburn and Nimkoff (1955) offer a modest version in their analysis of the relationship between the loss of family functions and technological change. Without doubt, the most ambitious historical perspective on family change has been that of Carle Zimmerman in his book *Family and Civilization* (1947). Zimmerman's analysis is seldom cited by today's family researchers intent on testing hypotheses with immediate practical implications and rooted to a specific time and place. When we ask "big" questions, however, such as "Where is society headed?" and "Will the family survive?" we find Zimmerman's theory of great relevance.

Zimmerman views social change as a dialectical process based on authority and power. The history of the human family can be understood by examining the *dialectic* between the family being the major site of authority over individuals or other institutions such as church and state being the major authority over individuals. Zimmerman argues that family and the state struggle for dominant authority over the individual. Failure to grasp this major struggle may be why others who have discussed theories of the family treat Zimmerman as an "institutional" theorist (e.g., Nye & Berardo, 1966/1981) rather than conflict theorist.

In Zimmerman's perspective, human history goes through cycles. At the beginning of a historical cycle, family authority evolves as paramount and unchallenged. This first of three phases is marked by the *trustee family*. Because family descent is a way of passing on wealth and status, the head of the family wields enormous power over the well-being of individuals. State and church control are limited because the trustee family controls the behavior of its members and transmits its values and systems of control from generation to generation. In this phase, the individual family member is subordinate to and dependent on the decisions of the head of the family. The family name and estate are ultimate in the trustee family.

The second phase of the cycle is marked first by the gradual increase in the abuse of authority by the unquestioned and uncontrolled head of the trustee family. Because there are no checks and balances to the head of the trustee family, church and state slowly evolve to offer some relief to the consolidation of authority and control in the trustee family. The type of family that is indicative of this second phase is called the *domestic family*. The domestic family represents a balance between the authority of the head of the family and the authority of church and state. Although the individual is buffered from the abuses of family authority by the state's increasing recognition of individual rights, the state and church also support and condone the family as an institution of social control because it passes on the values and discipline needed for civil society.

In the last phase of the historical cycle, the state wields most of the power and authority over individuals. Individual rights are supreme and the family group has little authority or control over its members. This phase is marked by what Zimmerman calls the *atomistic family*. The atomistic family is a loose social group and individual members are fully protected by the state from the authority of the family. Zimmerman stresses that this last phase is doomed to destruction because, to maintain a disciplined and civil society, the state is dependent on the family's socialization of the individual but has supplanted the family's authority so that adequate socialization and training can no longer occur. Once family authority is undermined and individuals are no longer trained, social control breaks down as does the civilization. In the vacuum of authority, the trustee family once again takes over control and discipline, and the cycle begins anew.

Zimmerman argues that civilization is now nearing the end of its second historical cycle through the three family types. Currently, we have evolved atomistic families and view the individual's rights and privileges as preeminent. Zimmerman's interpretation of history is, of course, not the only plausible analysis. There can be little doubt, however, that Zimmerman's work is one of the best examples of family historiography in the 20th century.

## DIALECTICAL DECONSTRUCTIONISM AND CRITICAL THEORY

*Critical theory* refers to a diverse cluster of scholars and scholarship united by their criticism of positivistic science and many established ways of knowing. It includes some phenomenologists such as Habermas (see Chapter 3) and Lyotard. Although its philosophical origins were from the Vienna Circle (see Thomas and Wilcox, 1987), critical theory has expanded to the point that it now is used most commonly to refer to critics of positivistic science and knowledge and has evolved into a broader perspective currently termed *postmodernism* (see Box 6.1).

*Deconstructionism* is most clearly identified with the work of the French scholar Jacques Derrida (1976). Deconstructionism is one of the many critiques of knowledge to emerge from the more general family of what was called critical theory in the 1980s (e.g., Thomas & Wilcox, 1987) and is currently identified with what scholars now call postmodern theory (see Cheal, 1991; White & Mason, 1999). Derrida's major focus has been to use a "dialectical" method in interpreting textual materials. In this sense, Derrida represents one particular development of *hermeneutics*. He advocates two readings of a text. The first reading constructs an everyday interpretation of it; the second reading deconstructs, or is critical of, all those assumptions developed in the initial reading. The rationale behind this technique is a form of radical *antifoundationalism* (e.g., White & Mason, 1999). Following from the work of the linguistic philosophers Wittgenstein and Austin, Derrida (1978) asserts that all communication acts are inherently "undecidable," or, in lay terms, they have multiple meanings. He argues that there is no way to exclude these several possible meanings to a communicative act. As a result, then, Derrida (1978) supposes that all possible meanings are equivalent because there is no way of definitively deciding among them. This view yields a kind of chaos or plurality of meaning for any communicative act.

The broader movement of deconstructionism has been widely discussed within the realm of literary criticism, but as yet there have

## Box 6.1    An Abbreviated Glossary of Postmodernist Ideas

**anarchy:** disorderliness

**antiessentialism:** absence of necessary truths and of general laws of nature; structure is in the mind

**antitheory:** no categories, no systems of ideas, no structures, no grounds for accepting or rejecting ideas

**artifacticity:** cultural productions such as theme parks and theme restaurants, video games, plastic Christmas trees

**constructivism:** reality is a human and social creation, collectively produced via interaction in groups

**contextualism:** reality is multilayered and framed within a background

**critique of modernity:** evolution and history are not progressive

**cultural cynicism:** culture is surprising, humorous, discontinuous, and perverse

**cultural diversity:** mixing architectural forms; mixing writing styles; mixing "is" and "ought"; mixing old and new

**decentering:** challenging dominant European American culture; a deliberate loss of cohesiveness, consensus, authority, certainty, and contentment; empowering the downtrodden

**deconstruction:** nothing is to be taken for granted

**discourse:** everything is just talk and opinion

**divergent thinking:** breaking out of conformist modes of action; being creative and unusual

**exceptioning:** seeking the nonnormal or the exception

**fluidity:** nothing is constant but change; everything is processual

**nonlinearity:** change is disruptive and transformative

**pluralism:** the appreciation of differences, complexity, and fragmentation; noncategorical thinking

**reflexivity:** the speaker is part of phenomenon spoken

**relativity:** ideas are relational and from a standpoint; there is no final authority for any argument

**subject–object connectedness:** knowledge and knower are interdependent

SOURCES: Adapted from Lemert (1993, parts 4 and 5) and Winton (1995, pp. 177–181).

been only a few applications to sociology (e.g., Game, 1991) and few direct applications to the family (Baber & Allen, 1992). Feminist deconstructionists currently focus on the deconstruction of the everyday view of female sexuality and the reconstruction of alternative meanings (e.g., Cixous & Clement, 1986). Deconstructionism is possibly the most extreme form of antifoundationalism and relativism, because Derrida and his followers feel that if one cannot nail down exactly the meaning of a communication act, then all meanings are on an equal footing. There appears to be no room for degrees of "decidability" in deconstructionism.

Deconstructionism is often linked to postmodernism. Postmodernism is directly linked to Jean-François Lyotard and the publication of *The Postmodern Condition* in 1979 (English translation, 1984). This work was the result of Lyotard's investigations into the status of knowledge commissioned by a university in the Canadian province of Quebec. The conclusion Lyotard (1979/1984) reaches is that all existing perspectives (narratives) on knowledge come from the rationalism of modernity. These perspectives seek to claim "legitimacy," whether for the claims of science as objective or the claims of democracy as just, equal, and free. Lyotard argues that these narratives give "modernity" its "project." Whereas Habermas argues that the project of modernity in science and culture needs to be renewed, Lyotard (1992) argues that it is dead (p. 18). According to Lyotard, we are entering a period in which there are only a plurality of ways of knowing (paralogy), with none having greater claim to veracity than any others. Cheal (1991) states of Lyotard,

> Unlike modernist theorists of knowledge, he does not view this situation negatively, as a "paradigm crisis." Rather, as a post-modernist, he positively embraces paralogy in a celebration of pluralism, and as a way of avoiding all forms of totalitarianism. (p. 157)

It remains somewhat unclear whether Lyotard (1979/1984, 1992) views postmodernism as a philosophy, as a historical era, or both. The descriptor postmodernist is increasingly attached to those who take an antifoundational and relativistic perspective on all knowledge. The term *postmodern* now refers to a set of terms (see Box 6.1) that may seem foreign to the uninitiated. Increasingly, these terms represent the backbone of a theoretical and methodological orientation.

Although we do not as yet have a major deconstructionist approach to the family, Cheal (1991) suggests that North American theories of the family cannot avoid being influenced by this train of thought. Gubrium and Holstein (1990) discuss their approach to definitions of the family as both phenomenological and deconstructionist.

# 164 FAMILY THEORIES

This would seem to indicate that this approach is having some impact on family scholarship. Indeed, many of these issues are discussed by Knapp (1997) and debated by his commentors (e.g., White, 1997) in a special issue of the journal *Family Perspective* on the topics of family theory and hermeneutics. In a recent paper, Allen (2000) argues that we are now in a postmodern era in the study of the family and that the rules of research have moved away from positivistic science. It remains to be seen if this movement, which has currently lost much of its momentum in Europe due to the rediscovery of U.S. pragmatism (e.g., Apel, 1981; Norris, 1989), will catch the imaginations of more than a handful of family scholars in North America.

## Empirical Applications

WIFE ASSAULT

One of the major empirical areas for the application of conflict theory has been family violence (see Johnson & Ferraro, 2000). The very nature of the subject matter, family violence, immediately implies that some variants of conflict theory rather than others will be more relevant. For example, because we are attempting to explain why some husbands assault their wives, theoretical variants of conflict theory that assist in predicting "conflict" seem more relevant than those variants that deal with negotiating, conflict management, and the unifying function of conflict (Caplow, 1968; Simmel, 1904). In general, conflict theory predicts that clashes and confrontations occur when there is competition for scarce resources. One way we can determine the potential for conflict is when one person or group does not have the same resources as another person or group. For Marx, the proletariat did not have the same resources as the bourgeoisie. For feminist theorists, patriarchy helped to ensure that men and women did not have the same resources. Thus, conflict theorists view social inequity as indicating the necessary conditions for conflict to arise.

Wife assault is difficult to observe and study. In North America, there is no uniform method for reporting and recording such incidents. Self-reports by both victims and perpetrators may be biased. Gelles and Straus designed and conducted the 1985 National Family Violence Survey, which probably represents the most complete data we have on wife assault and family violence. Wife assault can be measured as one of the following: pushed, grabbed, shoved; threw something at her; slapped her; kicked, hit, or punched; hit or tried to hit; beat her up; choked; threatened with knife or gun; used a knife or gun (Straus, 1994). Large studies are necessary because of the low incidence of family violence. As Gelles (1994) points out,

> Despite the fact that individuals are more likely to be hit, hurt, and even killed in the privacy of their homes and in intimate, as opposed to non-intimate relationships, the actual annual base rate of such victimization is still about 3 or 4 per 1,000 individuals. (p. 1)

Even though the number of victims adds up over the years, the annual rate of incidence is relatively low.

One version of conflict theory relevant here is based on gender inequality. Some feminist conflict theorists suggest that where gender inequalities exist there is a "patriarchal" social system that justifies and condones wife assault as one of many forms of the subjugation of women to men. Men basically are defending their greater resources from an underclass. Many of those resources are predicated on women "staying in their place." Yllö and Straus (1990) investigated this proposition using the National Family Violence Survey. They reported that the relationship between structural gender inequality (measured by each state's legal, political, and economic equality status) and wife assault is curvilinear. Those states with both the lowest and highest gender inequality showed the highest rates of wife assault. This suggests that feminists might be accurate in their interpretation but only for states in which there is great gender inequality. On the other hand, for states in which there is relatively high gender equality, perhaps Scanzoni's (1972; Scanzoni & Szinovacz, 1980) theory of sexual bargaining and the resulting social disorganization to traditional family roles would supply an explanation for the high rates of spousal abuse.

Straus (1994) tests three versions of conflict theory in an attempt to explain wife assault. The three versions of conflict theory he uses are gender inequality, income inequality, and social disorganization. His measures for gender inequality are the same as used by Yllö and Straus (1990). He uses a single measure of each state's income equality and a composite measure of each state's social disorganization, composed of items such as divorce rates, geographical mobility, and lack of religious affiliation. Straus (1994) reports that both gender inequality and social disorganization measures are significantly related to rates of wife assault. Income inequality, when age is controlled, is not directly related to wife assault. And although the proportion of the variance explained in wife assault is relatively modest (7%–13%), his findings suggest that these theories might be explaining different aspects of wife assault and might interact with income inequities.

Straus's (1994) research supplies an example of how conflict theory may be applied in research. His results should caution theorists about becoming too focused on a single, universal, explanatory source of conflict such as gender inequality. It may well be that there are different, independent but complementary explanations of phenomena such as wife assault. In the end, it may be that a broader, more abstract and inclusive theoretical perspective such as provided by Simmel (1904, 1950) would provide a unitary theoretical framework for these diverse sources of inequality and conflict.

## Implications for Intervention

Conflict theory's emphasis on conflict as endemic to social groups has served to focus attention on how conflict is managed. In the area of therapy, the micro versions of conflict theory emphasizing negotiations have inspired many "fair fighting" programs (e.g., Bach & Wyden, 1968).

These programs concentrate on the negotiation skills and style that allow for couples to negotiate and reach successful compromises. Conflict styles are often viewed as problematic in that some can escalate and lead to further conflict, whereas others tend to dampen further conflict.

Another area in which conflict theory has implications is resource management. Poduska (1993) focuses on the relationship between the management of resources and marital conflict. The management of financial resources is seen as intimately linked to the feelings of family members and the enhancement of relationships.

Many scholars and students would immediately align conflict theory's implications with the more "emancipatory" social movements encompassing general social change in addition to changes in the family. In the past 30 years, there can be little doubt that the most pervasive of these social movements has been the feminist movement. Other emancipatory conflict movements based on Marxian theory have been relatively ineffective when compared with the gains made by feminist movement (see Chapter 7).

## Critiques and Discussion

One of the major hurdles for conflict theory continues to be its emphasis on explaining conflict rather than order. This emphasis was undoubtedly justified in reaction to the stasis inherent in sociological structural–functionalism. Today, however, the emphasis on conflict often appears to highlight the sensational or negative rather than the dialectical process of conflict. For example, some scholars focus on gender or social class inequities without a clear picture of the dynamic process in which these inequities represent either a "thesis" or "antithesis." A very real danger for conflict theory is becoming focused on conflict as an existing social inequity rather than as a dynamic process.

Most of the theorists we have reviewed above avoid this problem. Simmel (1904) and Marx and Engels (1845–1846/1965) focus on the process. Scanzoni (1970) focuses in some detail on the mechanisms forging a synthesis between the inequity of patriarchy and the gender equality of the "equal partner" family.

Another challenge for conflict theory lies in explaining the relative permanence and stability of the social order. It is probably an understatement that norms, roles, and social structure appear to change slowly. Even conflict theorists such as Caplow, Bahr, Chadwick, Hill, and Williamson (1983) report that in the decades since Middletown was first studied and their subsequent return in the 1980s, the hallmark is that not much of importance has changed. If conflict is a dialectical process, it may be that it must be studied over fairly sizeable units of time as envisioned by Marx. The challenge, then, is for conflict theorists to demonstrate the applicability of conflict theory to more limited units of time, such as decades or years.

This challenge might partially be overcome by a greater emphasis on the details of the process of the dialectic. Between thesis, antithesis, and synthesis comes a lot of social interaction. For example, Scanzoni's (1972) work on renegotiating gender roles in the family is the type of detail work that fills in the gaps in the dialectic process. It is this more detailed work that may aspire to be more concrete and scientific than the more emancipatory view of the sweep of history.

What Turner (1998) has labeled the emancipatory viewpoint of some conflict theorists provokes some fairly hostile criticism. This criticism, however, is more subtle than it initially seems. Certainly, no scientist would assert that scientific knowledge might not have an emancipatory aspect to it; there is no disagreement on the issue of whether knowledge can be emancipatory. The issue is whether emancipation is the central aim of a theory (ideology) or whether the central aim is the production of knowledge (science). If the central role of theory is knowledge, then clearly knowledge claims must be judged by a set of criteria that is universally and equally applied to all such claims. In science, claims are subjected to the rules of logic, experiment, and replication. The fear of scientists is that if claims support the ideology, then they will be judged true because they are consistent with the ideology. One of the basic canons of science is that mere consistency of a finding with previous beliefs is insufficient to justify a claim. If such were the case, then findings would only need to support the prevailing ideology or "common sense." Indeed, the history of science is the history of the downfall of systems of thought such as the heliocentric universe, Newton's mechanics, Maxwell's daemon, and the eventual fall of Einstein's relativity theory.

On the other hand, historiography represents a particular form of analysis that lends itself to "seeing into the future." Hegel, Feuerbach, and Marx all believed that the historical processes they identified are inevitable. Furthermore, they believed that an actor's consciousness and knowledge of the process is part of the process. For example, class consciousness and conflict is a necessary and inevitable part of the process of extinguishing class conflict itself. Thus, our knowledge is viewed as a necessary part of the process. What scientists seem to be saying is, "Let scientific knowledge claims be subjected to scientific criteria, then if the knowledge is emancipatory within any historiography or ideology, so be it." "But," they would continue, "don't expect science to conform to the canon of consistency with the beliefs of ideology or even consistency with previous findings as the sole arbiter of the adequacy of a knowledge claim." In brief, knowledge may be emancipatory, but one of the criteria of knowledge should not be whether or not it is emancipatory.

Another criticism of conflict theory is the tendency to find one underlying theme or causal relation and then use that one cause to explain all of family and human behavior. Single-cause theories are suspect in this day and age of multivariate analyses and ecological consciousness. In defense of conflict theory, it must be pointed out that although there may only be one underlying cause, it keeps changing manifestations throughout history. For instance, although Marx viewed the "relation to the means of production" as being causal, the way it manifested conflict during various historical eras changed. Nonetheless, as we found in the research on wife assault, it may be that a more inclusive conceptualization of conflict that allows for multiple sources of conflict, such as gender and production, provides both inclusiveness and explanatory power.

## Conclusion

Conflict theory is diverse. It has both macrosocial and microsocial variants. But we cannot agree with the assessment by Farrington and Chertok (1993) that such diversity has contributed to the near demise of family conflict theory. Rather, what has contributed to that impression is a too-narrow focus on "conflict" rather than the process of conflict and management of conflict. There are several themes that allow us to see family conflict theory as a coherent and unified theory spanning time and history, micro- and macrolevels. Conflict is a process. The process is dialectical and must be studied over time. The way conflict is managed is part of the dialectical process of reaching a new synthesis. Of all the social groups we might study, the family provides the "laboratory" in which there is intense conflict and resolution, hate and love, and violence and support.

Conflict theory stands out in the pantheon of family theories as incorporating both time and history as a common process (the dialectic). As part of a historical process, conflict theory connects the study of contemporary families to families of the past. As grand and sweeping a vision as it provides, it nonetheless can be focused on the specific processes of negotiation and conflict management so that we can understand our day-to-day existence. Conflict theory, as Caplow (1968), Scanzoni (1970), and Straus (1994) have demonstrated, can be explicitly scientific. We believe the strengths of conflict theory far outweigh the criticisms launched against it. There is only one element that could destroy the potential of conflict theory to offer family researchers a vital, process-oriented theory that links family studies with the larger social system and historical processes. That one destructive element is if the theory is dragged into the quagmire of ideology and findings judged by "political correctness" rather than the canons of science. We are optimistic that this will not be the case.

## Suggested Readings

Farrington, K., & Chertok, E. (1993). Social conflict theories of the family. In P. Boss, W. Doherty, R. LaRossa, W. Schumm, & S. Steinmetz (Eds.), *Sourcebook of family theories and methods: A contextual approach* (pp. 357–381). New York: Plenum.
*This is a good survey of conflict theory, even though the authors express more reservations about the continued usefulness of conflict theory in family studies than we do.*

Knapp, S. J. (1997). Knowledge claims in the family field: A hermeneutical alternative to the representational model. *Family Perspective, 30,* 369–428.
*This entire issue is devoted to the thoughtful questions raised by Knapp and includes critical commentaries.*

White, J. M., & Mason, L. K. (1999). Post-positivism and positivism: A dialogue. *Family Science Review, 12,* 1–21.
*This is a good general introduction to some of the debates between positivism and its critics from critical theory and other postmodern theories.*

# 7

# The Feminist Framework

Jennifer and Heather hadn't seen each other since their university days. After bumping into each other in the grocery store, the two college chums decided to go catch up on what had transpired in each other's lives. "What are you doing now? Are you still painting?" asked Jennifer. "I'm a stay-at-home mom of three little ones" responded Heather. She continued that between meals, homework, laundry, and her volunteer work at her children's elementary school, she has little time to paint. "What about you?"

Jennifer paused for a second and then responded to Heather that after university, she did a law degree and is about to finally become a partner in a law firm downtown. "What about marriage, kids, family, any of that stuff?" Heather inquired. "Oh yes!" said Jennifer, "We have quite a household: My daughter Maggie is four, my husband, Cody, is also a lawyer, and we have a live-in nanny, Isabella, who makes it all possible."

Heather was impressed. "Gosh you're amazing to 'do it all'! I thought about staying at work, but when my first child was 6 months, I just couldn't leave him in someone else's care. Since that time, my family has become the most important thing in my life. Being a mom has become my central identity in life, and the other 'stay at homes' I know have all sacrificed a lot for their families."

Jennifer replied that she, too, was heavily invested in parenting. She had gone to great lengths to get their daughter into a very expensive day care only to find that her daughter didn't get the attention she felt she should get. "So we were delighted when we found Isabella. Her English is very good, and she is in the process of getting a driver's license so she can take Maggie to school and pick her up. Our only problem is that her work visa expires this summer, and we are not sure about renewal. She may have to return to her village in Guatemala."

Heather glanced at her watch and said, "Wow, I have to go soon to take the girls to ballet; it's my turn." Jennifer said, "Your turn?" "Yes," said Heather. "We moms organize car pooling so that we get some respite from the continual barrage of delivering to baseball, soccer, ballet, Olympics of the Mind, chess tournaments, and on and on. I am so grateful for the camaraderie and female culture that goes with the moms who volunteer at school."

Jennifer said, "I guess I haven't experienced that sort of thing since I'm at work and don't have the time. I guess these are all "stay at homes?"

"Yes they are." said Heather as she gathered her purse and packages to go.

Jennifer and Heather may both be feminists, but they represent different perspectives on feminism because of the choices, decisions, and directions their lives have taken. Jennifer represents a feminism that espouses equality and emphasizes work roles. On the other hand, Heather represents a feminism that emphasizes the nurturing mother role and the sharing culture of women. And, in between these two, is the nanny, Isabella, who represents an exploited woman of color. All of these are positions within feminist thought. The purpose of this chapter is to identify what unites these diverse positions into the feminist framework and then to highlight the variations within this framework.

## Intellectual Traditions

Identifying the dimensions that unite the various approaches to feminist theories is more problematic than it may appear. This is in large part due to the particular way feminist social thought has developed. Feminist thought has originated within a social movement for change. Theory in feminism can be described as both evaluative and empirical. The fact that feminist theories are empirical does not distinguish them from many other theories found in this book. The fact that they are is evaluative and ideological does.

Turner (1991, 1998) discusses this type of theorizing as "ideological" or "emancipatory." The role of such theory is not simply to establish explanation but to use theory as a tool in changing the world. Some theories contain a strong moral or evaluative element of what is right and wrong, fair and unjust. Needless to say, such evaluative approaches either implicitly or explicitly suggest "how" things should be changed. Furthermore, if theoreticians know how things "should be, they are in some ways "utopian" in their viewpoint. That is, they know what kind of society would be "ideal" and will work toward that "ideal" society. This "emancipatory" role of theory is shared by some of the frameworks we discuss, such as conflict theories, but is anathema to others because it brings into question the assumption of "neutrality" and "objectivity" often claimed by scientific realists.

Feminist theory originates from a social movement, and this fact helps us understand the number of variations. Over time, feminism has focused its attention on many different, although related, areas. For example, at the end of the 19th century, feminists concentrated on equal rights. As the social movement and its proponents shifted focus throughout the 20th century, attention turned to such diverse areas as female psychology, the culture of femininity, the basis for female nurturance, and mothering. Not all of these analyses necessarily agreed with one another. The outcome of this complex history is that there is a rich tapestry of perspectives that are difficult to paint with a single canvas.

In this section, we take a brief overview of the intellectual history that has been tied to this social movement. Many scholars studying feminism discuss the movement as historically divided into two phases. The first was from the 1880s to around the early 1920s, when many governments recognized universal suffrage. The depression of the 1930s followed by the war and later reconstruction of the 1940s represented a hiatus in the activities of the women's movement. The second phase is usually identified with the 1960s to the present. Even though these phases may be adequate descriptions of the social movement, they do not seem to help us understand the intellectual contributions throughout this time period.

Any intellectual history of feminism must begin with Mary Wollstonecraft's *A Vindication of the Rights of Woman* (1792/1975). Although Wollstonecraft was not the only voice to speak out for women's rights, her voice represents what has become the most significant statement of what Donovan labels "Enlightenment liberal feminism" (1985, p. 1). This early feminism was rooted in the rationalist thought of the Enlightenment. Among its tenets were a faith in rationality and a belief in natural rights. But Wollstonecraft's critique goes much further than merely subscribing to inalienable rights of individuals. She argued that women failed to develop their minds because the only avenue of obtaining power for a woman was through marriage. As a result, she explained that women were forced to "prostitute" themselves even though it was through the legal mechanism of marriage. This same sentiment was expressed by Marx and Engels in their communist manifesto almost 60 years later.

Another early intellectual contribution was from Frederick Engels's *The Origin of the Family, Private Property and the State* (1884/1946). Engels argued that the family was originally matriarchal and communal. Domestication of animals allowed for the rise of commodity exchanges and placed more economic power in the hands of men, thus destroying the equality of labor and rights that had existed previously. Engels described this evolution toward commodity exchange and eventually capitalism as the overthrow of the female sex. Female work became undervalued and patriarchy the rule. Although Engels's argument is based on a limited and dated ethnography of one tribal group, the arguments nonetheless represent one of the first analyses to openly identify female subordination as neither natural nor necessary. Much of Engels's writing was to inform later feminist scholars in both Marxist feminism and radical feminism (Donovan, 1985, pp. 65–90).

Charlotte Gilman's (1898) *Women and Economics* and *The Home* (1910) both assumed a social evolutionary perspective, as was common in the social Darwinism of that period. The ideas contained in *The Home* are perhaps the most radical. She argued that women are subjugated and kept in a state of arrested development in the home (Donovan, 1985, p. 48). She described the roles women filled—cook, nutritionist, provider of child care, and so on—and proposed that they should become trained professionals and be paid for their services. Such professionalization would allow for services to be offered at a community rather than family level. As a result, Gilman argues, women would be freed from the tasks of the home to develop and enter the public world. Gilman was one of the first scholars to identify the private versus public roles in the family. She believed that women would unite around feminism, and a truly cooperative social movement would evolve from this consensus.

After the attainment of universal suffrage, the onslaught of the Great Depression followed by World War II dampened much of the social movement's momentum. The intellectual contributions during this hiatus are important, however. Probably the most significant intellectual contribution during this period originated in the anthropological writings of Margaret Mead. The significance of Mead's work in such books as *Coming of Age in Samoa* (1928), *Growing Up in New Guinea* (1930), *Sex and Temperament in Three Primitive Societies* (1935) and, later, *Male and Female* (1955) is that she argued strongly that gender behaviors were largely cultural formations and definitions rather than any form of natural or genetic endowment. Her work clearly suggested that gender practices are relative to the cultural context and that often when we compare cultures, we find male behavior in one culture that shares similarities with female behavior in another culture.

Both Gilman and Mead had been social scientists. The next major intellectual influence came from a philosopher and literary figure Simone de Beauvoir in her work *The Second Sex* (1949). Simone de Beauvoir was influenced by the French existentialists, most notably Albert Camus and Jean Paul Sartre (de Beauvoir's companion for many years). Concepts such as the "subject–object dichotomy" and "authenticity," guided her analysis of gender relations. Donovan states that de Beauvoir

> realized that a dialectic obtains within a culture as well as within an individual: in a patriarchal culture the male or masculine is set up as the positive or the norm, where the female or the feminine is set up as the negative, the unessential, the abnormal, as in short, the Other." (1985, p. 122)

Her analysis of the root of this "otherness" for women lies in the reproductive capacities of women and the division of labor tied to those capacities. Although de Beauvoir rejects the acceptance of this "otherness" as "bad faith," she nonetheless recognizes the difficulty in rejecting what seems a biological imperative. Her solution is to charge women with becoming more "transcendent," for example, to engage in a career and education.

Critics of de Beauvoir such as Rabuzzi (1982) have suggested that she simply took the male model of work and career as "transcendent" and denigrated the female model in the very way she criticized in her analysis. Rabuzzi and other critics are quick to point out that the "culture" around traditional women's work should not be so denigrated and can be seen in a much more positive light than that which de Beauvoir used. It is, however, virtually uncontested that de Beauvoir's analysis occupies a central role in the reemergence of the women's movement after suffrage.

Although some intellectual historians of feminist theory might dismiss Betty Friedan's (1963) popular work *The Feminine Mystique* as modest, there can be little doubt that this *New York Times* best-seller refueled the feminist social movement and prepared the ground for other intellectual contributions to follow. Friedan struck a chord among American middle-class women living in the suburbs, who by all appearances had obtained the "American Dream" yet still suffered feelings of dissatisfaction. Friedan challenged the notions that the American Dream nuclear family in the suburbs was the most "functional" (Osmond & Thorne, 1993) and that it was the most psychologically fulfilling. The dissatisfaction of women living this "dream" had previously been labeled as neurotic from the perspective of Freudian psychology. Friedan, however, challenged the Freudian perspective that a well-adjusted woman was a passive object. Indeed, she saw this as labeling as neurotic any role for women other than one of inferiority. Friedan saw the situation as one in which women are oppressed by the male-dominated institutions surrounding them.

Shortly after Friedan, a host of feminist scholarship emerged. Three related works are Shulamith Firestone's *The Dialectic of Sex* (1970), Kate Millet's *Sexual Politics* (1970), and Juliet Mitchell's *Woman's Estate* (1972). All three criticize Freudian psychology's construction of women, but they diverge in important ways. Firestone sees woman's biology as being one of the primary problems in that reproduction and ownership of children produced a division of labor that subjugated women. Millet argues that contrary to Freudian psychology, biology is not destiny. Her analysis, however, raises questions for Firestone in that Firestone views female liberation as being achieved by freeing oneself from reproduction, that is, from the biological determinism of "motherhood." Mitchell (1971) focuses more on economic and social factors and somewhat chides Firestone for her emphasis on biology. All three of these authors agree that women's subjugation and oppression is closely tied to the family and its ideology.

Not all feminist theorists have so robustly rejected Freudian psychology. Indeed, the significant contribution of Nancy Chodorow in her book *The Reproduction of Mothering* (1978) relies heavily on the psychodynamics of "object-relations." Chodorow argues that the social roles of mother and father that are respectively characterized by nurturant affect and instrumentalism are not just due to patterns of socialization but to the psychodynamics of early childhood. In early childhood, the girl's identification with an affectionate mother and the boy's rejection of his mother's power over him provide the roots for both women's subjugation and men's misogyny. Female adults seeking affectively charged relationships are forced to turn from the affectively neutral male to the intimate bonding inherent in the mother–child relationship, thus *reproducing motherhood* from generation to generation. The reproduction of motherhood, because it demands nurturant affect rather than the rational, affective neutrality of the male workplace, reproduces the subjugation of women. Chodorow's work should not be interpreted as simply a diatribe against the role of mother, because she also pointed out the positive emotional dimension this role plays for women in an affectively neutral society. This was, in fact, a significant step for some feminists in realizing the importance of some aspects of traditional roles that might even be tied to female oppression.

In retrospect, the decade of the 1970s could be seen as one in which feminist theory was largely of one mind and a single voice. Although there was some variation, feminist thinking of the 1970s was to provide the foundation for the development of great diversity and variation in feminist theories in the decade of the 1980s. One starting point for this developing diversity sprang from the new work of one of the founders of the 1960s' movement, Betty Friedan.

Chodorow's insight regarding the importance of some traditional roles was not lost on Friedan. In 1981, Friedan sparked great controversy with the publication of her book *The Second Stage.* In this work, she clearly praises and acknowledges the many successes of the feminist movement since the initial publication of *The Feminine Mystique* (1963). Friedan argues, however, that in the fight to achieve "equality" of opportunity there lies an inherent danger of losing or even willingly giving up many of the positive aspects of traditional roles. Friedan does not argue that traditional roles shouldn't be changed, but that we don't want to be caught "throwing the baby out with the bath water." She especially focuses on the affective rewards of parenting and of intimate relationships found in the family. She argues that the second stage of the women's movement should be aimed at finding ways to successfully articulate the instrumental world of work with the affective world of family. She cautions that if feminists are forced to give up the very values and orientation that have made them different from men in order to fit into the male-fashioned work world, then success will be defined by some very great losses for women.

Friedan's position raised great controversy and also gave momentum to one variation of feminist thinking, "cultural feminism." This variation is distinguished by the position that what women value most may be intrinsically tied to and originate from traditional women's culture (Donovan, 1985, p. 62). This was just one of the variants to arise in the 1980s, however (e.g., Kourany, Sterba, & Tong, 1999). Various authors distinguish different variations of feminism. For example, Donovan (1985) identifies seven variations, Tuana and Tong (1995) identify nine variations, and Osmond and Thorne (1993) point to six variations. These variations have led to clashes of perspectives on such issues as the liberal feminist position on equality such as in military service clashing with the cultural feminists position the an integral component of female culture is the value of life and the pacific character of women as nurturers not destroyers (see Donovan, 1985, p. 62). As we shall see in our discussion of these theoretical variants, issues of ethnicity and culture have also been the subject of disputes between variant feminist theories.

The many voices that arose during the 1980s provided the impetus for the new developments in feminist theory that were to mark the decade of the 1990s. With many voices and theories that sometimes clash, the question for feminist theorists became "How can we include this diverse and sometimes contrary group of perspectives under the common umbrella of feminist theory?" This question has prompted scholars to address whether multiple and contradictory knowledge claims can simultaneously be held. Interestingly, in this regard one theoretical school of feminism appears to answer affirmatively and another one negatively. We discuss this question of the many voices of feminism in considerable detail in the next section dealing with the "assumptions" of feminist theories.

### Focus and Scope Assumptions

Although we have previously left the term *feminist theory* undefined, it is useful at this juncture to define it. Gordon (1979) defines feminist theory as "an analysis of women's subordination for the purpose of figuring out how to change it" (p. 107). Although there are definitions, such as that by Wood (1995), emphasizing similarity between males and females, such definitions tend to be identified with only the *liberal* school of feminism. Gordon's definition is extremely useful. As Osmond and Thorne (1993) point out, Gordon's definition presents three themes that are common to feminist theory. These themes are the "emphasis on women's experience, the identification of oppression, and the emancipatory purpose of feminist theory" (Osmond & Thorne, 1993, p. 592). These themes also express the basic scope and focus assumptions of feminist theories.

*Women's experience is central.* One of the core assumptions of feminist theory is that women's experience is real and provides the foundation for knowledge claims in feminist theory. This assumption does not rule out other forms of evidence or data but provides a strong epistemological statement as to how such claims will be judged. Tuana and Tong (1995) state that in the history of philosophy, there have often been serious reservations raised about women's capacity to think and reason "rationally" (p. 1). The emphasis on women's *experience* is in part a way of legitimizing and empowering the insights that women have. However, this assumption goes much further to a deep distrust of the kind of thinking that has systematically excluded the experiences and claims of women especially in such realms as children, violence, and moral decisions. As Tuana and Tong point out,

> This emphasis on women's experience—on women's ways of knowing and making moral decisions as well as perceiving reality and controlling their destiny—builds on the understanding that from time to time, what women feel, think, or do will differ from what men feel, think or do. (1995, p. 1)

*Feminist theory has many voices.* If women's experience is central, then there is probably more than one way of looking at any given problem, issue, or knowledge claim. It is the centrality of women's experience that partially offers a foundation for the diversity we find in feminist theorizing. Women from different cultures, places, and times may have vastly different experiences, which are accorded the same status and respect.

> "Women's experience" is not shorthand for some sort of monolithic "groupthink" but for a vast array of thoughts, feelings, and activities mediated through the lenses of each individual woman's race, class, sexual preference, ethnicity, religion, age, physical condition, and states of mind." (Tuana & Tong, 1995, p. 2 )

As we have already alluded, the first assumption—that we can judge the adequacy of a statement by referring it to "women's experience"—is seemingly at odds with the second assumption that women's experience is diverse. This problem has not gone unnoticed by feminist theorists. For example, Harding (1987) puts it as follows:

> It is a vast overgeneralization to presume that all Africans, let alone all colonized peoples, share distinctive personalities, ontologies, ethics, epistemologies, or worldviews. But is it any worse than the presumption that there are commonalities to be detected in all women's social experiences or worldviews? (1987, p. 297)

Harding proceeds to point out that the argument that feminist theory has many voices is problematic for the development of stable concepts and a theoretical structure. Other feminists such as Smith (1992) have argued that women's experience does provide a strong epistemological foundation, yet others argue that the "many voices" notion throws feminist thinking into the intellectual flux of *relativism.* That is, feminist claims would have no more authority in challenging patriarchal or biased knowledge than any other group based on one characteristic such as class, race, ethnicity, or age (Harding, 1987, p. 298). Duran (1998) succinctly states the quandary:

> Without some kind of notion of empirical confirmation, claims to have had any kind of experience—including an experience of victimization—cannot be confirmed. The contemporary efforts on the part of many reactionary political forces to delegitimize a great deal of what has transpired in the history of various minority groups should disabuse us of any notions we may have that confirmation is not important. (p. 181)

Duran continues that the underrepresentation or trivialization of such events as the Holocaust suggest the need for a notion of knowledge claims and evidence that goes beyond relativism. Although there is no simple resolution to this debate, it is useful to acknowledge that this debate is critical to the continued credibility and growth of feminist theory.

*Feminist theory is emancipatory.* Feminist theory is closely linked to the feminist movement. This movement has identified patriarchy as being one of the major sources of oppression and inequality in the lives of women. Turner (1991) describes theories that describe, evaluate, and prescribe social action as emancipatory theories. He states that in this perspective,

> Theoretical knowledge cannot, therefore, merely describe events. It must expose exploitive social arrangements and, at the same time, suggest alternative ways to organize humans in less oppressive ways. Social theory cannot be neutral; rather, it must be emancipatory. (p. 182)

Feminist theory, then, does not simply have to meet criteria about validity but also is judged by whether it is emancipatory. Although this might seem a somewhat foreign assumption to some, to others this third assumption is not that different from the demand that theoretical knowledge should be useful. Only with this meaning, "useful" theory is that which liberates women from patriarchal oppression. Indeed, one way out of the relativism inherent in allowing many voices within a theory is to raise this emancipatory criterion as a pragmatic test of a theory's empirical adequacy.

## Concepts

### GENDER AND SEX

Feminist scholars have routinely made the distinctions that *sex* refers to the biologically determined component and *gender* to the cultural and learned component (e.g., Fox & Murry, 2000). This distinction has carried with it the tacit assumption that much of what we identify as gender because of its social nature is more malleable than sex. Osmond and Thorne (1993, pp. 604–606), following Harding (1987) and Scott (1988), discuss three dimensions of gender. First, there is individual gender or gender identity. This dimension of gender focuses on the ways by which we acquire our personal construct of gender—what is masculine and feminine. Second, there is structural gender or gender as a social status. This is gender as a class or category that is part of a hierarchical organization. So, for example, to say that women are second-class citizens would be using this meaning of structural gender. Last, there is cultural gender that focuses on the symbols attached to social gender and their construction. For example, the religious symbols around Eve the Temptress versus the Virgin Mary or the adage that "cowboys don't cry." It is in this cultural realm that scholars have examined the way our language constructs gender.

The discussion of sex and gender has proved to be complicated. First, there is some doubt that any meaningful nature–nurture distinction can be made in this regard. The acquisition of social constructs is so interactively tied to biological maturation that we may not be able to tease these processes apart nor correctly label which effects are due to which processes. A second problem is that one's gender identity probably interacts in complex ways with the other dimensions of gender, structure, and culture, so that these distinctions may lack clarity.

Despite criticisms, gender has remained one of the most popular concepts in feminist scholarship. It has been used as the basic dimension for identifying differences, gender relations, culture, and language. It represents the basic dimension for feminist analysis.


FAMILY AND HOUSEHOLD

Many feminist scholars do not define the family as most other social scientist would—as an empirical entity with members and kin relationships between those members. Rather, the family is more often treated as an "ideology" or as a conceptual fabrication used to justify and maintain certain patterns of privilege. Ferree (1990) states that examining the family from a gender perspective "requires distinguishing between household, which are the coresidential units in which people empirically can be found, and family, the ideology of relatedness that explains who should live together, share income, and perform certain common tasks (Andersen, 1991; Rapp, 1982)" (Ferree, 1990, p. 870). In this perspective, family is defined not by its membership nor by the fact of coresidence, but by the prevailing ideology that suggests that a certain division of labor or type of coresidence is normal or natural. Thus, part of family would be the understandings that in family certain work is "women's work" or in custody disputes that mother custody is preferred because of some inherent maternal ability. Family, then, is an ideology and normative set that is ripe for the analysis of gender-based distinctions and inequalities.

## PUBLIC AND PRIVATE

The idea that women's and men's experience is divided into fairly distinct sectors is viewed by feminists as a means to organize people into social classes based on gender. During the industrial revolution, women were increasingly "protected" from the exploitation of capitalism and poor working conditions by eliminating them from any role in the paid labor force and relegating their work and industry to the private sphere of the home. The private sphere of the home was removed from public accountability not only in terms of work but also in terms of public social norms. What was illegal or nonnormative in terms of public behavior could be tolerated in the private. Thus, the exploitation of women and children continued in an even less regulated environment where men could escape public sanction for beating, violence, and even rape because it was in the private sphere of the family. Indeed, in the 20th century the family became the dominant ideology tied to the private sphere. For example, what might be a criminal assault in public could be concealed and even forgiven in private. Hence, the dichotomy of private and public spheres is seen by feminists as being an ideology that supports and maintains a gender-based class system (see Osmond and Thorne, 1993, pp. 608–612).

## SEXISM

This concept shares similarities with concepts about age and race, ageism and racism. In fact, we can adapt the definition of racism by Pierre van den Berghe for our definition of sexism.

> Sexism is any set of beliefs that organic, genetically transmitted differences (whether real or imagined) between human groups are intrinsically associated with the presence or absence of certain socially relevant abilities or characteristics, and hence that such differences are a legitimate basis of invidious distinctions between groups socially defined as sexes (adapted from van den Berghe, 1979, p. 11).

This definition clearly states that when someone believes a trait such as sex is genetically determined and relatively immutable and then makes harmful or damaging attributions about all individuals with that trait, such beliefs would be labeled "sexist" and behavior guided by such beliefs would be "sexism." It should be noted that the veracity of the beliefs is not the determinant but only the harm or damage associated with the class distinction. Thus, to say all girls cannot play in a soccer league is to make a potentially harmful distinction based on class inclusion and would be an example of "sexism." It would also be sexist by this definition to say "All women are nurturing" or "All women are peace loving."

Other key terms are "inequality" and "oppression." In fact, they are usually the major dependent variables in feminist theories. These ideas are important in order to appreciate that it is not enough to simply understand gender differences. The differences that matter are those that subordinate women to men, and such inequality is not natural or inevitable but the result of social forces that "push down" or subjugate women relative to men.

## Propositions

Feminist theory has been inclusive of women's differing experiences and perspectives. As a result, some theoretical statements that we include below express the perspective of one group of feminist scholars but not others. Indeed, some of the propositions listed below would spark controversy among these groups. We highlight the differences in perspectives in Variations, which follows this section. For this section, we attempt to present a reasonably consistent and coherent theory, which we believe captures the major propositions and logic in this area of discourse.

*Gender structures our experience.*

Although biological sex may account for some differences between males and females, every culture raises these few differences to a heightened status in the social construction of gender. For example, in North American culture, women stereotypically have had longer hair than men. The sex difference is that females' hair on average grows faster than males' and that females do not inherit alopecia. Yet from this rather simple difference entire industries are spawned to highlight, manage, and accentuate this difference in cosmetology, hair dressing, and fashion. Thus, the experience of females and males is socially constructed to be different in all cultures.

*Gender structures all societies.*

Gender is used as a basic class distinction in all societies. Looking around at the world in which we live, we see babies wrapped in pink or blue blankets, we see washrooms designated by gender, and we see girls soccer teams and boys soccer teams. Gender, like age, represents one of the most basic social class distinctions. Although some might argue that the division is sex and not gender, we would simply point out that being in the appropriate washroom is more a function of attire and deportment than it is related to biology, as any transvestite can attest. Thus, it is cultural symbols and meaning that construct this social class.

*Women as a class are devalued and oppressed.*

Andreas (1971), as well as many other feminists, has pointed out that gender as a class distinction is not simply an organizational principle but represents invidious distinctions that privilege one class (men) while oppressing another (women). The basic structure of all societies seems organized by the principle that females are inferior— physically, mentally, or both—to males. As a result of such distinctions, referring back to the definition of sexism, all societies are sexist to some degree. Some feminists state this fact as being the dominance of *patriarchy*. Sexism could occur even in the absence of patriarchy and be aimed at either gender, however.

*As a result of sex, gender beliefs, and historical and continuing sexism and oppression, there exists a "female culture."*

Centuries of patriarchy and sexism have resulted in female identity being formulated in opposition and as an antidote to oppression. The result has been the development of a "female culture" founded on a much different vision of the world than usually supplied by patriarchy. For example, Donovan (1985) lists some attributes of this vision as being "pacifism, cooperation, nonviolent settlement of differences, and harmonious regulation of public life" (p. 32). In this perspective, the social construction of gender combined with gender class distinctions has given rise to a culture that represents an alternative to the patriarchal, bellicose, and competitive world view that seems to dominate the world today.

*The family is not monolithic.*

Feminist such as Eichler (1988) have pointed out that, in large part, the ideology of the public and private spheres has been buttressed by the vision of the family as unitary and monolithic. By portraying the family as a monolithic single type of organization governed by unchanging social norms, scholars in sociology and other disciplines have established the status quo as a moral norm. Young women and men are led to believe that to be a "family," certain norms and timetables must be followed; otherwise, one will not have a family as we now know it—that is, the reconstruction of their own family of orientation in their family of procreation (see Chodorow, 1978). This view is often couched in language that would assign particular immutable social functions to the organization of the family and imply that if the family changes, society, as we know it, would founder. Feminist scholars have been at the leading edge of research on family diversity in terms of sexual preference, organization of family roles and labor, and culture and ethnic variability.

*The family is a central institution for the reproduction of oppression.*

Feminists view the concealment of diversity within and between families as part of the construction of gender because it allows a portrayal of gender roles as fixed and immutably defined by the tradition of patriarchy. As a result, the family as an institution is often viewed as one of the central organizations responsible for the reproduction of oppression through socialization and social expectations (Taylor, 1997). As Ferree (1990) notes, feminists recognize both the need for changing constraining sex roles and that "Families are also institutions of support and resistance for women as they confront other forms of social oppression" (1990, p. 868). Thus, feminists carefully examine the institution of the family with an eye to not "throwing the baby out with the bath water."

One last caveat in regard to these propositions is required. Such propositions are not laid out in many other feminist works. The reason for this is twofold. First, as we have already noted, there exist some disagreements between different theoretical variants. Second, much of feminist scholarship has either rejected positivist approaches or viewed such approaches with suspicion. One of the suspicions has been that in the search for nomothetic general laws, not only have women been poorly represented, but diversity and variation have been seen as standing in the way of generalizations—and hence poorly represented. Although we believe that both of these reasons bear consideration, we also believe that feminist theory is sufficiently well developed that some general propositional inventory is appropriate and assists student and scholar in more fully understanding this theoretical framework. One example of a more propositional approach to feminism will be discussed later (Lorber, 1998).

## Variations

There are many variants of feminist theory. Like other theoretical frameworks, these variants have developed for numerous reasons. Some variants latch onto one substantive dimension of feminist theory such as mothering or patriarchy. Macroscopic and microscopic analyses also explain some of the variants. And finally, some of the variants are tied to broader theories such as psychoanalysis or Marxist theory. In the following section, we review what we believe are the most significant of the variations for the study of the family. Our discussion follows the distinctions made by feminist scholars such as Osmond and Thorne (1993), Tuana and Tong (1995), and Donovan (1985).

### LIBERAL FEMINISM

Liberal feminism is tied to the Enlightenment philosophy of rationalism and human rights (Donovan, 1985). The rationalist belief that "all men are created as equal" was easily envisaged as extending to both genders. The major thrust of this perspective is on achieving gender equality. Barriers to gender equality are viewed as any law, institution, or person that discriminates on the basis of gender. Thus, most of the efforts of liberal feminism have been directed at equality of opportunity and the removal of barriers that would work against such equality.

Although this variant does not directly appear in any particular feminist theory of the family per se, it nevertheless informs many research perspectives. For example, much of the research on the division of labor in the household has taken as an implicit assumption that equality of labor is desirable (Hochschild & Machung, 1989; Scanzoni, 1972). When researchers report inequitable hours of labor in the home for working wives and husbands, they immediately assume that this is far from desirable (Acock & Demo, 1994). This perspective has a firm basis in Enlightenment rationalism and informs our views of fairness and justice.

Although many would find the tenets of liberal feminism appealing, these same tenets have contributed to various contentious debates. One example is the break between liberal feminists who support the inclusion of women in the armed forces and cultural feminists who have opposed this move on the grounds that women's pacific nature and culture are at odds with the militarism of this traditional male bastion. Another example of the contentiousness of the liberal feminist stance is that it ignores any true biological differences between sexes. Most liberal feminists tend to see few if any real differences between males and females. Most differences are viewed as not fixed but rather as malleable by socialization. Other variants question these assumptions, however. They are perhaps most strongly questioned by cultural and psychoanalytic schools of feminism, where biological differences such as breast-feeding are viewed as interactively creating roles and identities that are universal for females. This debate really ignites when we discuss whether "extra" rights are required for maternity leave as opposed to paternity leave or other workplace benefits.

Many of these issues have led some liberal feminists to become more radical in their thinking. Gender is a long-term, historical construction. It is a more complex issue than simply one caused by a denial of equal rights, and it will not be cured by equality of opportunity alone. One need only point to the failure to ratify the Equal Rights Amendment in the United States, where women voters were a major factor in the defeat. Clearly identities, social roles, and social structure are deeply embedded in our world.

## RADICAL MARXIST/SOCIALIST FEMINISM

One of the most cogent and impressive analyses in this area is contained in the work *The Dialectic of Sex* by Shulamith Firestone (1970). Firestone (1970) begins her analysis with an acknowledgment of her debt to Engels's (1884/1946) analysis in *The Origin of the Family, Private Property and the State* and her evaluation that Engels and Marx failed to go deep enough in their analyses:

> Engels did observe that the original division of labor was between man and woman for the purposes of childbreeding; that within the family the husband was the owner, the wife the means of production, the children the labor; and that reproduction of the human species was an important economic system distinct from the means of production. (p. 5)

Where Marx and Engels went wrong, according to Firestone, is that they did not plumb the depths of the nature of reproduction and sex but instead envisioned these as part of the underlying economic class conflict. Firestone proposes a view of history based on sex rather than economic relations. She supposes that unlike economic class, "sex class" sprang directly from a biological reality: Men and women were created different and not equally privileged (p. 8). She argues that for most of human history, the family (and women) has been characterized by four fundamental points. First, before the very recent development of birth control, women were at the mercy of their biology in terms of pregnancy, lactation, and care of infants and thus were dependent on others for survival. Second, human infants take a long time to become self-sufficient and are dependent on adults for their survival. Third, basic mother–child interdependency has shaped the psychology of every woman and child. Fourth, and last, the basic reproductive division of labor provides for the most fundamental class distinction—that of sex. From these four points, Firestone (1970) argues that "sex class" underlies other social divisions by economic class or race. She suggests that male patriarchy as well as female socialization in the family have encouraged the social partitioning of labor so as to justify not only social inequality but inequality of opportunity. Her argument does not lack for either historical, cross-cultural, or contemporary examples of inequity based on gender.

Firestone notes that the root source of the inequity is biological in origin. As long as women get pregnant, bear children, and breast-feed, they are tied to the very elements that justify the division of labor:

> Nature produced the fundamental inequality—half the human race must bear and rear the children of all of them—which was later consolidated, institutionalized, in the interests of men. Reproduction of the species cost women dearly. (p. 232)

Firestone (1970) suggests a program to correct the damage that has been done to both males and females by the excessive sexual division of labor. The central point in her program is that females should be freed of the tyranny of biological reproduction. She argues that only when we use reproductive technology to free women from biological reproduction will the division into sex classes cease. She goes even further and argues that removing biological reproduction and creating economic independence of both women and children "would be enough to destroy the family, which breeds the power psychology" (p. 236). Firestone's program thus envisions the reorganization of reproduction in addition to the more traditional Marxian focus on the reorganization of production. She believes that the changes she envisions are already under way as technology slowly replaces the functions of the family and care of infants becomes increasingly performed by "professional caregivers." In the end, she believes that "revolt against the family could bring on the first successful revolution" (p. 274).

Firestone (1970) probably represents the more radical wing of Marxist-feminism, but other scholars have followed up on various aspects of these ideas. For example, Berk (1985) deals with the family as the major component in the reproduction of gender relations and the division of labor. Ferree (1990), in her review of feminists' contributions to the family literature, cites the family ideology that can be used to legitimate appeals for female self-sacrifice (p. 870). Osmond and Thorne (1993) point out that feminist scholars have been critical of what constitutes "family" because they are "critical of that ideology and alert to contemporary disputes . . . (i.e., over surrogate mothering, the control of reproduction, child custody, and legal provisions for domestic partnerships)" (p. 618). Although all feminist scholars are not necessarily Marxist-feminist or as radical as Firestone (1970), the issues that she raises are indeed central.

CULTURAL FEMINISM

Linda Alcoff (1995) defines cultural feminism in the following passage:

> Cultural feminism is the ideology of a female nature or female essence reappropriated by feminists themselves in an effort to revalidate undervalued female attributes. For cultural feminists, the enemy is not merely a social system or economic institution or a set of backward beliefs but masculinity itself and in some cases male biology. (pp. 435–436)

Although this quote serves to orient us toward cultural feminism, it does not identify the characteristics that are most often seen as essentially female. Different positions exist within this framework, yet the traits of pacifism, nurturance, and expressiveness are often listed. Aggressiveness is often identified as a male trait, linked to testosterone, that is the antipathy of femaleness.

Donovan (1985) traces the history of cultural feminism back to 1923 and documents the dispute between liberal and cultural feminists as a component in the failure to ratify the Equal Rights Amendment. Indeed, it is a centerpiece of cultural feminism that equality may be a hindrance and threat to preserving female culture and its values. If equality means becoming like males in terms of power, politics, and war, then most cultural feminists would reject it. Furthermore, the strong vein of pacifism and environmental concerns that runs in cultural feminism would favor not equality but protection and special attention.

Cultural feminists are not exactly clear about whether the origins of female culture are biologically or socially constructed. The work of psychoanalytic feminists such as Nancy Chodorow (1978) has suggested that it is a complex weave of culture and genes that interact to create the femaleness that cultural feminists treat as central. Although many women are leery of claiming "differences'" that deserve special treatment, there are certainly new calls for this in regard to female education and relationship development (Gilligan, 1982).


OTHER VARIATIONS

There are numerous other variations that could be considered such as psychoanalytic feminism, anarchist feminism, phenomenological feminism, and so on. Several of these variants could be joined with the ones above. For example, environmental feminism (e.g., Gaard, 1993) might be best linked to cultural feminism. There are also variants identified with multicultural feminism that are especially germane to family studies. The realization that the North American family is not a monolithic institution but contains great diversity of family types and structures can in part be credited to feminist scholars (e.g., Eichler, 1988). Accompanying this idea is the insight that ethnic, religious, and racial identities help to create much of this diversity in form and structure. For example, Dilworth-Anderson, Burton, and Johnson (1993) argue that most of the existing theories about families need to be reframed to predict and understand minority families. More recently, Allen (2000) has argued that family scholarship needs to direct research toward diversity and be more sensitive to the presence of diversity in families. In addition, multicultural feminism raises issues such as the exploitation of immigrant women from underdeveloped countries who labor as nannies and caregivers for dual career families in North America. These women may relinquish many personal freedoms as they enter a semivoluntary legal arrangement between their sponsor family and immigration officials. Furthermore, many women from other cultures may desire to continue what they regard as their cultural practices, while other North American feminists may see these as "sexist" practices. Perhaps, the most volatile example of this has been the "right" of women in parts of Africa to practice clitorectomy as a religious and cultural symbol of devoutness. Such examples raise the serious issue of feminist ideology versus respect and tolerance for religious and cultural diversity.

Lorber starts *Gender Inequality* by saying that "feminism is a social movement whose goal is raising the status of women" (1998, p. 1). She focuses with equal emphasis in every chapter on both theories and politics, however, identifying 11 varieties of feminist theory, clustered into three larger categories, "reform," "resistance," and "rebellion." For each of the more specific 11 theories, one per chapter, Lorber begins by listing "sources" of gender inequality, "remedies," and "contributions." The sources (or causes) are of most interest to our theoretical understanding of gender inequality. For example, "low pay for women's jobs," and "lack of affordable child care for mothers who work outside the home" are two of the six primary sources according to the "liberal" variety of reform feminist theory (p. 19).

On the basis of Lorber's clear and well-organized presentation, it does not take much imagination to see causes and effects linked in propositions. For example, we could say that the lower the pay for women's jobs, the greater the gender inequality. Of course, some refinements might be necessary to make certain propositions more plausible. In the case of "low pay," we'd probably want to treat women's pay relative to men's. Otherwise, if pay is low for both, there would be little gender inequality.

A second refinement might involve the dependent variable, or what we need to explain. We seem to be forced to make a choice between seeing gender inequality as currently being constant at a high level or as variable across time and place. Many feminist theorists may wish to avoid the choice and see both as true. So it helps to see inequality as pervasive to inspire concern about it. But it also helps to see inequality as variable, at least in principle, or else no remedy is possible. Thus, the refinement that may make the most sense is to treat gender inequality as nonnormally distributed in the present (usually high), but with the distribution capable of being changed if action based on the sources or causes either has been or will be undertaken.

The underlying issue here is that we cannot readily explain constants by referring to their causes. We can ask questions such as "Why is the divorce rate high?" and we can speculate on the reasons, but we cannot have full confidence in a reason unless there are past, current, or future instances in which the cause loses force and the divorce rate changes. In terms of feminism, and returning to the "low pay" example, we can't be sure that this postulated source of inequality is operative unless the pay is or becomes higher in some place or time and the inequality level decreases. Any theory, feminist or not, is utopian if it tries to explain a "better world" but that world has never yet existed. The better world can be predicted, but the prediction must eventually be correct for the theory to have explanatory power. To put it another way, we don't need a theory of inequality so much as a theory that can explain equality, inequality, and all shades in between.

## Empirical Applications

### GENDERED DIVISION OF LABOR

One of the most obvious applications for feminist theory has been in the area of the division of household labor between husbands and wives. Thompson and Walker (1995) conclude that feminist scholarship has moved to the center of research in this particular domain. The context of much of the study of division of labor is the 30 or more years of feminist action resulting in initiating reforms in the areas of work and education. There appears a clear departure from these advances when we examine the "private sphere" of the division of labor in the household. Indeed, some authors have characterized this as a "stalled revolution" (Hochschild & Machung, 1989).

Hochschild and Machung (1989), as well as other researchers (e.g., Acock & Demo, 1994), have documented the fact that when researchers use hours of housework as a measure of the division of labor within the household, we find some estimates that wives spend almost double the time that husbands spend on household chores and child care (see Coltrane, 2000; Perry-Jenkins, Repetti, & Crouter, 2000). In addition, satisfaction with the division of labor in the household has proven to be a strong predictor of overall satisfaction with the balance between work and family (White, 1999). Attitudes about giving and receiving support in the household are also strongly correlated with marital quality (Vannoy & Phillber, 1992). Pyke and Coltrane (1996) found that husbands with an egalitarian gender role were more likely to share household chores.

A persistent anomalous finding in regard to the unequal number of hours spent by spouses on home labor is in regard to the perception of fairness. According to Acock and Demo (1994), wives typically report that they are satisfied with the fairness of the division of labor in the household. Acock and Demo argue that this may be due to the comparison with others where any assistance is viewed as a bonus. Other researchers such as Hawkins, Marshall, and Allen (1998) have argued that a sense of fairness is linked to the wives feeling appreciated by husbands. Finally, several researchers have demonstrated that among wives that sense unfairness in the division of labor, there is lower marital quality (e.g., Blair & Johnson, 1992; Greenstein, 1996; Voydanoff & Donnelly, 1999).

Note that all of these researchers have assumed that "hours spent" in housework is a valid indicator of the division of labor. Shaw (1988) reported that men were more likely to report household tasks as leisure and women to report it as work. Greenstein (1996) points out that within the household there are gendered tasks. An inference is that to avoid measurement bias, "chores" should not overemphasize one group over the other. In addition, economic approaches might stress the "economic value" of the task as a measure of the division of labor over sheer quantity of hours, because nowhere else in our society is labor solely quantified by hours. In general, then, there remain questions about the validity of some of the measures.

Regardless of the measurement problems, there is little doubt that sharing in the household labor is a function of egalitarian ideology (Pyke & Coltrane, 1996). Even early feminist scholars pointed out that equality of opportunity in the world of work and education can be stalled by the organization of the private sphere of the household. Indeed, feminists have argued that patriarchy is sustained by the household division of labor. Not only do males benefit from the inequality of work, but this inequality in the private sphere helps to guarantee the perpetuation of gendered class structure in the public sphere. Female ascension in the work world is short-circuited as a result of added labor in the private sphere (see Shelton & John, 1996). In addition, Thompson (1992) argues that ideology determines perceptions of fairness in that women who expect less than equal arrangements in domestic labor would tend to view inequality as fair. Certainly, research in the area of the division of labor in the household supports this suspicion. However, it should be acknowledged that there are other competing theories, such as social exchange, that may offer an equal or superior explanation of these data (Shelton & John, 1996).

In a recent essay, Barbara Ehrenreich (2000) speculates that housework is moving from the private sphere to the public in what she calls the "capitalization" of housework. She explains that more dual-earner families are hiring maid services to do the previously contested housework. The hidden dimension of this is that it represents a traditional class, gender, and ethnic division of labor. For example, she reports that between 14% and 18% of households employed an outside service for cleaning in 1999, but a recent report cites a 53% increase in demand between 1995 and 1999 (2000, p. 62). She cites a 1998 Bureau of Labor Statistics report that 37% of private cleaners and servants were Hispanic, and another 19% were Black or Asian (p. 63). Furthermore, Ehrenreich (2000) reports that one study found that the median earnings for household cleaners and servants was "$12,220 in 1998 which is $1,092 below the poverty level for a family of three" (p. 64). If nanny and household cleaning services are added together, this area of the "private sphere" seems increasingly within the sphere of the "public" capitalistic exploitation of women of color. If this is so, then the suggestions by liberal feminists such as Gilman (1910) that women be freed from home-based tasks by professionals trained in homemaker roles may be at the expense of an underclass of women of color.

MEASURING DIVERSITY IN FEMINISM

In a recent analysis of a national survey, Russo (1998) found that only 27% of the female respondents self-identified as feminist. Even more surprising was the diversity of answers about attitudes ascribed to feminists. Although feminism may have started out as a largely unified perspective (see Donovan, 1985), it currently is marked by great diversity. Although there have been many scales developed to measure the attitudes toward feminism since the original attempt by Kirkpatrick (1936), there have been few attempts to categorize the various dimensions of attitudes by the theoretical variant of feminism that they represent.

Henley, Meng, O'Brien, McCarthy, and Sockloskie (1998) developed a scale to measure diversity of feminist attitudes that would identify the various schools of thought. These researchers identified six perspectives or schools: conservative, liberal feminism, radical feminism, socialist feminism, cultural feminism, and women of color feminism. Items were developed to cover the major topics addressed by each school. Henley et al. initially used 306 items to develop the scale. After two samples and a third combined analysis, a factor analysis showed support for the scale discriminating all of the schools of feminism with the exception of liberal feminism. Liberal feminism appeared more defused throughout the feminist attitude spectrum.

The importance of the attitudinal scale is that it is the first that recognizes the diversity of feminist perspectives and that is inclusive of that diversity. In addition, this scale allows researchers to begin to ask questions such as, "Is a person's identification with one school of feminist thought related to the person's age group, social class, or occupation?" Such questions have previously been posed by feminists. Now Henley et al. have helped provide the measures to answer such questions.

Similar research can be applied to the other theories in this book. In any case, it is important to make a distinction between the attitudes toward feminist theories by taking a sample of public opinion and by surveying family scientists. In one survey of more than 100 family scholars with theorizing experience, the attitudes toward feminist theory were not negatively related with the attitudes toward any other theory but rather were statistically independent (Klein & Janning, 1997). This suggests that some feminist scholars are attracted to certain elements of other theories whereas others are not. Likewise, some family scholars who identify with other theories are attracted to certain elements of feminism, and others are not.

## Implications for Intervention

Unlike many academic theories about the family, feminist theory does not draw a strict line of demarcation between action, practice, and theory. From the outset, feminists attempted both to analyze the causes of oppression and instigate social action to reduce or eliminate it. Thus, it is not difficult to identify many implications for intervention. Here we focus on what we regard as the three major areas: family policy, family therapy, and family scholarship.

One of the principal areas for intervention is in the realm of family policy. One of the major insights gained from feminist analyses is that the family is not one monolithic consensual unit. Furthermore, economic conditions outside of the family unit are linked to the internal dynamic of power and privilege within the family. As a result of these insights, feminist scholars can be credited with giving impetus to policy reforms in diverse areas. For example, Goldner (1993) lists some of these areas of policy reform as wage discrimination, sexual and physical violence, sexual harassment, reproductive freedom, acknowledging and accounting for unpaid work, and quality day care. It is doubtful that the attention these areas have received during the last 40 years would have been forthcoming without the strong advocacy of feminists.

A second area for intervention is family therapy. Goldner (1993) argues that "insofar as family life remains symbolically and materially 'women's sphere', it is women who are held primarily responsible for marital and family problems" (p. 624). She goes on to connect systems and cybernetic theories of family therapy with the maintenance of the myth that families are a monolithic unit composed of interacting parts that then views conflict and disagreements as a threat to family harmony and equilibrium. Not only is a return to the status quo (equilibrium) valued, but women are made to feel both responsible and guilty for departures from the oppressive *status quo*. Goldner views the solution to this problem to be the development of feminist therapy that attempts to correct the conservative political stance inherent in traditional family therapy.

The third implication for action is in family scholarship and the research process. Feminists have been critical of family research that continues to conceal gendered relations within the private sphere of the family. Walker and Thompson (1984) and Thompson and Walker (1995) have addressed the "status" of feminism in relation to research on families. Although their most recent appraisal (1995) cites gains for feminist research, they conclude that, with the exception of household division of labor, feminist research on families remains at the margins of family research: "In most domains, authors consider gender to be irrelevant to their understanding of family life" (p. 847). Allen (2000) argues that family studies should be more inclusive of the diversity of family forms. In addition, she advocates a more "reflexive" methodology in which subjective values are acknowledged and incorporated into the research process. Her proposals reflect two common feminist themes: a critique of positivistic scientific approaches and inclusiveness of marginalized and underrepresented groups. Feminists continue to argue that the assumptions and processes of research are partially responsible for marginalizing women's roles and issues as well as those of other groups.

## Critiques and Discussion

Any theoretical perspective that is critical of the status quo is likely to garner reactions and critiques from those that might feel threatened by change. It is useful to avoid such simple reactions. Furthermore, it is somewhat difficult to address criticisms to such a diverse grouping of schools of thought. Often we can find diametrically opposed positions characterizing feminist schools, such as cultural feminism versus radical feminism. The discussion here only addresses issues that the schools of feminism tend to share and that are relevant to the nature and purpose of theory.

The first criticism that is often raised is that feminist theory is not a theory at all but an ideology. This criticism is often founded on the assumption that the sole purpose of "theory" is to explain phenomenon. Calls to action and advocacy of values such as those inherent in much of feminist theory are viewed as a moral or valued perspective rather than an attempt to explain phenomena. Thus, critics argue that feminism is not a theory at all but a political ideology.

Undoubtedly, there is some evidence for this criticism when we find unsupported claims made because they are deemed morally justified. The same accusation could be made about other emancipatory theories such as Marxian conflict theory, however. Furthermore, if ungrounded comments from some theoreticians were prima facie evidence that a theory did not exist, most existing theoretical frameworks would be equally tainted. It seems to us that the more valid question is not whether values or morals are interwoven with the theoretical perspective but whether this theory offers theoretical propositions that can be empirically disproved. To put this another way, we would focus not on where the theory comes from (context of discovery) but solely on whether it supplies disconfirmable propositions about family phenomena (context of justification).

In many ways, feminism falls short of this criterion of providing clear propositions for testing. This fact alone would suggest that it is not yet a theory in the traditional scientific sense. Nonetheless, it joins

many of the other theoretical frameworks in this book in having
concepts and some suggestive propositions that are not yet clearly
specified. Indeed, our assessment is that feminism is a theoretical
framework with great potential. The obstacles to developing this
potential, however, are not inconsequential. First and foremost is the
rejection of the traditional model of the justification of knowledge
claims by empirical testing. As long as feminists reject the methods
and goals of theoretical propositions, it is doubtful that they will produce a theory that is disconfirmable. The caveat here is that successive
generations of feminist scholars may be more receptive to producing
knowledge claims that are subjected to empirical testing. As Duran
(1998) points out, the success of feminists has in part been due to their
ability to produce empirical evidence to support claims of discrimination and inequities. This same strength can be used to develop empirically testable theory.

Closely aligned to this problem is the problem inherent in the
feminist epistemology of *experience* (e.g., Haack, 1998). The claim
that experience provides the basis for knowledge is not controversial.
It should be noted that science should not care where good ideas come
from but should focus on whether the ideas can be subjected to disconfirmation. It is at this point that some feminists might argue that
subjective experience should count in the disconfirmation of statements. If this were so, we would not be teaching evolution in many
school systems where subjective religious beliefs would hold sway
over propositions that have been subjected to empirical tests. Indeed,
this is a danger for the progress of feminism because it would make
popularity and political sway the arbiters of fact rather than science.
It can be argued that with all its frailties, science has proved useful for
feminist goals and arguments.

Standpoint epistemology and the impossibility of resolving disputed claims is another area of criticism. Standpoint epistemology
argues that each group's or person's standpoint is valid (e.g., Smith,
1992). To adopt this position, however, it is necessary to assume a
relativistic perspective on knowledge. The relativistic perspective then
fails to provide a way to resolve contradictory knowledge claims other
than by "might makes right," where might is determined by popularity, money, or power.

As we have seen from the diversity of the feminist schools of
thought, the notion that feminist are defined by a value commitment
to knowledge that liberates women from patriarchal oppression provides further difficulties. We are left asking whose values determine
"true" liberation. For example, the cultural feminists opposed women
entering the armed services because such integration was seen as

undermining the pacifist values of feminism. On the other hand, liberal and radical feminist supported this move as following their value on equality of opportunity. More clashes will occur over issues such as universal day care as opposed to maternal care. With fertility falling in all of the developed world, a potential area for conflict will be whether women in the labor force should be treated as equal in all regards to males in the labor force or whether special concessions should be made for women due to child birth and lactation. Again, we must ask every value-driven theorist how to decide whose values are the correct ones.

To make a theory of gender inequality useful as a family theory, ideas about the family must be included. One possibility is to attend to the familial aspects of the inequality itself. So we might focus on the power and division of labor among wives and husbands, mothers and fathers, or daughters and sons instead of all women and all men. The other major possibility is to locate at least some the causes of gender inequality within family variables or processes.

Lorber's (1998) work is again instructive. She is most interested in all manifestations of gender inequality, so most family scholars would need to adopt a narrower focus. What about causes? Across her 11 varieties of feminist theory, Lorber provides 38 different sources or causes. Some examples of causes are a lack of affordable child care (as we noted earlier) and "limitations on reproductive choice" (liberal theory), "exploitation of women in unwaged work for the family" (Marxist/Socialist theory), "inadequate maternal and child health care" and "patriarchal family structures and cultural practices harmful to women and girls" (development theory), and "work and family based on two and only two genders" (social construction theory). If Lorber is correct, only a small portion of all gender inequality is explained by features of family life. Of course, we might wish to argue that familial causes are correlated or otherwise intertwined with extrafamilial causes, but making good sense of such a complex web of explanatory factors is a project still underway.

Finally, the core concepts of feminism need to be more fully developed. Notions of psychological and structural gender need to be linked together. For example, Straus (1994) found support for the link between spousal abuse rates and the status of women for each state in the United States. There is the need for careful theoretical exposition moving from this structural level of patriarchy to individual family violence. The need for such exposition is not exclusive to feminism but is a critique that could be addressed to many social theories. However, feminist scholars have proved themselves particularly adept at producing insights linking different levels of analyses. Once feminism takes as one of its goals the production of knowledge claims that are logically coherent and empirically testable, much progress should be made. It is this potential that should excite scholars in family studies.

## Conclusion

Is feminism dead? Russo's (1998) recent analysis of survey data reported that of the women in her sample who self-identified as feminist, 33% agreed with a statement saying that pushing equal rights has gone too far and 38% agreed that the United States would be better off if people worried less about how equal people are. Of the sample, only 27% of the females identified themselves as feminists!

Although in the critique section we argued that the major threat to the theoretical framework of feminism is its lack of investment in the goals of science and the production of empirically testable knowledge claims, overall there may be an even larger threat: becoming irrelevant as a social movement. Many authors have catalogued the successes of the feminist movement in winning legislated workplace equality and equality of opportunity (e.g., Friedan, 1981). Yet in many ways the rhetoric of the movement seems mired in the 1970s. When the movement is relevant, it is often because special interest groups focus on very specific goals (women of color). So the movement is both increasingly diverse and specialized on the one hand, and, on the other hand, when it is univocal, it seems out of date. As one of our students expressed it, feminism is a movement unaware of its success. Indeed, the current and successive cohorts of students take for granted these successes and cannot comprehend a time when males and females were less equal.

Even if the social movement is waning in popularity, the intellectual contribution from feminist scholars remains strong and vibrant. The intellectual contribution is not isolated to feminist theory but participates in the way other theories are developed and applied. For example, Foschi and colleagues (1996, 2000; Foschi, Lai, & Sigerson, 1994) have extended the social psychological theory of "expectation states" into the realm of the application of double standards of competence for men and women. She and her colleagues experimentally investigated how lower status based on characteristics such as ethnicity, social class, and gender contribute to stricter levels of competence being applied to these individuals. Foschi's work shows a concern with "feminist issues," but her intellectual contributions are buttressed by strong theoretical and empirical science. Also imagine the implications for theory if the social movement of feminism ever succeeds, if gender inequality is substantially reduced or eliminated. Would there continue to be a need for feminist theory if there is nothing left to explain? At best, what would be left to explain is how equality historically arose. Realistically, however, we do not expect anything approaching gender equality to be just around the corner, so feminist theory has an open and vibrant future.

We would argue that one way a univocal feminism can be increasingly relevant is to produce a set of theoretical propositions grounded in the unique value orientation that views gender as a multifaceted and multileveled explanatory paradigm.

## Suggested Readings

Fox, G. L., & Murry, V. M. (2000). Gender and families: Feminist perspectives and family research. *Journal of Marriage and the Family, 62*, 1160–1172.
*This is a decade review of family research from the feminist perspective.*

Nelson, H. L. (Ed.). (1997). *Feminism and families.* New York: Routledge.
*A very clear discussion of the role of families in feminist theory.*

Osmond, M., & Thorne, B. (1993). Feminist theories: The construction of gender in families and society. In P. Boss, W. Doherty, R. LaRossa, W. Schumm, & S. Steinmetz (Eds.), *Sourcebook of family theories and methods: A contextual approach* (pp. 591–622). New York: Plenum.
*This chapter provides a more general perspective on the diversity and forms of feminist theories.*

# 8

# The Ecological Framework

"Mom, why does Dad take us to school and pick us up when all the other kids' mothers do that?" Katrina's mother answers that the father lost his job, and it's easier for her, the mother, to find work. Hidden in the mother's response to Katrina is a complex explanation. Recently, most of the growth in jobs has been in the service sector of the economy. Traditionally, men have been employed in the primary-extractive and secondary-manufacturing sectors of the economy. In North America, both of these traditional male employment sectors have been automated and streamlined to cut costs and compete in the global economic market. Katrina's dad, a civil engineer, was one of the victims of this realignment. At the same time, Katrina's mom, who also has a good education and had worked in banking previously, easily got a job in the growing service sector of the economy. This family is adapting to economic and social changes that are creating a realignment of family roles and responsibilities.

The most basic notion in the ecological approach is *adaptation*. The family in the example above is adapting to changing social and economic conditions. The notion of adaptation in ecology is far reaching. This concept reaches down to our biological roots and up to large-scale interactive processes at the level of populations of organisms. The concept of adaptation can be applied to an individual organism's successful adaptation to a specific environmental *niche* or to global changes such as increases in ultraviolet radiation. Indeed, adaptation is the central concept of ecology.

Some of you may ask what this has to do with families. A concern with families and the environment is at the heart of what *ecology* means and of the ecological social movement that has become so active during the later part of the 20th century. The term *ecology* was coined in 1873 by Ernst Haeckel, a German biologist (see Clarke, 1973). It was developed from the Greek root *oik*, which means "place of residence."

Haeckel used the German *oekologie* in which the prefatory *oe* makes the term universal as "everyman's house or environment" (Clarke, 1973). As Clarke points out, although "Haeckel, a male biologist, saw that a science of everyone's house environment needed to be developed, the female chemist, Ellen Swallow Richards, slowly began to take up residency in the structure" (p. 40).

Ellen Swallow Richards was the first female student at MIT and one of the pioneers of water purity analysis. Her many published books include studies in the areas of water analysis, minerals, and sanitation, and she also published works on the cost of food and shelter and the chemistry of cooking. Indeed, it was Richards who founded and served as first president of the American Home Economics Association. She believed that the family and home were central to the ecological movement: "Science has to apply its knowledge to [improve] that unit of the community, the home; for upon the welfare of the home depends the welfare of the commonwealth" (Clarke, 1973, p. 141). Although Richards's hard-nosed scientific empiricism has been challenged and rejected by some prominent contemporary home economists (e.g., Brown, 1984; Bubolz & Sontag, 1993), there can be little doubt that her viewpoint favored the development of interdisciplinary ecological and environmental sciences in the broadest of senses.

Richards lived in an era (1842–1911) when unbridled industrialization triumphed, but her keen scientific eye saw the hidden costs. She documented the loss in water quality in studies that were instrumental in leading to the first U.S. water quality standards. Although the 19th century was intellectually illuminated by Darwin, day-to-day life was governed more by corporate greed. For example, in the early 1870s, the Boston Milk War was fought between milk businesses and an embryonic consumer movement. The businesses routinely diluted milk with water, and when a group of citizens organized a consumer protection association to deliver untainted milk to Boston, their drivers were beaten, their horses crippled, and the milk tainted (Clarke, 1973, p. 42). Increasingly, industry claimed areas of production that had previously been the principal role of women in the home. As a result, many women felt a loss of purpose, and the "manufacture" of previously "homemade" products was fertile ground for avaricious interests. Richards documented to the Massachusetts State Board of Health, Lunacy and Charity in the first-ever scientific survey of the state's food supply that many common foods contained additives that were harmful. She reported that out of 33 samples of baking soda, 9 contained alum, 5 contained ammonia, and others contained large quantities of starch (Clarke, 1973, p. 103). Rather than tight legislative controls, Richards favored the education of the major group of consumers—women:

> It is because I believe in the possibility of control of [the environment] and even economic conditions that I urge so strongly the dissemination of what knowledge we have. . . . [Otherwise] a cry for state interference will come in that day when it is clear that the carelessness of men threatens to extinguish the race. (quoted in Clarke, 1973, p. 211)

To further our education about our environment, Richards, in 1907, reiterated her proposal for a new science:

> Human Ecology is the study of the surroundings of human beings in the effects they produce on [other] lives. . . . The features of the environment are natural, as climate; and artificial, produced by human activity such as noise, [dirt], poisonous vapors, vitiated air, dirty water and unclean food. (quoted in Clarke, 1973, pp. 215–216)

Shortly after Richards died, Robert Wollcott and C. V. Shreve founded the Ecological Society of America in 1916 (Clarke, 1973). By 1919, the society had acquired *Ecology* as a journal outlet for its publications. By 1917, the society's membership was 307, and by 1973 the membership had swollen to 5,148 (Hinckley, 1976). Although the membership includes scholars from almost every field of science, in 1920 the president of the society, Barrington Moore, urged that human ecology be taken to represent an especially important aspect of ecology. Since this time, human ecology has developed mainly in association with the academic discipline of sociology (e.g., Burgess, 1925; Hannan & Freeman, 1984; Hawley, 1986; Park, 1925).

## Intellectual Traditions

The early studies in human ecology (e.g., Burgess, 1925; McKenzie, 1924; Park, 1925; Park & Burgess, 1921) derived much of their intellectual and conceptual foundation from the work of plant ecologists. In contrast to the notion that the United States was a "melting pot," these sociologists detected homogeneous spatial ordering and change that could readily be described in the language of plant ecology, especially ecological succession and species dominance. These early scholars were preoccupied with the spatial arrangement of the urban setting, particularly Chicago, and this explains why some students identify human ecology with this spatial approach and what has become known as the Chicago school of human ecology. But as Hawley (1986) points out, this spatial approach was superseded by a concern with population ecology. Population ecology united social demography with the bioecological study of populations so that spatial orderings became one of a myriad of ways a population adapts to a particular environment. To understand why and how human ecology became generally linked to population ecology, it is necessary to trace some of the historical currents that only came together in the mid-20th century.

Although the field of ecology is relatively new, significant scholarly work in the area of humans and their environment preceded the nomenclature identifying the field. Most notable in this regard is the work of Thomas Malthus (1766–1834). Malthus lived in a time when the prevailing notion was that a growing population increased the power of a country. Surplus population could be used to feed mercantilism and populate colonies. Before Malthus's (1798/1872) *An Essay on the Principle of Population*, the folk wisdom regarding food sources might be summed up as a reliance on nature to provide "no more children than teats" (Peterson, 1969, p. 146). Malthus (1798/1872) proposed that in an unconstrained situation population would increase at a geometric rate (2, 4, 8, 16 . . .) and food production at an arithmetic rate (1, 2, 3, 4, 5 . . .). He pointed out that in reality the relationship between food and population was always constrained by either preventative checks (e.g., moral restraint) or positive checks (e.g., wars, famine). Clearly, preventative checks tend to focus on fertility, whereas positive checks tend to focus on mortality. Regardless of the controversial nature of the predictions of overpopulation that can be derived from Malthus, his work served to bring an ecological focus to the emerging studies of economics, sociology, and demography by highlighting the interaction of environmental and biological variables with social and human variables.

Ecology, as a science, must trace its paternity to Charles Darwin (1809–1882). The early focus by Malthus on the interaction of biological and social variables was given broad substance and theoretical form in the work of Darwin. He published his most famous work, *On the Origin of Species by Means of Natural Selection*, in 1859. It was in this work that his ideas of natural selection and evolution first appeared, only slightly ahead of the simultaneous exposition of these ideas by Alfred Wallace. Basically, Darwin argued that a species or population evolved principally by the process of natural selection or elimination of those members of the population that were less adapted to survive in their environment. Although evolution is a population process, elimination or selection takes place at the individual level.

The rudimentary understanding of this process led both Darwin and later social Darwinists to maintain arguments favoring eugenics and bordering on biological determinism. For example, Darwin argued that many times we

> do our utmost to check the process of elimination; we build asylums for the imbecile, the maimed, and the sick; we institute poor laws; and our medical men exert their utmost skill to save the life of everyone to the last moment. . . . Thus, the weak members of civilized societies propagate their kind. . . . It is not surprising how soon a want of care, or care wrongly directed, leads to the degeneration of a domestic race; but excepting in the case of man himself, hardly anyone is so ignorant as to allow his worst animals to breed. (Darwin, 1880, pp. 130–134, quoted in Martindale, 1960, pp. 163–164)

Statements that confused acquired characteristics such as being maimed (in the above passage), poor, or uneducated with traits that are inheritable is a disturbing characteristic of early social evolutionists. Much of this confusion arose because the exact mechanisms by which traits were passed to later generations were not identified until the publication of Mendel's (1865/1965) work on genetics at the turn of the century.

If ecology traces its paternity to Darwin and his central notion of adaptation, then human ecology must trace its kinship through Gregor Mendel. This is especially true for those forms of family ecological theory that unite ontogenetic development with environmental interaction (e.g., Bronfenbrenner, 1979) and those family theorists who believe that much of family behavior is explained by biological factors (van den Berghe, 1979). Mendel first presented his ideas in two lectures in 1865, but his ideas were not "discovered" by the scientific community until the turn of the century (e.g., Brannigan, Wanner, & White, 1981). When Mendel's work was finally understood, it provided a theoretical understanding for the genetic mechanisms that drive evolution. Mendel proposed that genes attached to chromosomes transmit the genetic information to offspring. Attached to the chromosome were two alleles, one of which might be dominant and therefore expressed in the offspring's phenotype (visible physical characteristics); the other might be recessive but nonetheless remain part of the offspring's genotype (genes that are potentially transmittable). From his experiments, Mendel could show that although it was impossible to predict an individual-level genetic outcome, it was possible to predict the proportions or probabilities for a reproducing population. Mendel's work was seminal for both laboratory genetics and population genetics, but it was population genetics that carried the greatest implications for evolutionary theory and ecological theory.

Population genetics received its early impetus from the simultaneous work of Hardy (1908) and Weinberg (1908). They developed an equation for predicting allele frequencies for subsequent generations of a population based on the assumption that the only factor operating in the population is the initial distribution of alleles. Thus, their model assumed no evolution. The degree to which their predictions were inaccurate could be used as a measure of evolution. The discrepancy between their prediction and the actual observed allele frequencies could be explained by four evolutionary factors: natural selection, mutation, gene drift, and gene flow. In relatively large and immobile populations, the principal factors are natural selection and mutation (see Turner, 1991).

The mathematical nature of population genetics attracted statisticians and demographers. For example, Karl Pearson (1857–1936) served as editor of both *Biometrika* and *The Annals of Eugenics* and, like Galton (1869/1952) before him, felt that human progress and development was largely related to natural selection (Martindale, 1960). Another famous statistician, Ronald Fisher (1958), mathematically demonstrated that natural selection and not mutation is the major explanatory factor in evolution. He argued that variation in a gene pool was inextricably linked to natural selection and adaptation. Without sufficient variation in the gene pool, there is insufficient range from which to select an adaptation. Despite the fact that both Fisher and Pearson favored eugenics as a way to ensure the promulgation of the "fittest" genes, their statistical contributions confirmed that natural selection and adaptation are the central mechanisms in the process of evolution (Turner, 1991).

The genetic emphasis in human ecology found natural extensions into the area of human development. The first genetically based theories about human development were simple extensions from evolutionary theory summarized as "ontogeny recapitulates phylogeny." It did not take long to disprove the simple notion that human development followed the evolutionary tree as a progression of phylogenetic evolution. But this early approach launched the developmentalists' early concern with two basic dimensions of development. First, they were concerned with the development of the organism that was genetically transmitted and universal to the human species (ontogenetic). Second, they were concerned with clearly demarcating the "stages" they assumed all development would traverse. For example, theorists such as Piaget (1952) proposed invariant developmental stages through which all humans would progress in the development of their cognitive capacity. Such approaches, however, failed to acknowledge the contribution of the social and physical context in which the organism was developing. At roughly the same time, a more contextual approach developed from the work of Lewin (1935) that emphasized the interaction of the developing person with the environment. Lewin's work greatly influenced the development of a ecological theory of human development by Bronfenbrenner (1979). Bronfenbrenner's ecological approach then greatly influenced family researchers such as Belsky (1990) and family theorists (e.g., Bubolz & Sontag, 1993; Garbarino, 1992). Today, the ecological approach that originated from developmentalists is one of the most influential models in regard to theorizing about the family and the development of its members.

The human ecology framework brings together these diverse influences. From evolutionary theory and genetics come the view that humans develop as individual biological organisms with capacities limited by genetic endowment (ontogenetic development). From population genetics comes the perspective that populations change mainly by means of natural selection. At the individual level, this implies that individuals demonstrate their fitness by adapting to their changing environment (family adaptation). From ecological theories of human development come "contextualized" and "interactional" theories of human development that emphasize the family. From the human ecology of Richards comes the notion that humans can, through education, understand their interactions with the environment and can direct their consumption (and production) to the benefit of the overall environment (family resource management). And most important for the scientist and scholar is the startling idea from evolutionary theory that a phenomenon needs to be examined at different levels of analysis. What we see as failure and death for an individual organism may be linked to success and adaptive fitness for the population (sociobiology). It is this idea that often leads ecologists and conservationists to suggest solutions that seem counterintuitive, such as killing some deer in a herd so that the population will survive. And lurking just under the surface of this view that we can control natural selection and thus evolution are the proposals favoring eugenics that are far too often driven by sexism and racism.

## Focus and Scope Assumptions

*Individuals and groups are both biological and social in nature.* Like systems theory, ecological theory is a relative newcomer on the social science scene. Ecological theory is distinguished from other theories, such as systems theory, in its emphasis on the biophysical environment and especially the concept of *adaptation*. In systems theory, environment may be a heuristic device, whereas in ecological theory, environment is both spatial and biophysical. This basic assumption leads ecological theory to a more biological and geographic orientation and a less mechanistic perspective on human groups.

This first assumption links the dual nature of humans as constructions of both biology and culture. This dual nature of humans has given rise to some of the world's greatest literature, such as Goethe's *Faust*, and has also occupied generations of academics in the fruitless debate over whether human characteristics are due to biology (nature) or environmental influences (nurture). Today, we have not so much resolved this debate as moved beyond it. We now recognize that even an embryo in the mother's womb is affected by environmental factors such as sounds from the environment and the health status of the mother. Furthermore, a supposed genetic trait such as intelligence requires the interaction of a nurturing environment as shown in the example of kwashiorkor (infant protein deficiency) and cognitive development (IQ). The particular nature of human development ensures that the development of most human traits depends on a nature–nurture interaction rather than on one or the other. Although some academics persist in attempts to identify the additive amounts of contribution made by the nature side and that exact amount made by the environment, most now readily admit that the entire multiplicative process beginning with the formation of a DNA strand depends on interactions with the environment. As van den Berghe (1979) puts it, our behavior can be understood "as the product of an extraordinary complex of interaction between genotype and environment" (p. 5).

*Humans are dependent on their environment for sustenance (air, water, food, etc.).* The assumption of dependency follows from the first assumption in that humans can only survive in environments in which their biological needs can be met. Of course, human culture has developed so that we can survive in fairly inhospitable environments with the assistance of technology. But even technology has its limits, as in the case of water supply.

*Human beings are social and thus are dependent on other human beings.* Another way to state this assumption is to say that most of what we think of as truly "human" seems social in nature—for example, language.

*Humans are finite and their life cycle coupled with their biological needs for sustenance impose time as both a constraint and resource.* This assumption most directly points to the fact that over any individual's life, there is species-common change and development (*ontogenetic development*). In addition, we must remember that time is a factor in the evolution of a population. Furthermore, because we are finite, time becomes a crucial resource for understanding social organization and individual behavior.

*Human interactions are spatially organized.* Populations of humans organize their interactions within their environments. The organized interactions show up as distinct spatial arrangements. Anyone who has ever looked down on the Earth from an airplane is struck by the spatial organization of human activities. But we are not dissimilar from the many other social animals that demonstrate distinct spatial organization as a way of channeling interactions with the environment (e.g., ants, baboons, wolves).

*Human behavior can be understood on several levels.* The two levels that are most often used in human ecology are the *population* and *individual*. For example, populations of organisms show spatial organization and represent particular frequency distributions of genes. Individual organisms may adapt or fail to adapt to their environment. Changing the level of analysis can radically alter our perspective, however. The failure of an organism to successfully adapt, leading to that individual organism's death, may seem a negative outcome at the individual level, but for the population, this same outcome might represent the evolution of a healthier gene pool or the survival of the group faced with food scarcity.

## Concepts

### ECOSYSTEM

Although there are many varieties of ecological theory, most of these would identify the concept of "ecosystem" as central to ecology. Hawley (1986) defines ecosystem as "an arrangement of mutual dependencies in a population by which the whole operates as a unit and thereby maintains a viable environmental relationship" (p. 26). In Hawley's view, an ecosystem is necessarily a subset of the larger environment. The notion of ecosystem contains the elements of wholeness and the interdependency of parts. For example, we might talk of an urban ecosystem, a desert ecosystem, or a polar ecosystem. Each ecosystem, although attached to other ecosystems, has a set of characteristics that demarcate it as a whole. Bubolz and Sontag (1993) suggest that "a family ecosystem consists of a given family system in interaction with its environment" (p. 431).

ECOLOGICAL LEVELS

One of the levels of analysis commonly used in evolutionary theory is *population*. Hawley (1986) argues convincingly that a population is not simply an aggregation of all those people or units sharing a common characteristic. If population referred to such simple aggregations, we might be tempted to talk meaningfully of the population sharing the characteristic of "wearing blue jeans." Hawley defines a population as an aggregate having unit character by virtue of internal organization. In his sense of the term, we could discuss the population of Canada but not the population of "wearers of blue jeans." Hawley's definition of population moves the term away from the identification of a mere statistical aggregation and imbues it with theoretical meaning. Population processes are dissimilar to individual-level processes as seen in the example that a population may have a death rate yet continue over time, whereas an individual who dies fails to continue over time.

There are perhaps many ways to view the levels of an ecosystem (see Bulcroft & White, 1997); however, one of the most popular formulations is that offered by Bronfenbrenner (1979). Bronfenbrenner (1979) suggests that the family is one among many "nested" ecosystems in which the individual develops and interacts. Bronfenbrenner (1979) examines these "nested" systems on four levels of analysis: the *microsystem*, the *mesosystem*, the *exosystem,* and the *macrosystem.* The *microsystem* involves the direct and concrete interactions of the developing person with significant others (1979, p. 22). The *mesosystem* is defined by the interrelations of two or more microsystems, such as work and family (p. 25). The *exosystem* refers to systems that are not in direct interaction with the developing person but have indirect effects on the person's micro- or mesosystem. Last, the *macrosystem* provides the general cultural context in which lower-order systems are environed (p. 26). These distinctions have become widely accepted in ecological theory of the family.

NICHE

Every ecosystem contains *niches.* The interdependencies in an ecosystem are not between specific individuals but between specific niches occupied by individuals or even a species. Associated with each niche is a patterned and relatively stable set of activities. These activities provide "functions" for the maintenance or adaptation of units in the environment or those occupying a specific niche. For example, in a marsh environment, the activity of beavers serves the *function* of water regulation. In the human family, the role of father often has been tied to the function of provider. According to Hawley (1986), these niches represent functions for the ecosystem. Thus, "the mutual dependencies comprising a system (ecosystem) are seen to be linkages among recurring activities" (p. 32). The idea of niche is similar to Bronfenbrenner's (1979) notion of molar activity and to the social psychological construct of social roles.

ADAPTIVE RANGE

An organism that occupies a niche in an ecosystem can be characterized as having an *adaptive range*. The organism's ontogenetic development gives it a range of behavior, but the organism cannot adapt outside of this range. For example, a 2-year-old is not going to be able to understand the principle of conservation of matter because of his or her developmental stage (e.g., Piaget, 1952). Human intelligence represents a broad adaptive range because we apply technology (culture) to problems we would be hard pressed to adapt to organically (e.g., space travel, underwater exploration).

ONTOGENETIC DEVELOPMENT

Every unit within an ecosystem may undergo change that comes about from its own internal structure. Change that is a result of the internal organization and dependencies of parts is called development. For humans, the most important biological part of such developmental change is aging and *ontogenetic development* (see Chapter 4, Concepts). The most important social part of this internal development is experience or maturation. As Piaget (1952) and others have noted, ontogenetic development and social development are inextricably linked. Indeed, Bronfenbrenner (1979) challenges the very assumption that development can be discussed meaningfully as just occurring within the organism. He argues that development is always a relationship between the organism and its immediate environment.

NATURAL SELECTION AND ADAPTATION

Before Fisher's (1958) proof that mutation could not possibly be a major factor in evolution, there were thought to be two major sources of evolutionary change, mutation and natural selection. Now we usually consider only natural selection and its correlate, adaptation. Indeed, the concepts of natural selection and adaptation are simply different sides of the same process. Natural selection is a concept about the outcome of adaptation. If an organism or population successfully adapts (survives) to changes in its ecosystem (interrelations among niches), then it has not been "selected." If the organism does not adapt, then it has been "selected." If a population undergoes changes, it is because some poorly adapted organisms were "selected out," and the remaining organisms represent a more adaptive set of alleles for the population. The classic example here is that of the species of white moths in late-19th-century coal-dependent Britain. The few dark-colored moths in this population survived the change to a coal-blackened environment, whereas their white relatives became readily visible against the gray, coal-covered environment to every hungry bird.

In ecological theory, natural selection is often treated as a population process and adaptation as an individual-level process. But natural selection and adaptation, population and individual, gene pool and gene can all be viewed as components of evolution and ontogenetic development. An organism's development over time is constrained by its genetic endowment. Whether a particular organism can adapt to changes in its environment depends on the adaptive range provided by its genetic endowment. If one type of organism is selected out of the population, then the gene pool changes. Thus, the adaptive range provided in the ontogenetic development of the organism interacts with the changing environment to produce the outcome of selection and adaptation.

## Propositions

Human ecological theory has not produced one uniform and consensual set of theoretical propositions. At the most abstract level are the general propositions developed by Hawley (1986), which are difficult to apply to the family. Some family ecologists such as Bubolz and Sontag (1993) do not cite propositions and seem to advocate goals that might not be conducive to developing propositional theory in science. Bronfenbrenner (1979) has suggested several sensitizing concepts and highlighted many possible propositions. Bronfenbrenner focuses on the forces that propel and impede human development rather than focusing on the family. For Bronfenbrenner, the family is one of many microsystems for the developing individual. The propositions we list here are principally drawn from the school of thought developed by Bronfenbrenner and his followers. We believe, at this time, much can be gained by integrating the exiting propositions, where possible, from all of these sources.

The family is a social organization embedded in a larger kinship network (Hawley, 1986, p. 73). The family occupies a niche in all social systems by providing for the sustenance and nurturance of its internal members while providing the larger society with the reproduction of economic and social organization. It is Bronfenbrenner (1979) who most clearly envisions the individual's development within the ecosystem:

> *The individual grows and adapts through interchanges with its immediate ecosystem (the family) and more distant environments such as school.* (Bronfenbrenner, 1979)

The individual child is always in a relationship with another person from conception onward. Bronfenbrenner asserts that in the study of development the dyad is the smallest unit of analysis. Although the child develops ontogenetically, this development is always in the context of these relationships. Thus, the child's development is interactional. However, any point of development can be measured by the developmental status of the individual.

> *The developmental status of the individual is reflected in the ability of the individual to initiate and maintain a new level of adaptive range and to maintain these behaviors in the absence of directions from others.* (Bronfebrenner, 1979, p. 55)

As Hawley (1986) points out, when individuals or populations adapt and develop, they change their interactions with their environment. Thus, the developing organism changes the relationships in the ecosystem.

> *Ecosystem change occurs as new information is converted to new functions (specialization) or increased specialization of old functions.* (Hawley, 1986, p. 60)

and

> *When one member of a dyad undergoes developmental change, the other member of the dyad will also be likely to undergo change.* (Bronfenbrenner, 1979, p. 65).

As the child develops, his or her functions in the family change from being mainly supported and maintained (what Hawley terms *commensalistic*) to increasingly symbiotic and interdependent functions such as household production and consumption (what Hawley terms *corporate*). The family as a production and consumption unit provides individual services and relates to other units as a social and economic household unit. In this process, the child takes on increasingly specialized roles according to his or her developmental maturation and age-graded norms.

> *Changes in specialization involve changes in relationships among functions.* (Hawley, 1986, p. 60)

and

> *Different settings have different distinctive patterns of roles, activities, and relationships for persons in those settings.* (Bronfenbrenner, 1979, p. 109).

For example, husband-and-wife dyads become increasingly specialized in the role (niches) of mother and father with the arrival of a child. These roles are commensalistic rather than corporate. As the child matures and becomes increasingly specialized as a consumer and producer (corporate), the parents become less specialized in the commensalistic arena and more specialized in the corporate area of consumption and production.

> *Complex units develop on each of two axes: on the basis of complementary differences (corporate units) and on the basis of common environmental requirements (commensalistic units).* (Hawley, 1986, p. 86)

and

> *Family organization is the processing system through which energy and information are transformed into life-supporting (consumption or commensalistic) activities and life-enhancing (socializing and corporate) activities.* (Bubolz & Sontag, 1993, p. 431)

As children mature in their corporate roles and become more interdependent, they tend to follow the normative system that gave rise to their parental ecosystem. Thus, children tend to reproduce the family organization of their family of orientation but under the new constraints of an ecosystem that has changed with the passage of time.

Hawley states that "closure" of a niche is a relative concept, but that when a unit is involved in the biophysical environment, such as with the more commensalistic or family-oriented tasks of raising small children, closure is maximized and helps to ensure the stability of the system. Thus, we would expect more resistance to information regarding role change while children are young.

We have only presented a few of the many propositions in human ecology. Indeed, we have not presented the more abstract population-level propositions developed by Hawley. The propositions we cite above reveal a picture of human ecology theory as driven by the realization that human ecological systems are different mainly in that human ecology "finds its fullest expression in the commitment to organization as the adaptive mechanism" (p. 126). In the sense that the family is the central social organization, we can see that human ecologists must view the family as a core adaptive mechanism, whether examining the ecosystem from the perspective of individual development (Bronfenbrenner) or from the perspective of macro-organization (Hawley).

Let's apply these propositions by returning to our initial example of Katrina's dad taking her to school. Recall that Katrina wanted her mother to take her to school as the other kids' mothers did. The family is reorganizing roles because of complex social and economic changes, yet these changes do not in themselves predict the particular direction and form of the reorganization. For example, Katrina's parents could decide that roles should be discontinued by sending Katrina off to other relatives. Katrina is responding to the fact that her family is reorganizing their roles because "changes in specialization involve changes in relationships among functions" (Hawley, 1986, p. 60). Katrina's mother and father have had to adapt to a complex economic environment. Part of this adaptation is that the father's role is being redefined to occupy some of the niche vacated by the now-employed mother. But rather than eliminate these roles, the family preserves its functions because the family corporate unit "tends to replicate the structural properties of the parent ecosystem" (Hawley, 1986, p. 86).

Furthermore, the family unit tends toward closure regardless of the openness of the ecosystem (see p. 86), testifying to the inherent conservative nature or inertia of family organization. Part of this inertia comes from the commensalistic nature of the organization. As Katrina matures, however, she will have to do more to assist the family because her dad will also be looking for a job in addition to his expanded household role and her working mother will not be free from aspects of her mother role. In Bronfenbrenner's (1979) formulation, "Different settings have different distinctive patterns of roles, activities and relationships for persons in those settings" (p. 109). And Hawley might say, "Increases in intensity of specialization of any given function are accompanied by increases in intensity of specialization of all complementary functions" (p. 85). In this regard, we can also see the school system changing, in that neither mom nor dad may be available to help with supervision and transportation of fieldtrips and so on.

Indeed, "Ecosystem change occurs as new information is converted to new functions (specialization) or increased specialization of old functions" (Hawley, 1986, p. 60). Thus, the changes that Katrina's family and other families are experiencing may have ramifications for the educational system. And, in the longer run, the demonstration that such "adaptation" is necessary may lead Katrina's generation to reduce the number of children they have so that reorganization is more easily accomplished. Such curtailing of fertility would lead to population-level changes.

In the final analysis, we cannot completely explain what is happening to Katrina's family without examining the complex causes in the higher-order systems. Yet the rudiments of the ecological approach can be seen in this example. Basic principles are the connectedness and embeddedness of various ecological levels and the continual need for adaptation to the constant currents of change.

## Variations

### HUMAN DEVELOPMENTAL ECOLOGY

Urie Bronfenbrenner (1979) tied together ideas from ecological theory and Kurt Lewin's (1935) field theory to formulate the ideas in his book *The Ecology of Human Development*. Bronfenbrenner argues that the child always develops in the context of family-type relationships and that development is the outcome not simply of the ontogenetic factors but of the interaction of the person's genetic endowment with the immediate family and eventually with other components of the environment. Although this central argument does not originate with Bronfenbrenner, his work represents one of the most recent systematic statements of this perspective. As a result, the ecological approach to human development has proven influential in guiding research by family scholars, developmental psychologists, and researchers in education.

From the macroscopic perspective of Hawley's (1986) propositions, the ecological approach to human development could be interpreted as focusing on Hawley's propositions linking changes in specialization to changes in relationships among functions (p. 60). Although there is no contradiction between Bronfenbrenner (1979) and Hawley (1986), Bronfenbrenner's contribution is significant and should not be trivialized as simply filling in details for Hawley's macroperspective on human ecology. The distinction between the two complementary approaches lies in what they explore. Hawley (1986) examines the linkages between parts of the ecosystem and the general laws that govern the interrelations of these parts. Bronfenbrenner (1979) examines individual human behavior as a consequence of the interaction between the environment and the person.

Bronfenbrenner's (1979) work stands in sharp contrast to those psychologists who would explain individual behavior solely by examining individual traits or abilities. Bronfenbrenner argues that a person's behavior is a function of the interaction of the person's traits and abilities with the environment $(B = f\{PE\})$. This view supposes that a person's traits interact with the environment to create individual behavior that cannot be explained by simply adding the effects of the person's traits to the effects of the environment. The classic example of this is early toilet training. The child does not gain voluntary muscular control in this regard until about 18 months of age. Socialization before this time is likely to frustrate both the child and parent. It is only when the ontological development and the environmental socialization coincide that the desired outcome is reached. The causes of the behavior, toilet training, cannot be seen as additive, because socialization before muscular control will have little effect, and muscular control without proper socialization will also have little effect in attaining the target behavior. It is the interaction of these two components $(P \times E)$ that produces the behavior. And it is this interactionist perspective that distinguishes Bronfenbrenner's (1979) view of human development from the more ontological individual approaches. He defines his position as follows:

> The ecology of human development involves the scientific study of the progressive, mutual accommodation between an active, growing human being and the changing properties of the immediate environment in which the developing person lives, as this process is affected by relations between these settings, and by the larger contexts in which the settings are embedded. (1979, p. 21)

Bronfenbrenner views the individual as being embedded in a microsystem (role and relations), a mesosystem (interrelations between two or more settings), an exosystem (external settings that do not include the person), and a macrosystem (culture). His idea of ecological change is very similar to Hawley's (1986) notion linking changes in niche specialization to changes in relationships among functions. In Bronfenbrenner's (1979) definition of an "ecological transition," a "person's position in the ecological environment is altered as the result of a change in role, setting, or both" (p. 26). Later, Bronfenbrenner (1989) expanded this notion and discussed a model in which there are "differences in developmental processes and outcomes associated with different ecological niches" (p. 200). For example, as a child develops, he or she is brought into roles with caregivers other than the mother: day care, preschool, peers, and eventually the school system. All of these interactions may represent significant ecological transitions for the developing child in that there are new roles (niches) and interactions with the immediate environment and increasingly distant environments. The child–school mesosystem is further affected by other exosystems and the macrosystem by forces such as economic pressures and political decisions. Bronfenbrenner's (1979, 1989) approach encompasses the entire environment of the developing person while maintaining a focus of the microsystem (roles and relations) and mesosystem interactions as having the greatest direct effects on the child.

The most important refinement Bronfenbrenner (1989) has made is to include *time* as a more integral part of his theory. This incorporation of time has led to two major additions to the theory. First, Bronfenbrenner now views his ecological theory as applying "throughout the life course" of the individual (p. 188). Second, he has added the notion of the *chronosystem,* which incorporates time as the developmental history of the individual (events and experiences) and its effect on development. The need for the addition of time 10 years after the original statement of the theory might in part be due to changes that occurred during the 1980s. The decade of the 1980s witnessed some significant theoretical and methodological innovations in regard to the occurrence and timing of life course events (see Chapter 5). These refinements also give Bronfenbrenner's (1979, 1989) theory a greater similarity to other life course theories covered in Chapter 5 and may suggest a gradual merging into more of an emphasis on "development" than "ecology." For example, followers of Bronfenbrenner such as Moen, Elder, and Lüscher (1995) clearly move to a more life course perspective. On the other hand, Garbarino (1992) focuses more on families and the context in which they exist. Because these may be seen as complementary levels of analysis within ecological theory, such diversity may only increase the already powerful influence of Bronfenbrenner's developmental ecological approach on family scholarship.

## FAMILY DEMOGRAPHY AND ECOLOGY

Peterson (1969) defines demography as "the systematic analysis of population phenomena" (p. 1). He goes on to point out a basic distinction among classes of demographers. On the one hand, there is "formal" demography, the study of population as a self-contained process using sophisticated mathematical models. On the other hand, there is "population analysis," which includes variables from the social setting such as norms, natural resources, and economic growth as both independent and dependent variables (Peterson, 1969, p. 3). Population analysis is a theoretical variant of human ecology.

Since its inception, demography has been necessarily concerned with the study of many "family" variables such as nuptuality and fertility. Demographers from the time of Malthus recognized that variables such as fertility were influenced by social custom and organization and that differences in the rules of organization would affect fertility patterns. But a concern with family variables does not necessarily suggest that demography occupies a niche in the human ecology of families.

The claim that demography occupies a theoretical role in the human ecology of the family would strike many demographers as unusual or questionable. The case for this theoretical contribution is quite strong, however. From the turn of the century, sociologists and demographers of rural life have been concerned with the life cycle of the family. Paul Glick (1947), a family demographer, formalized this life cycle approach to data on families in his article, *The Family Cycle* (see Chapter 4). Demographers have also been interested in how families are integrated with other organized sectors of society, such as work and education. Hogan (1978) examined the effects of event sequences, including finishing education, starting a first job, and marriage. Oppenheimer (1988) examined family change and economic change. Sweet, Bumpass, Call, and others from the University of Wisconsin Center for Demography and Ecology launched a longitudinal panel study, the National Survey of Families and Households, focused on families and family forms in the United States (Sweet, Bumpass, & Call, 1988). Most recently, Teachman, Tedrow, and Crowder (2000) focus on changes to the structure of American families during the last decade.

Demographers study macroscopic levels of analysis such as social organizations, institutions, and populations. The principal theoretical orientation they have provided is their focus on how these social groupings are interwoven in time and space for any given society. Some demographers have moved to global levels of analysis in their attempt to understand social phenomena such as the connection between fertility and rates of female labor force participation (e.g., Westoff, 1978). Demography, then, occupies the niche in ecology that is focused on population characteristics and population change.

SOCIOBIOLOGY OF THE FAMILY

Since the writings of Darwin, various attempts have been made to explain social behavior as a consequence of evolution. Recently, most such attempts for a biological explanation of social behavior have been labeled *sociobiology,* following E. O. Wilson (1975). Sociobiology was preceded by the eugenics of Pearson (1909) and Fisher (1958) and early ethologists such as Konrad Lorenz (1966). Pierre van den Berghe (1979) is responsible for the most systematic application of sociobiology to the family.

Sociobiologists of the family accept that human behavior is a complex interaction of genes and environment (van den Berghe, 1979, p. 205). They do not offer a simplistic biological determinism of social behavior. Rather, the key concept used in sociobiology is *inclusive fitness,* or kin selection. Inclusive fitness refers to individuals behaving in ways to maximize their own or their relatives' reproductive success (1979, p. 19). This means that the individual attempts to maximize the transmission of his or her genes to the succeeding generation. Because a sibling carries 50% of one's own genes, the success of a sibling in reproduction is related to one's own success. The principle of inclusive fitness is used to explain much of human family behavior within the constraints of natural selection on the gene pool and the configuration of the environment. For example, van den Berghe discusses two parental strategies for maximizing reproductive success. One strategy is to have few children and invest a lot in the care and socialization of these few. The other strategy is to have many children but with the necessary reduction in the parental investment of time and energy per child. He points out that the two strategies have different strengths and weaknesses depending on the environment. In an unstable and hostile environment, high fertility might prove more successful, whereas lower fertility with high parental investment is more appropriate for stable populations close to the carrying capacity of the environment (1979, p. 26). Thus, the explanatory biological principle of inclusive fitness is always used within a particular environment.

An interesting example of how sociobiologists attempt to explain family phenomena is the application of inclusive fitness to pair bonding and marriage. Humans do not practice random mating or mating driven by female estrus. Rather, in most human societies, we find that relatively permanent heterosexual couples are the rule. To explain why this is so offers some difficulty for sociobiology. Van den Berghe (1979) argues, "Females invest more in offspring, have less of an incentive to be promiscuous, and have a greater concern to bind a male to themselves than vice versa" (p. 46). Males, on the other hand, have less at stake in the nurturance of individual children and more to gain by maximizing the contribution of genes to a larger number of females. Thus, according to van den Berghe (1979),

Courtship (the rituals preceding the formation of a pair-bond) is primarily a method by which females assess and choose males and whereby males woo females. A woman subjects her suitors to tests that enable her to make the best possible choice of a provider—a mate likely to contribute maximally to her fitness. A man seeks to convince his prospective mates that he qualifies, but since he can also increase his fitness by being fickle, he will seek to deceive women. (p. 46)

For van den Berghe, females ultimately invest in their offspring because they carry the child, and the results of any promiscuousness are borne by them. Males may pursue a different strategy for maximizing their inclusive fitness in part because they may not have to directly bear the responsibility of care and nurturance. Indeed, until the recent development of DNA testing, paternity was difficult to prove compared with maternity. The so-called double standard for the sexual conduct for males and females is founded on this difference in reproductive strategy.

Sociobiology raises questions about social change. For example, in the explanation of pair bonding, we may ask about the effect of easily available and effective birth control for women. Would this lead to promiscuity? According to van den Berghe's argument, birth control would not lead to promiscuity as an inclusive fitness strategy for females because it would allow sex but not reproduction. Women would continue to bear the responsibility of childbirth. From the other side of the equation, we might ask why males would have ever become "providers" and "social fathers" when their best strategy for inclusive fitness appears to be promiscuity. Van den Berghe's analysis tends to represent marriage as a female institution in which males have little investment.

Although sociobiologists may have difficulty providing explanations of some areas of family behavior, they provide very clear explanations of areas that have proven difficult for other theorists. One of these is the basic question, "Why do people have children?" From an exchange perspective, children are costly and provide few rewards. Sociobiology provides the unequivocal argument that having children maximizes inclusive fitness. Yet lurking around the corner are problems for this explanation because social change brings about the introduction of new and effective reproductive technologies not directly tied to the biological individual.

Also, keep in mind that many sociobiologists do not assume a deliberate and conscious attempt by members of any species to reproduce their genes per se. All that is required, other than an assumption that humans desire to copulate and raise children, is an appreciation for existing behaviors in a population being the result of differential reproduction. The principles of evolution work regardless of attitudes about our own or anybody else's genes. Social patterns that don't reproduce themselves disappear. What is most difficult is predicting which social patterns will be maladaptive before they disappear.

Troost and Filsinger (1993) aptly characterize this area of theory as an emerging perspective. A recent review by Booth, Carver, and Granger (2000) supports this contention. Indeed, recent research has tended to move toward examination of hormonal differences and on the inheritability of divorce. To date, however, much of this research has been based on correlational type surveys and does not seem well integrated into the work of contemporary endocrinologists. In addition, this newer research effort does not seem to identify with explanations regarding inclusive fitness but clearly puts more emphasis on specific hormones as mediating between the individual's genetic endowment and the individual's behavior. The direction of this emerging area places greater emphasis on the biological underpinnings of humans and human society and on the fact that this biological substrate must be part of any complete ecological theory.

## HOME ECONOMICS AND HUMAN ECOLOGY

From its inception, home economics has been a form of human ecology. Richards's vision was that only through intelligent consumption and management of household resources could our society combat the waste and pollution of unbridled capitalism. She envisioned an application of scientific knowledge and principles to home management. These sentiments were given a more concrete framework by Paolucci, Hall, and Axinn (1977), who fostered the idea that families could affect significant outcomes at the macroscopic level by the management and control of their decisions.

Deacon and Firebaugh (1988) developed an ecological framework for family decision making. They view the family as a system interacting with its environment. Resources and some demands for family resources originate outside of the family. The family system is composed of individual personal subsystems and the family managerial subsystem. The family managerial subsystem contains both planning and implementing functions and results in demand responses and changes in resources as system output. Deacon and Firebaugh emphasize the embeddedness of the family system in the larger ecosystem and the interchanges that take place between these various levels. They stress resources, values, and information in family resource management and decision making that remain true to Richards's original vision.

Bubolz and Sontag (1993) argue that Richards's vision of a scientifically based, family consumption unit missed the fact that family decisions ultimately reflect values. A proactive home economics profession, they argue, must likewise reflect a set of values. In this sense, because home economics is a practitioner field and not simply a field of studies, it cannot follow the value neutrality that Bubolz and Sontag identify with positivistic science. Thus, Bubolz and Sontag, as well as others such as Brown (1984), have rejected science as the appropriate model for knowledge and practice and favor a hermeneutic approach that includes the subjectivity of experience and valuing. Among the issues Bubolz and Sontag see as central to human ecology theory are a number of value-laden questions such as "What changes are necessary to bring about human betterment?" and "What should be done to realize such universal values for the common good as economic adequacy, equity in access to resources and opportunities, increased freedom and justice, and development of peace?" (p. 429). It is interesting to contrast this approach with that of traditional scientists, who would first question if a universal set of values does indeed exist and want to see evidence that these values are universal.

In some senses, Bubolz and Sontag's (1993) version of home economics is caught in a dilemma common to the "helping" professions. Home economics is dedicated to both the study of the ecosystem and to helping people. On one hand, home economists would like to build a theory of human ecology. On the other hand, they require that such a theory contain a statement of values, such as "equity in access to resources," so that practitioners have a clear notion of what the "common good" and "human betterment" represent. Scientists have in part attempted to remain value neutral because the juxtaposition between an accurate description and prediction of the "way things are" has largely been thought to be independent of our thinking about the "way things should be." The name change of the American Home Economics Association to the American Association of Family and Consumer Sciences might signal the beginning of a resolution to the science versus service dilemma.

## Empirical Applications

### EFFECT OF DAY CARE ON YOUNG CHILDREN

The research on day care and its effects on young children has proved to be one of the most effective applications of ecological theory of the family. The ecological formulations of Bronfenbrenner (1979) have guided most of this research. Major studies include

Belsky, Gillstrap, and Rovine (1984) in the United States and Goelman and Pence (1987) in Canada. Researchers in the Pennsylvania Infant and Family Development Project (Belsky et al., 1984) examined infant–mother attachment by using variables drawn from the micro-, meso-, and exosystems developed by Bronfenbrenner (1979; see Bretherton, 1993, p. 287). Findings from the work by Belsky and colleagues (1984) and the myriad other studies examining the ecological factors of child care appear to contradict previous research in the area of child care.

Belsky (1990) characterizes the newer research findings, first noting that the macrosystem environment in which these studies were conducted has changed over time: "Less than one-third of all mothers with an infant under one year of age were employed in 1976" but "by 1985 virtually one out of every two such women were working" (pp. 894–895). Belsky summarizes the current state of the literature:

> Children in any variety of child care arrangements, including center care, family day care, and nanny care, for the first year of life, are at elevated risk of being classified as insecure in their attachments to their mothers at 12 or 18 months of age and of being more disobedient and aggressive when they are from 3 to 8 years old. (p. 895)

Belsky and Eggebeen (1991) analyzed the National Longitudinal Survey of Youth and found greater noncompliance among children whose mothers were extensively involved in work early in the child's life. Although Belsky's (1990) claim has been accepted by some academics, a significant number of critics offer empirical support for the position that either other factors might account for the differences in attachment or that no significant differences exist (see Demo & Cox, 2000; Greenstein, 1993). The point here is not that ecological theory is a shortcut to quick answers regarding maternal attachment. Indeed, the inclusion of ecological variables makes analyses more complex, but in the long run the findings will be more valid because these contextual variables are included.

## CHILD MALTREATMENT

Garbarino and Sherman (1980) argue that when the parent–child relationship is embedded in a community in which other adults with greater resources interact with the parent–child dyad, there is less child maltreatment than in socially isolated parent–child dyads. In *High-Risk Neighborhoods and High-Risk Families: The Human Ecology of Child Maltreatment*, Garbarino and Sherman (1980) cite ethological studies with isolated gorilla mothers and their infants and cross-cultural studies that suggest parental rejection of the child is inversely associated with social embeddedness. Garbarino and Sherman matched two neighborhoods, one high and one low in child risk, by racial composition and socioeconomic status. They state that about 40% of child maltreatment is associated with socioeconomic status, but there remain additional differences in child maltreatment. The hypothesis these researchers examined is that when socio-economic status is controlled, child risk is associated with neighbor-hood characteristics.

The results support their contention that neighborhood charac-teristics are associated with levels of child maltreatment risk. Garbarino and Sherman describe the high-risk neighborhoods as being different from the low-risk neighborhoods on several dimen-sions. In low-risk neighborhoods, the children played with other children, and parents lent a helping hand with "coverage" of children so that stressed parents could recover. In high-risk neighborhoods, the children did not play with other children, and the parents expressed doubts that the neighborhood was a good place to raise children: "Family life is threatened from within and without. . . . A family's own problems seem to be compounded rather than ameliorated by the neighborhood context, dominated as it is by other needy families" (1980, p. 194).

Garbarino and Kostelny (1992) likewise view child maltreatment as a community problem. The presence of informal support networks in the community militates against child maltreatment. But as ecolo-gists such as Burgess (1925) have pointed out, there is a tendency for neighborhoods to homogenize. This process leads Garbarino and Sherman (1980) to conclude that "we have repeated findings that ecological niches can 'make or break' risky families. The challenge to researchers and policymakers is to make the best of it" (p. 196).

### Implications for Intervention

Westney (1993) points to several possible implications of ecological theory for practitioners. First and foremost is that ecological theory sensitizes practitioners and others to the multiple levels and complex interactions between various ecological units. For example, parent education might entail not just what the parent can do for the child but in addition could be extended to parent–child interactions with the neighborhood and schools. The ecological perspective is inherently multidisciplinary in its implications. In addition to family scientists, nutritionists, urban planners, and traffic engineers have an important role within the ecological model.

Campbell (1993) suggests that one especially important area of application for ecological theory is in health care delivery. Policymakers in more and more countries are critically examining the escalating costs of health care. For some of these countries, part of the solution is to move from a "general hospital" program of disease treatment to a community- or family-based model emphasizing health as well as treatment. In community-based treatment, more emphasis is placed on the family as both a provider of services and as a treatment unit. In family practice, physicians may team up with nutritionists and family therapists to provide service aimed at the family (Bloch, 1983). In addition, the family may require special supports as it takes on increasingly higher loads of caregiving (e.g., Gatz, Bengtson, & Blum, 1990). Ecological theory provides many of the biosocial and physical concepts to inform and assist practitioners in this area.

### Critiques and Discussion

Regardless of the appealing logic of ecological theory and its seeming breadth and inclusiveness, there are some rather severe criticisms of both the logic and substance of this approach. The criticisms we broach here are not ones that can be dismissed by claims that the theory is too new or that these are simply areas that have not been adequately filled in as yet. Rather, many of the criticisms are directed at the logic of the explanation in general.

One of the basic notions in Hawley (1986) and Bronfenbrenner (1979, 1989) is that growth comes about by interchanges with the environment. Equally important is the question "How does decline and decay come about?" Hawley's (1986) *Human Ecology* contains chapters on growth, evolution, and expansion in time and space; chapters on decay, disintegration, and death are notably absent. Bronfenbrenner (1979) focuses so exclusively on child development that statements about environmental interaction and growth appear natural. Even with his later admission that the life course as well as child development need to be included in the model, there is no discussion of degeneration (Bronfenbrenner, 1989). Some ecological scholars address these issues and indeed go some distance in resolving the oversight. Most notable is the work by Hannan and Freeman (1984), who use the idea of structural size and attendant inertia to predict the ability of organizations to adapt to changing environments and the natural selection that results from their adaptive failure. These authors link the properties of the organization with adaptation and selection. The need remains to incorporate concepts such as aging and continuous decay into the ecological model.

Another major problem for ecological theory is the need to specify when ontogenetic causation changes to sociogenetic causation. For example, a child may not learn toilet training at 2 months of age for reasons of ontogenetic maturation, but at some point in the life course of the organism, the same outcome (toilet training) switches from being ontogenetic to sociogenetic. Another way of thinking about this is that there comes a time when the organism's responses are no longer determined by the organism's internal development but largely by processes exogenous to the organism. The process of this changeover and its stages have not yet been identified by ecological theorists. Hawley (1986) provides a partial solution in his notion that an organization (such as a family) can switch from commensalistic to corporate functions. Bronfenbrenner (1979) incorporates this notion in relating the child to successively broader ecosystems. Yet the exact process and identity of this switch from genetic to social causality eludes us.

Somewhat similar to the above criticism is the question of levels of analysis. The problem is that there are few rules to guide the scholar as to when one level of analysis is appropriate rather than another. For example, if behavior is explained by gene pool variance, then when behavior changes rapidly, we would expect rapid changes in the gene pool. Now, imagine that violent crimes increase in a city in a short period of time, such as 3 years. We would be tempted to explain those changes in crime by changes in the gene pool or population, yet it is doubtful that gene pools change so rapidly with normal levels of migration. What, then, is the appropriate level of analysis, the individual, the group, the organization, or some other level?

A problem with the sociobiological variation of ecological theories is its limited predictive value. For example, we usually have to wait many generations before seeing whether a behavioral pattern is fit or adaptive. For this reason, empirical evidence is usually applied to outcomes that have already occurred rather than to outcomes that take place and are observed in the near-term future.

Ecology, many critics claim, is a sensitizing metaphor. For example, in home economics some proponents show embedded circles as diagrams of ecological levels and interfaces, but critics claim these represent pretty circles but no theory. A theory must identify the process by which change occurs. Even Bronfenbrenner (1989) concedes that this is a rather large flaw in the theory. In his original contribution, Bronfenbrenner (1989) identified behavior as a function of the person interacting with his or her environment $(B = f\{PE\})$. Bronfenbrenner says,

> The all-essential key to scientific discovery is missing. In all the preceding pages, what is there to substitute for the fateful "f" in the formula? What is the process that the person and the context are to generate? (p. 241)

Bronfenbrenner also states that he is working on this problem, but as yet it remains a major question for ecological theorists.

Bronfenbrenner's (1989) task is complicated by the criticism that the logic underlying ecological theory is basically tautological or circular (Turner, 1991). For example, evolution is a form change brought on by adaptation and selection to change that in turn was brought on by evolution. One needs to ask if this is not defining change by change. It may not be a problem if there is sufficient precision and detail in the theory so that generalities such as "change" become more precisely specified as "evolution," "adaptation," and "development."

The notion of biological or ontogenetic development of the organism represents a richness that many sociological theories neglect. This allows for the inclusion of both internal and external dynamics of change. But the biological arguments from sociobiology and some ontogenetic arguments share a common flaw. Critics argue that because many of these claims and explanations are ex post facto in nature, any number of other plausible theories might also be true (including sociogenetic theories). The way out of this criticism is to abandon claims that may appear reasonable on the surface but fail to lead to empirically testable predictions. For example, the claim that the male strategy for inclusive fitness is to maximize sexual partners might lead to cross-culturally testable hypotheses. But if this strategy is nothing other than a preference that is extremely malleable by the environment, then it would undoubtedly lead nowhere. This is what has happened to those ridiculous claims about the true "nature of man" and "natural law" theories. At the present time, the inclusion of biological factors holds great promise but also represents the threat of dragging ecological theory into the quagmire of ad hoc and ex post facto explanations that has been the bane of sociobiology.

Finally, there is criticism of building a value-laden human ecology theory (Bubolz & Sontag, 1993). It seems there is a choice to be made between producing a social science theory or a general value orientation. On one hand, it can be argued that all scientific theories entail some value orientation, and this may be the case. The problem we see is different. First, by definition, social science theories describe and predict. A value orientation may simply not meet the meaning or function of a scientific theory. There are philosophical theories, religious theories, theories of literature, and ideologies, none of which are scientific theories. Also, a value orientation may simply not be a social science theory. Second, value-oriented theories may be able to produce predictions, but we wonder whether predictions would be judged by their accuracy or by their desirability or value correctness. For example, Galileo's ideas were suppressed because they were politically incorrect, not because of the inaccuracy of his predictions.

## Conclusion

In the final analysis, the ecological approach is at a youthful stage of its development. It has the necessary breadth and depth to offer a perspective on humans that is both biological and social. The possible unification of work from sociobiology with the ecology of human development and Hawley's (1986) more organizational ecology offers some intriguing prospects for studying both individual family members, the family as a group, and the general ecological context in which those groups function. It might well be that ecological theory will provide not only family scholars but social scientists in general with the most powerful theoretical propositions possible. At present, however, we can only say that this promise remains a potentiality. As Turner (1991) says in regard to Hawley's (1986) formulation, "Human ecology, then, is a theoretical perspective worthy of further development" (p. 151).

## Suggested Readings

Moen, P., Elder, G. H., Jr., & Lüscher, K. (Eds.). (1995). *Examining lives in context: Perspectives on the ecology of human development.* Washington, DC: American Psychological Association.
*This compilation of papers supplies a vivid topography of the developmental perspective in ecological framework.*

Troost, K., & Filsinger, E. (1993). Emerging biosocial perspectives on the family. In P. Boss, W. Doherty, R. LaRossa, W. Schumm, & S. Steinmetz (Eds.), *Sourcebook of family theories and methods: A contextual approach* (pp. 677–710). New York: Plenum.
*This is a very good introduction to the biosocial perspective.*

# 9

# The Current State and Future Course
# of Family Theory

We have now traversed a considerable amount of theoretical territory. You have been introduced to the basic elements of theory in Chapter 1 as well as several family theories in Chapters 2 through 8. Now it is time for a comprehensive overview of family theory. A comprehensive overview is, however, not only a daunting task but may well be impossible. The reason such a task might prove impossible is simply that a theory is never finished!

In the preceding chapters, we have presented theories as *products* of human thought. Although this is certainly one useful way to learn about theories, an overemphasis on the product may lead you away from the power of theories as tools to assist us in understanding our world. A tool analogy may help you appreciate our point here. Imagine you have a screwdriver. You can hold it up and examine it from different angles, note the color, the type of point, and so on. In this sense, you are examining the screwdriver as a product and a human construction. But your image of the screwdriver changes when you use it to screw in a screw, pry open a paint can, weed the garden, and so on. You might even find other new and helpful ways to use the screwdriver. Your appreciation changes when you use this tool to do things. The same is true of theories.

Any of the family theories you find in this book can be used for myriad tasks. These theories can be used to predict, to interpret, to explain, to formulate questions, to integrate research, to make deductions, and to lead us into novel areas of research. When we use them, we gain an understanding of theories that is unlike the rarefied experience of holding them up in isolation as objects for academic scrutiny.

Like the tools developed for carpentry or gardening, theories are often modified as they are used and as a result of their use. A researcher who tests a series of theoretically derived hypotheses may find some disconfirmed and others not disconfirmed, and these continue to be plausible. The researcher may then suggest modifications in the theory to make the theory more consistent with the findings.

Although researchers often focus on a theory's ability to predict, theories are also used to interpret events that have already occurred. This after-the-fact (ex post facto) interpretation is what many of us consider to be the central component of explanation. We would like a good story about why or how something happened or usually happens. These interpretations of past events may also lead to modifications in theories. As we attempt to explain why Kyle and Sara are getting divorced or why our grandparents are extraordinarily frugal, we may find other dimensions and variables that are needed to make our story a plausible one.

Yet another way theories are modified is when practitioners use a theory to guide an educational, political, or therapeutic intervention. Often practitioners discover inadequacies in theories that researchers might miss. All of these tool users of theory may assist in modifying and improving family theory. This is the process of theory construction and reconstruction.

In presenting you with various family theories as *products,* we do not want to mislead you into thinking that these theories are finished artifacts of human thought. Nothing could be further from the truth. Because they are useful tools, theories are constantly being modified and refined. We are not saying that the core concepts and relations change constantly, but even those core concepts are not exempt from the process of theory building.

## Theory Construction

The process of theory building is often called *theory construction.* Theory construction is a process that cannot be easily communicated as a set of rules or an architectural blueprint. Theories develop deductively, inductively, and by a combination of these two processes (what C. S. Peirce termed *abduction;* see Buchler, 1955; Wallace, 1968).

### FORMATIVE AND REFINEMENT STAGES

Roughly speaking, all theories go through two stages, a formative stage and a refinement stage. During the formative stage, the basic metaphor of the theory comes into sharper focus. This metaphor may eventually be so precise as to be expressed as propositions or even as mathematical models. During the refinement stage, the theory is increasingly subjected to testing, criticism, and application. As a result of these different activities, the theory will either become more refined, divide into variants, or fall into disuse along with the other theories on the trash heap of scientific history (e.g., early heliocentric theories of the universe).

All of the theories in this book are beyond the formative stage. You can readily identify the metaphor of these theories, such as "clash" and "opposition" in conflict theory and "time-dependent change" in family developmental life course theory. Furthermore, these theories are sufficiently precise to offer us propositions and models. As we suggested in Chapter 1, however, theories may emerge from postpositivist thought or other sources that are at this time not clearly identifiable. The theories in this book are clearly recognizable as theories in the second phase of theory construction.

The refinement stage is a difficult period in the life of a theory. Imagine that scientific theories, like ourselves, have a birth, a life course, and eventual death. The history of science clearly attests to the fact that there are no "true" scientific theories, at least not everywhere and forever. Even the theories currently occupying hallowed ground in physics, such as relativity theory, will eventually fall or be modified to achieve greater explanatory power and greater capacity to deal with the anomalies that plagued preceding versions and alternative theories. There is no one critical scientific test that leads to a theory falling into disuse.

Even if we consider theories with little if any empirical support, such as Freudian psychological theory, we find that the powerful metaphor in these theories continues to serve certain functions, such as therapeutic application. But when a theory cannot meet the standards of empirical plausibility demanded by science, it can no longer be regarded as a scientific theory but only as a general orientation. Thus, the theory that the Earth is flat was at one time widely accepted by the best minds of their time, but the theory has fallen into disuse and no longer can be regarded as an acceptable scientific theory.

We have said that all of the theories in this book are in the refinement stage of development. Now we may ask if there is any way of comparing the adequacy and utility of one theory over another. The answer to this question is complex. If two theories are equally logical and have the same scope and breadth of explanation, then we could say that the theory that explains the most variance in a set of dependent variables is more adequate. But none of these "ifs" are ever exactly true. For example, is dialectical logic more "logical" than symbolic logic or Boolean algebra? There is really no answer here. As we have seen,

**Table 9.1**        Criteria for Evaluating Family Theories

1.    **Internal consistency:** a theory does not contain logically contradictory assertions.
2a.   (tie) **Clarity or explicitness:** the ideas in a theory are expressed in such a way that they are unambiguous. They are defined and explicated where necessary.
2b.   (tie) **Explanatory power:** a theory explains well what it is intended to explain.
4.    **Coherence:** the key ideas in a theory are integrated or interconnected, and loose ends are avoided.
5a.   (tie) **Understanding:** a theory provides a comprehensible sense of the whole phenomenon being examined.
5b.   (tie) **Empirical fit:** a large portion of the tests of a theory have been confirmatory or at least have not been interpreted as disconfirming.
7.    **Testability:** it is possible for a theory to be empirically supported or refuted.
8.    **Heuristic value:** a theory has generated or can generate considerable research and intellectual curiosity (including a large number of empirical studies, as well as much debate or controversy).
9.    **Groundedness:** a theory has been built up from detailed information about events and processes observable in the world.
10.   **Contextualization:** a theory gives serious consideration to the social and historical contexts affecting or affected by its key ideas.
11.   **Interpretive sensitivity:** a theory reflects the experiences practiced and felt by the social units to which it is applied.
12a.  **Predictive power:** a theory can successfully predict phenomena that have occurred since it was formulated.
12b.  (tie) **Practical utility:** a theory can be readily applied to social problems, policies, and programs of action (i.e., it is useful for teaching, therapy, political action, or some combination of these).

SOURCE: Klein (1994).

family theorists tend to attempt explanations of different levels of analysis and different dependent variables depending on the basic assumptions they make. And although scientists properly make demands about empirical testability and internal logical coherence, they do not and cannot justifiably claim that one set of assumptions is correct and all of the other sets are wrong.

We have been very cautious here about making final judgments about the adequacy of any theory, but the members of the scientific community do look to certain standards for discriminating between theories as they exist at a given point in time. Table 9.1 lists and defines in descending order of importance the 13 most frequently endorsed criteria, from a longer list of 32 criteria, based on a survey of a diverse group of over 100 family scientists (Klein, 1994).

Of course, not everybody would agree that all of the 13 criteria listed in Table 9.1 are equally important. In this particular study, a set of criteria composed of explanatory power, empirical fit, testability, and predictive power tended to be endorsed by the same scholars. The other standards were more randomly distributed among the participating scholars. It is clear that family scholars rely on many different considerations to judge their own theories or those of their colleagues.

We cannot say for sure how each of the major theories in this book would compare if we were trying to determine their relative adequacy. Surely all of these theories must be fairly adequate or they would not have such long traditions or have survived into the refinement stage. It is also the case, however, that perfection is never achieved in family science, let alone the rest of life. We should expect each theory to have both strengths and weaknesses.

What we do know from Klein's (1994) study is that scholars who prefer certain family theories sometimes also prefer certain standards for judging them. The clearest example of this is that the family systems theorists favored "practical utility" more than other theorists. They also were more likely to favor standards that were not popular enough in general to appear in Table 9.1. Such standards are those more clearly associated with a critical philosophy of science than the other philosophies. This is rather interesting, for we mentioned earlier that Burr (1995) labeled family systems theory as being most consistent with an interpretive philosophy. Apparently, many family systems theorists would themselves place their theory more comfortably within the critical–emancipatory philosophy.

We encourage you to nurture your own opinions about which family theories are better and in what specific ways. Because we have argued that the result is most likely to be that all of the theories in this book come out fairly strong and nearly equal overall, you may have to try a different way to find theories you would consider extremely adequate and extremely inadequate. Instead of starting with the more general theoretical frameworks, begin with a few specific books or articles by researchers who create or use a theory for a particular topic. By seeing how theories are applied at this very specific level, it should be easier for you to form opinions. Remember, however, that a few successes or a few failures are usually not enough to make sweeping judgments about an entire theoretical tradition or framework.

STRATEGIES

The final aspect of theory construction we cover deals with methods. As in building a house or empirically studying families and family members, there are strategies and techniques for building theories. If inappropriate methods are used, the house will collapse or information about the families in them will not be instructive. Although there might be no one best way to build a theory, a number of ways have been discussed and used by family theorists.

Hill (1971) outlined five principal theory construction strategies early in the theory construction era. Each has been fairly popular (e.g., Burr, Hill, et al., 1979, Vols. 1 & 2), and each is still used today.

*1. Deducing Family Theories From More General Theories.* We have mentioned several times that most of our current family theories have been derived from more general theories in the social sciences. As new general theories are developed in the future, we would expect some to be eventually applied to families. It is also worth noting, however, that deriving inspiration from a general theory is possible without using formal deductive logic. Indeed, if you return to the lists of propositions in Chapters 2 through 8, you will see little evidence of formal deductive logic. This suggests that more work lies ahead for those who are deductively inclined, even if they start with current general theories. For example, it is not easy to start with propositions about individuals making rational choices and formally deduce other propositions about how small groups of interacting individuals such as families make rational choices.

*2. Codifying Partial Theories.* Many current theories about families are "partial" or incomplete in either of two ways. One is that they may only address part of a phenomenon. For example, a theory about dating among adolescents may tell us little about whether they get married, and it may not apply to divorced older adults who also are dating. Hill (1971) suggested that we could take several theories that are incomplete in this sense and combine them into, for example, a more comprehensive theory of mate selection or something even more general such as relationship formation.

The other way in which theories are partial is that their explanations apply to a limited number of instances. We are especially likely to notice this when researchers test a theory and discover that they can explain only some of the differences that they observe. Again, the strategy needed to improve the situation is to combine the partial theories. If there are, for example, two or more theories of helping behavior among middle-aged siblings, but each omits explanatory variables found in one of the others, the theories might well be eligible for combination.

Although combining theories that are partial in either respect may be done intuitively, a more rigorous way is to first *codify* them, that is, clearly identify all of the assumptions, concepts, and propositions and then try to link them in various ways that are logical and plausible. Hill (1971) also argued that merely formalizing partial theories would represent progress. Clarity is thereby gained, and users of these theories benefit.

*3. Borrowing From Other Fields of Study.* Because it is relatively difficult to invent any truly new idea that has never before been imagined, borrowing ideas is a fairly common practice. For example, systems theorists borrowed the idea of entropy from physics. Family development theorists borrowed the "career" concept from theories about labor force participation. Given that there are many specialized areas of study in the sciences, there is practically no limit to sources of ideas that might be transferred to the domain of the human family and molded into an existing or new theory.

It is also the case that family theorists often borrow from each other. Indeed, it has become such a common practice in the past few decades for theorists and researchers to blend elements of different family theories that it is becoming increasingly difficult to appreciate the origins and general themes in the newer theories. We return to this "food blender" phenomenon when we discuss the future in the next section. For now, it is enough to say that borrowing from each other's theories about the family is one good way for researchers to build a more comprehensive picture of families.

*4. Inducing From Empirical Research Generalizations.* Some empirical research is guided by preexisting theory; other research is not. In either case, particular studies tend to yield not only specific results but also more general statements that summarize the findings. Hill (1971) suggested that we could identify a somewhat topically bounded field, collect several reports of studies in that field, and, by inspecting them for similarities and differences, build a theory.

Because research is an ongoing process and some topics may be more popular than others during a given period, it is likely that this strategy would result in only partial theories. Assuming that these partial theories eventually became sufficiently adequate, however, we could shift to the second strategy above and continue the theory construction process.

*5. Integrating Concepts and Building Taxonomies.* The vocabulary of scientific concepts is always large and always growing. Some concepts get discarded or replaced along the way, of course, but certainly in an area of study with a growing population of theorists, researchers, and practitioners, the pool of potentially valuable concepts tends to grow as well.

Today, as in earlier decades, it is an enormous task just to learn the meanings of all of the technical terms that can be used in theories. Unlike the English language generally, there is no Webster's *Dictionary* for concepts about the family. There are many glossaries in many books, but there is no single common glossary that everyone is trained to understand. The fact that family theorizing is also conducted by non-English-speaking people obviously adds to the complexity of the nomenclature.

In our judgment, we have reached the point, or perhaps merely remained at the point, at which words themselves are unreliable indicators of meaning or theoretical posture. For example, many family scholars use the word *system* without having any allegiance whatsoever to family systems theory. The same could be said about many other key concepts found in our theories.

Hill's (1971) advice remains relevant today. By carefully studying our terminology and the various meanings of our concepts, we might be able to distill the crucial ideas or invent new ones. Taxonomies are similar to typologies, except that taxonomies employ hierarchies of ideas arranged from more inclusive to less inclusive. For example, affection between two family members may have several subtypes, one of which might be physical. Then, within physical affection, there might be several subtypes, such as hugging, and so on. As we develop multiple taxonomies for different kinds of concepts, we might be able to find connections between or within the taxonomies that lead to new theories.

We have focused on five of the main strategies that are used to construct family theories, although it is likely that the inventory of useful strategies will itself continue to grow as family scholars search for ways to improve the stock of knowledge. One helpful way to learn more about these strategies is to locate one or a few theoretical works in the literature, and then, instead of the usual practice of trying to figure out the content or product, study the work processually—that is, see if you can identify the strategies and steps that the theorist used to craft the argument.

## The Future of Family Theory

It would be presumptuous of us to forecast what family theories and theorizing will be like as the 21st century unfolds. Perhaps if we had a good theory about how the social sciences develop over time, we would be willing to make predictions. Many such theories have been formulated by historians (e.g., Kuhn, 1970), sociologists (e.g., Crane, 1972; Mullins, 1973), and psychologists (e.g., Maslow, 1966; Toulmin, 1972). No such theory has yet been used to explain why family science has developed as it has, although there are some suggestive hints in the works we cited toward the end of Chapter 1.

We already have discussed some strategies of theory construction that have been commonly used, and it is reasonable to expect that they will continue to be used. As for other aspects of the future, we prefer to pose challenges rather than predictions. Thus, our discussion is oriented toward problems more than solutions. In our view, three major challenges lie ahead.

CONTINUED THEORY TESTING AND REFINEMENT

It hardly seems worth saying that we need more research and more development of existing theories, for this appears to be both obvious and a perpetual challenge. We have some particular ideas in mind here, however, that may not be so obvious.

First, we note that a large proportion of family research today is not geared to test theories. It is unnecessary to cite examples, for all you have to do is scan a recent mainstream journal, and you will quickly learn this. Much family research is descriptive rather than explanatory. Although as we have repeatedly emphasized, theories do have descriptive aspects; a theory that cannot explain is not very useful. When family research does include an explanatory component, the kinds of theories tested are not often those we have covered in this book. Rather, they tend to be models or narrowly focused or topically specific theories. Often, only isolated hypotheses are tested, and such hypotheses have no direct or clearly articulated connection to a more general explanation.

Finally, although we cannot pursue the details here, the methods researchers use are frequently inappropriate for testing theories. A common example is that researchers may start with a dynamic theory but use static forms of data collection and statistical analysis to test the theory.

What we are suggesting, therefore—and this is by no means an original idea—is that we need more theory-driven research and better fit between our theories, our research methods, and our data (cf. Lavee & Dollahite, 1991).

The second part of this challenge concerns refinement. This sounds rather unambitious, not especially difficult, and not particularly rewarding. In fact, we suggest that it is precisely the unattractive quality of refining what already appears to be well developed that leads scholars to eschew this important task. It is much more glamorous to work on something that nobody else has worked on before.

Because this is a book for newer professionals just entering the field, there may be no better place to begin than to take a fairly well-developed theory or part of a theory and push it in a slightly new and improved direction. Once you have mastered this small step, then you can with greater confidence try something more ambitious.

### GETTING "FAMILY" INTO FAMILY THEORY

Family theorists sometimes face questions regarding the viability of family theory. One of the most interesting of these is the question, "Is family theory necessary, or can we use any social science theory about groups to explain behavior in the family group?" This question suggests that theories designed expressly for the family may not be necessary or even desirable. Any social science theory dealing with groups may be fruitfully applied to the family. Of the seven major theories we have discussed in this book, only family development theory was expressly formulated to deal with the family. All the other theories have drawn much more heavily from disciplines such as sociology, psychology, and economics. Indeed, we can ask, "Do we need family theory? Or can general social and behavioral science theories be applied to the family?"

The basic assumption behind the argument that general theories about social groups can be applied to the family is that the family group does not differ from other social groups in any but trivial ways. It seems to us, however, that the family is not simply like any other social group, such as a work group or a friendship network. The family differs from other social groups in several important ways. We pointed out these unique properties in Chapter 1, and we encourage you to inspect them again.

Clearly, the behaviors of family members have the potential for longer-lasting effects both in the longevity of the family group and the historical and intergenerational nature of kinship. We argue that the family group is so different from other social groups that theories explicitly formulated about the family are likely to be necessary. We also expect that sociological and psychological theories will continue to be useful for family research and theory building.

Some existing theories have been useful to explain individual behavior in families not because of family variables but because of individual variables. Other theories have been useful to explain how families are swept along on the powerful social tides of the larger society. These theories rely on the family being a group within the larger society but not a uniquely familial group. Psychological theories gain their usefulness by shedding light on how individual and relationship level variables are related to the family group. Macrolevel social theories provide insights about how institutional and social-structural pressures may affect the family group.

What appears to be missing, however, is a theory focused on the family group as a group rather than a collection of individuals (micro) or one of many social organizations buffeted and determined by social processes (macro). Both micro- and macro-orientations fail to acknowledge and deal with the mesolevel phenomena of the family group. We believe that such mesolevel family theories are necessary to explain the unique and important properties of the family group. Genuine mesolevel theory aimed at the family as a unique form of social group seems elusive, but we anticipate greater attention to this problem in the future.

INTEGRATING

There always seems to be a tension, in family science as well as other sciences, between keeping things separate and pulling them together. The case for separation is straightforward. If phenomena really are different, it is important to know this. We illustrated this argument above by reemphasizing that because families are unique, we need special theories that fit family realities. The risk of ignoring differences is confusion, although some would argue that it is confrontation between incompatibilities that ignites creativity and change (e.g., dialecticians). In any case, one challenge in the future will be to create these family-focused theories.

An emphasis on pulling things together has been much more pronounced during the history of family theorizing. When we discussed strategies for theory construction, our emphasis was on organizing the theories and fragments of theories that exist and creating new theories out of them. There also is a much more profound kind of theoretical unification, which has periodically been the topic of great debates. The question is, "Should we attempt to take many or perhaps even all of our existing theories about families and create a 'grand synthesis'?"

If such an effort were possible and successful, it would be a remarkable feat, not unlike the unified theory of matter in physics. But this idea of one encompassing theory of family life repeatedly meets with resounding resistance. Only occasionally is the resistance voiced by theorists with a fanatical devotion to their "favorite" family theory. Instead, most of the objections are raised by what could be called the "oil-and-water" contingent.

A favorite story of the anti-integrationists (e.g., Burr, 1995, pp. 73–74; Winton, 1995, pp. 186–187) is the one about six blind men who each approached an elephant from a different direction. Asked to describe the beast, each emphasized that part he touched. They all had different accounts, and none of the accounts had anything to do with elephants. What is the lesson here? Perhaps these authors are attempting to say that each theory gives us an aspect of reality and that all of these are true in some regards. But this analogy also might lead us to believe that all of us are blind, and we create our own realities based on our unique experiences. Our blindness presumably prevents us from expanding the horizons of our knowledge. Furthermore, it might lead us to believe that there are no generally accepted criteria for establishing which theoretical propositions are better in regard to a phenomenon. Seemingly, if every theory or every theorist is blind, there is no way to integrate them. To try would be like trying to mix oil and water or any other set of insoluble compounds.

The fable of the blind men has some merit. It follows quite naturally from an interpretive philosophy of science, and it makes sense from within that perspective. But it is not the only way to think about theories or even about families. In the case of theories, we are alerted to look for incompatibilities, for instance, between the assumptions in different theories. Yet finding inconsistencies does not mean that we must accept them as givens or as evidence that theorists of different stripes have nothing to say to each other.

As for families, it is certainly plausible to argue, as some symbolic interactionists and others have argued, that every member of a family has a different interpretation of the invisible elephant that is their family. But even these family theorists are willing to argue that this does not prevent family members from creating a pragmatic set of shared understandings to give them some kind of identity as a family.

Thus, we would not claim that either family theorists or family members are blind. Indeed, we all know enough to conclude that we have an elephant (or family) that is our subject matter. The real argument seems then to focus on our ability to integrate statements from different theories and to be able to distinguish the better explanation among competing explanations of the same phenomena. In our view, science has always followed this course (see Table 9.1). So, contrary to the "oil and water" perspective, we see integration as desirable and attainable.

Most family theorists avoid the yes-or-no debate over integration. They steer a more moderate course, which is eclecticism. To be theoretically eclectic is to take pieces selectively, as the situation seems to warrant, from different perspectives, and blend them into something a little different. The result is not oil and water but a milk shake.

During the nearly two decades of the conceptual frameworks era described in Chapter 1, a major lesson was learned by most family scholars. The big advantage of trying to array perspectives according to their similarities and differences is the discovery that novel combinations are sometimes possible. This spirit has continued with full force as we have moved into the refinement period of family theorizing. Eclectic theorizing is likely to continue as a principal activity in the future as well. In fact, if it continues much longer, the landscape of family theory may be nothing but milk shakes. Theories like those in this book will be ingredients, not the end products.

Even among those who are seeking mesolevel family theory, a more selective kind of integration may bear fruit. Within some of the variants of the existing theories, we find some possible ways we might develop such a theory. For example, the structural conflict approach of Caplow's (1968) "coalition theory" allows the theorist to analyze group properties such as cohesion by means of variables such as the impermanence of coalition partners. If your opponent of today might be your ally of tomorrow, then we would assume greater cohesion than where allies and opponents are relatively permanent. Although coalition theory may assist in developing the structural aspects of the family group, it still neglects the time dimension and historicity of the family. Thus, although existing theoretical variants are not devoid of approaches to the mesolevel of the family, they need further development and integration by family scholars.

## Conclusion

As we look back on the seven theories in this book and their many variants, we are struck by the amazing richness of the ideas. Not only do these theories deal with different levels of analysis, but within any level of analysis they often deal with different dependent variables. Although we have said that we perceive a relatively underdeveloped area in mesolevel theories about the family group, we are nonetheless impressed by the power and breadth that these seven theories provide researchers and practitioners.

At the conclusion of a work such as this, it is only natural that we should ask, "What has this book achieved?" Of course, it is gratuitous for the authors to answer this question. Time, colleagues, and successive generations of students will supply the answer in due course. But we hope that if this book achieves nothing else, it will serve to give you a glimpse of the "life of ideas" in which scholars participate. In this book, we believe we have introduced you to the world in which academics interested in understanding families dwell, that is, the life of ideas about families.

If we look at the history of science, it is not a particular research finding or project that survives the test of time, nor even the reputations of people who produce them. Only basic ideas and theories survive over time. For most scholars, these ideas are what initially compelled them to join the academic enterprise and, indeed, it is this life of ideas that still furnishes the most significant but intangible rewards for many of us. We hope the theories and ideas you have encountered here will become integrated with the knowledge you have from other sources. As these ideas come together for you, forming a more complete picture of your world, your family, and especially other families, you should experience the same intrinsic rewards that we believe reside in the life of ideas.

## Suggested Readings

Burr, W. R. (1995). Using theories in family science. In R. Day, K. Gilbert, B. Settles, & W. Burr (Eds.), *Research and theory in family science* (pp. 73–90). Pacific Grove, CA: Brooks/Cole.

Winton, C. A. (1995). *Frameworks for studying families.* Guilford, CT: Dushkin.
*These sources offer somewhat different and contrasting approaches to categorizing theories.*

# References

Adams, B., & Steinmetz, S. (1993). Family theory and methods in the classics. In P. Boss, W. Doherty, R. LaRossa, W. Schumm, & S. Steinmetz (Eds.), *Sourcebook of family theories and methods: A contextual approach* (pp. 71–94). New York: Plenum.

Acock, A. C., & Demo, D. H. (1994). *Family diversity and well being.* Thousand Oaks, CA: Sage.

Alcoff, L. (1995). Cultural feminism versus post-structuralism: The identity crisis in feminist theory. In N. Tuana & R. Tong (Eds.), *Feminism and philosophy: Essential readings in theory, reinterpretation, and application* (pp. 434-456). Boulder, CO: Westview Press.

Aldous, J. (1978). *Family careers.* New York: John Wiley.

Aldous, J. (1990). Family development and the life course: Two perspectives on family change. *Journal of Marriage and the Family, 52,* 571–583.

Aldous, J. (1994). Someone to watch over me: Family responsibilities and their realization across the family lives. In E. Kahana, D. Beigel, & M. Wykle (Eds.), *Family caregiving across the life span* (pp. 42–68). Thousand Oaks, CA: Sage.

Aldous, J. (1996). *Family careers: Rethinking the developmental perspective.* Thousand Oaks, CA: Sage.

Aldous, J., & Hill, R. (1967). *International bibliography of research in marriage and the family, 1900–1964.* Minneapolis: University of Minnesota Press.

Allen, K. (2000). A conscious and inclusive family studies. *Journal of Marriage and the Family, 62,* 4–17.

Allison, P. (1984). *Event history analysis: Regression for longitudinal event data.* Beverly Hills, CA: Sage.

Andersen, M. (1991). Feminism and the American family ideal. *Journal of Comparative Family Studies, 22,* 235–246.

Anderson, E. (1993). The application of systems theory to the study of family policy. In P. Boss, W. Doherty, R. LaRossa, W. Schumm, & S. Steinmetz (Eds.), *Sourcebook of family theories and methods: A contextual approach* (pp. 353–355). New York: Plenum.

Andreas, C. (1971). *Sex and caste in America.* Englewood Cliffs, NJ: Prentice Hall.

Apel, K. (1981). *Charles S. Peirce: From pragmatism to pragmaticism* (J. Krois, Trans.). Amherst: University of Massachusetts Press.

Arcus, M., Schvaneveldt, J., & Moss, J. (Eds.). (1993). *Handbook of family life education* (Vols. 1 & 2). Newbury Park, CA: Sage.

Baber, K., & Allen, K. (1992). *Women and families: Feminist reconstructions.* Newbury Park, CA: Sage.

243

Bach, G., & Wyden, P. (1968). *The intimate enemy: How to fight fair in love and marriage*. New York: William Morrow.

Bagarozzi, D. (1993). Clinical uses of social exchange principles. In P. Boss, W. Doherty, R. LaRossa, W. Schumm, & S. Steinmetz (Eds.), *Sourcebook of family theories and methods: A contextual approach* (pp. 412–417). New York: Plenum.

Baltes, P., & Nesselroade, J. (1984). Paradigm lost and paradigm regained: Critique of Dannefer's portrayal of life-span developmental psychology. *American Sociological Review, 49*, 841–846.

Bartz, K., & Nye, F. I. (1970). Early marriage: A propositional formulation. *Journal of Marriage and the Family, 32*, 258–268.

Bateson, G., Jackson, D., Haley, J., & Weakland, J. (1956). Toward a theory of schizophrenia. *Behavioral Science, 1*, 251–264.

Becker, G. (1981). *A treatise on the family*. Cambridge, MA: Belknap.

Belsky, J. (1990). Parental and nonparental child care and children's socioemotional development: A decade review. *Journal of Marriage and the Family, 52*, 885–903.

Belsky, J., & Eggebeen, D. (1991). Early and extensive maternal employment and young children's socioemotional development: Children of the National Longitudinal Survey of Youth. *Journal of Marriage and the Family, 53*, 1083–1110.

Belsky, J., Gillstrap, B., & Rovine, M. (1984). The Pennsylvania Infant and Family Project. 1: Stability and change in mother-infant and father-infant interaction in a family setting at one, three, and nine months. *Child Development, 55*, 692–705.

Belsky, J., & Rovine, M. (1990). Patterns of marital change across the transition to parenthood. *Journal of Marriage and the Family, 52*, 5–20.

Bengtson, V. L., & Allen, K. R. (1993). The life course perspective applied to families over time. In P. Boss, W. Doherty, R. LaRossa, W. Schumm, & S. Steinmetz (Eds.), *Sourcebook of family theories and methods: A contextual approach* (pp. 469–499). New York: Plenum.

Berger, P., & Kellner, H. (1964). Marriage and the construction of reality. *Diogenes, 46*, 1–25.

Berk, S. (1985). *The gender factory: The apportionment of work in American households*. New York: Plenum.

Beutler, I., Burr, W., Bahr, K., & Herrin, D. (1989). The family realm: Understanding its uniqueness. *Journal of Marriage and the Family, 51*, 805–816.

Blair, S., & Johnson, M. (1992). Wives' perception of the fairness of the division of household labor: The intersection of housework and ideology. *Journal of Marriage and the Family, 54*, 570–581.

Blau, P. M. (1964). *Exchange and power in social life*. New York: John Wiley.

Bloch, D. (1983). Family systems medicine: The field and the journal. *Family Systems Medicine, 1*, 3–11.

Blumer, H. (1962). Society as symbolic interaction. In A. M. Rose (Ed.), *Human behavior and social processes* (pp. 179–192). Boston: Houghton Mifflin.

Blumer, H. (1969). *Symbolic interactionism*. Englewood Cliffs, NJ: Prentice Hall.

Blumstein, P., & Schwartz, P. (1983). *American couples*. New York: William Morrow.

Bohannan, P. (Ed.). (1970). *Divorce and after: An analysis of the emotional and social problems of divorce*. Garden City, NY: Doubleday.

Booth, A., Carver, K., & Granger, D. A. (2000). Biosocial perspectives on the family. *Journal of Marriage and the Family, 62*, 1018–1034.

Boss, P. (1987). Family stress. In M. B. Sussman & S. Steinmetz (Eds.), *Handbook of marriage and the family* (pp. 695–723). New York: Plenum.

Boss, P. (1988). *Family stress management*. Newbury Park, CA: Sage.

Boss, P. (1993). The reconstruction of family life with Alzheimer's disease: Generating theory to lower family stress from ambiguous loss. In P. Boss, W. Doherty, R. LaRossa, W. Schumm, & S. Steinmetz (Eds.), *Sourcebook of family theories and methods: A contextual approach* (pp. 163–166). New York: Plenum.

Boss, P. (1999). *Ambiguous loss: Learning to live with unresolved grief*. Cambridge, MA: Harvard University Press.

Boss, P., Doherty, W., LaRossa, R., Schumm, W., & Steinmetz, S. (Eds.). (1993). *Sourcebook of family theories and methods: A contextual approach*. New York: Plenum.

Bowen, M. (1978). *Family therapy in clinical practice*. New York: Aronson.

Brannigan, A., Wanner, R., & White, J. (1981). The phenomenon of multiple discoveries and the re-publication of Mendel's work in 1900. *Philosophy of the Social Sciences, 11*, 263–276.

Bretherton, I. (1993). Theoretical contributions from developmental psychology. In P. Boss, W. Doherty, R. LaRossa, W. Schumm, & S. Steinmetz (Eds.), *Sourcebook of family theories and methods: A contextual approach* (pp. 275–297). New York: Plenum.

Brinkerhoff, M., & Lupri, E. (1989). Power and authority in the family. In K. Ishwaran (Ed.), *Family and marriage: Cross-cultural perspectives* (pp. 213–238). Toronto: Wall & Thompson.

Broderick, C. (1971). Beyond the five conceptual frameworks: A decade of development in family theory. *Journal of Marriage and the Family, 33*, 139–160.

Broderick, C. (1993). *Understanding family process*. Newbury Park, CA: Sage.

Broderick, C., & Smith, J. (1979). The general systems approach to the family. In W. Burr, R. Hill, F. I. Nye, & I. Reiss (Eds.), *Contemporary theories about the family* (Vol. 2, pp. 112–129). New York: Free Press.

Bronfenbrenner, U. (1979). *The ecology of human development*. Cambridge, MA: Harvard University Press.

Bronfenbrenner, U. (1989). Ecological systems theory. In R. Vasta (Ed.), *Annals of child development* (Vol. 6, pp. 187–249). Greenwich, CT: JAI.

Brooks, D., & Wiley, E. (1986). *Evolution as entropy: Toward a unified theory of biology*. Chicago: University of Chicago Press.

Brown, M. (1984). Home economics: Proud past-promising future. *Journal of Home Economics, 76*, 48–54.

Bubolz, M., & Sontag, S. (1993). Human ecology theory. In P. Boss, W. Doherty, R. LaRossa, W. Schumm, & S. Steinmetz (Eds.), *Sourcebook of family theories and methods: A contextual approach* (pp. 419–448). New York: Plenum.

Buchler, J. (Ed.). (1955). *Philosophical writings of Peirce*. New York: Dover.

Buckley, W. (1967). *Sociology and modern systems theory*. Englewood Cliffs, NJ: Prentice Hall.

Bulcroft, R., Forste, R., & White, J. (1993, November). *An integrated model for studying the decision to breast-feed, duration of breastfeeding, and consequences for child health and development*. Paper presented at the National Council on Family Relations, Theory Construction and Methodology Workshop, Baltimore, MD.

Bulcroft, R., & White, J. M. (1997). Family research methods and levels of analysis. *Family Science Review, 10*, 2–19.

Burgess, E. W. (1925). The growth of the city: An introduction to a research project. In R. Park, E. Burgess, & R. McKenzie (Eds.), *The city* (pp. 47–62). Chicago: University of Chicago Press.

Burr, W. R. (1973). *Theory construction and the sociology of the family*. New York: John Wiley.

Burr, W. R. (1995). Using theories in family science. In R. Day, K. Gilbert, B. Settles, & W. R. Burr (Eds.), *Research and theory in family science* (pp. 73–90). Pacific Grove, CA: Brooks/Cole.

Burr, W. R., Day, R., & Bahr, K. (1993). *Family science*. Pacific Grove, CA: Brooks/Cole.

Burr, W. R., Hill, R., Nye, F. I., & Reiss, I. (Eds.). (1979). *Contemporary theories about the family* (2 vols.). New York: Free Press.

Burr, W. R., Leigh, G., Day, R., & Constantine, J. (1979). Symbolic interaction and the family. In W. R. Burr, R. Hill, F. I. Nye, & I. Reiss (Eds.), *Contemporary theories about the family* (Vol. 2, pp. 42–111). New York: Free Press.

Campbell, T. (1993). Applying a biosocial perspective on the family. In P. Boss, W. Doherty, R. LaRossa, W. Schumm, & S. Steinmetz (Eds.), *Sourcebook of family theories and methods: A contextual approach* (pp. 711–713). New York: Plenum.

Caplow, T. (1968). *Two against one: Coalition in triads.* Englewood Cliffs, NJ: Prentice Hall.

Caplow, T., Bahr, H., Chadwick, B., Hill, R., & Williamson, M. (1983). *Middletown families: Fifty years of change and continuity.* Minneapolis: University of Minnesota Press.

Carter, E., & McGoldrick, M. (Eds.). (1988). *The changing family cycle: A framework for family therapy* (2nd ed.). New York: Gardner.

Cheal, D. (1991). *Family and the state of theory.* Toronto: University of Toronto Press.

Chodorow, N. (1978). *The reproduction of mothering.* Berkeley: University of California Press.

Chomsky, N. (1965). *Aspects of the theory of syntax.* Cambridge, MA: MIT Press.

Christensen, H. (1964). Development of the family field of study. In H. Christensen (Ed.), *Handbook of marriage and the family* (pp. 3–32). Chicago: Rand McNally.

Cixous, H., & Clement, C. (1986). *The newly born woman* (B. Wing, Trans.). Manchester, UK: Manchester University Press.

Clarke, R. (1973). *Ellen Swallow.* Chicago: Follett.

Coleman, J. S. (1990). *Foundations of social theory.* Cambridge, MA: Belknap.

Collins, R. (1975). *Conflict sociology: Toward an explanatory science.* New York: Academic Press.

Coltrane, S. (2000). Research on household labor: Modeling and measuring the social embeddedness of routine family work. *Journal of Marriage and the Family, 62,* 1208–1233.

Cook, J., Tyson, R., White, J., Rushe, R., Gottman, J., & Murray, J. (1995). Mathematics of marital conflict: Qualitative dynamic modeling of marital interaction. *Journal of Family Psychology, 9,* 110–130.

Cooley, C. H. (1902). *Human nature and the social order.* New York: Scribner's.

Cooley, C. H. (1909). *Social organization.* New York: Scribner's.

Coser, L. (1956). *The functions of social conflict.* Glencoe, IL: Free Press.

Cowan, P. A., & Cowan, C. P. (1992). *When partners become parents: The big life change for couples.* New York: Basic Books.

Cox, M. J., Paley, B., Burchinal, M., & Payne, C. C. (1999). Marital perceptions and interactions across the transition to parenthood. *Journal of Marriage and the Family, 61,* 611–625.

Crane, D. (1972). *Invisible colleges: Diffusion of knowledge in scientific communities.* Chicago: University of Chicago Press.

Cromwell, R., & Olson, D. (Eds.). (1975). *Power in families.* New York: Halstead.

Crouter, A. C., Bumpus, M. F., Maguire, M. C., & McHale, S. M. (1999). Linking parents' work pressure and adolescents' well-being: Insights into dynamics in dual-earner families. *Developmental Psychology, 35,*1453–1461.

Daly, K. (1996). *Families & time: Keeping pace in a hurried culture.* Thousand Oaks, CA: Sage.

Dannefer, D. (1984). Adult development and social theory: A paradigmatic reappraisal. *American Sociological Review, 49,* 100–116.

Dannefer, D., & Perlmutter, M. (1991). The life course perspective in current sociobehavioral research on development. *Research on Aging, 16,* 112–139.

Darwin, C. (1880). *The descent of man.* New York: D. Appleton.

Darwin, C. (1859/1901). *On the origin of the species by means of natural selection.* London: J. Murray.

Davis, K. (1947). Final note on a case of extreme isolation. *American Journal of Sociology, 52,* 432–437.

Deacon, R., & Firebaugh, F. (1988). *Family resource management: Principles and applications.* Needham Heights, MA: Allyn & Bacon.

de Beauvoir, S. (1949/1953). *The second sex.* New York: Knopf.

Demo, D. H., & Cox, M. J. (2000). Families with young children: A review of research in the 1990's. *Journal of Marriage and the Family, 62,* 876–895.

Derrida, J. (1976). *Of grammatology* (G. Spivak, Trans.). Baltimore, MD: Johns Hopkins University Press.

Derrida, J. (1978). *Writing and difference* (A. Bass, Trans.). Chicago: University of Chicago Press.

Dewey, J. (1929). *Experience and nature.* LaSalle, IL: Opencourt.

Dilworth-Anderson, P., Burton, L. M., & Johnson, L. B. (1993). Reframing theories for understanding race, ethnicity, and families. In P. Boss et al. (Eds.), *Sourcebook of family theories and methods: A contextual approach* (pp. 627–645). New York: Plenum.

Doherty, W., Boss, P., LaRossa, R., Schumm, W., & Steinmetz, S. (1993). Family theories and methods: A contextual approach. In P. Boss, W. Doherty, R. LaRossa, W. Schumm, & S. Steinmetz (Eds.), *Sourcebook of family theories and methods: A contextual approach* (pp. 3–30). New York: Plenum.

Donovan, J. (1985). *Feminist theory.* New York: Frederick Ungar.

Duran, J. (1998). *Philosophies of science/feminist theories.* Boulder, CO: Westview.

Duvall, E. (1957). *Family development.* Philadelphia: J. B. Lippincott.

Ehrenreich, B. (2000, April). Maid to order: The politics of other women's work. *Harper's Magazine,* pp. 59–70.

Eichler, M. (1988). *Families in Canada today: Recent changes and their social policy consequences* (2nd ed.). Toronto: Gage.

Ekeh, P. (1974). *Social Exchange Theory.* Cambridge, MA: Harvard University Press.

Elder, G., Jr. (1974). *Children of the great depression: Social change in life experience.* Chicago: University of Chicago Press.

Elder, G., Jr., Modell, J., & Parke, R. (Eds.). (1993). *Children in time and place: Developmental and historical insights.* New York: Cambridge University Press.

Elman, C. (1998). Intergenerational household structure and economic change at the turn of the century. *Journal of Family History, 23,* 417–437.

Emerson, R. (1976). Social exchange theory. In A. Inkles, J. Coleman, & N. Smelser (Eds.), *Annual review of sociology* (Vol. 2, pp. 335–362). Palo Alto, CA: Annual Reviews.

Engels, F. (1946). *The origin of the family, private property and the state.* New York: International Publishers. (Original work published 1884)

Falicov, C. (Ed.). (1988). *Family transitions.* New York: Guilford.

Farrington, K., & Chertok, E. (1993). Social conflict theories of the family. In P. Boss, W. Doherty, R. LaRossa, W. Schumm, & S. Steinmetz (Eds.), *Sourcebook of family theories and methods: A contextual approach* (pp. 357–381). New York: Plenum.

Featherman, D. (1985). Individual development and aging as a population process. In J. Nesselroade & A. Von Eye (Eds.), *Individual development and social change: Exploratory analysis* (pp. 213–241). New York: Academic Press.

Featherman, D., & Lerner, R. (1985). Ontogenesis and sociogenesis: Problematics for theory and research about development and socialization across the lifespan. *American Sociological Review, 50,* 659–676.

Ferree, M. (1990). Beyond separate spheres: Feminism and family research. *Journal of Marriage and the Family, 52,* 866–884.

Firestone, S. (1970). *The dialectic of sex*. New York: William Morrow.

Fisher, R. (1958). *The genetic theory of natural selection*. New York: Dover.

Fitzpatrick, M. A. (1988). *Between husbands and wives*. Newbury Park, CA: Sage.

Foa, U., & Foa, E. (1980). Resource theory: Interpersonal behavior as exchange. In K. Gergen, M. Greenberg, & R. Willis (Eds.), *Social exchange: Advances in research* (pp. 77–94). New York: Plenum.

Foschi, M. (1996). Double standards in the evaluation of men and women. *Social Psychological Quarterly, 59*, 237–254.

Foschi, M. (2000). Double standards for competence: Theory and research. *Annual Review of Sociology, 26*, 21–42.

Foschi, M., Lai, L., & Sigerson, K. (1994). Gender and double standards in the assessment of job applicants. *Social Psychological Quarterly, 57*, 326–339.

Fox, G. L., & Murry, V. M. (2000). Gender and families: Feminist perspectives and family research. *Journal of Marriage and the Family, 62*, 1160–1172.

Friedan, B. (1963). *The feminine mystique*. New York: Norton.

Friedan, B. (1981). *The second stage*. New York: Summit Books.

Gaard, G. (Ed.). (1993). *Ecofeminism: Women, animals, nature*. Philadelphia: Temple University Press.

Galton, F. (1952). *Hereditary genius*. New York: Horizon. (Original work published 1869)

Game, A. (1991). *Undoing the social: Towards a deconstructive sociology*. Buckingham, UK: Open University Press.

Garbarino, J. (1992). *Children and families in the social environment* (2nd ed.). New York: Aldine De Gruyter.

Garbarino, J., & Kostelny, K. (1992). Child maltreatment as a community problem. *Child Abuse and Neglect, 16*, 455–464.

Garbarino, J., & Sherman, D. (1980). High-risk neighborhoods and high-risk families: The human ecology of child maltreatment. *Child Development, 51*, 188–198.

Gatz, M., Bengtson, V., & Blum, M. (1990). Caregiving families. In J. Birren & W. Schaie (Eds.), *Handbook of the psychology of aging* (3rd ed., pp. 405–426). New York: Academic Press.

Gelles, R. (1994). Introduction to special issue on family violence. *Journal of Comparative Family Studies, 25*, 1–6.

Gerth, H., & Mills, C. W. (Trans. & Eds.). (1946). *From Max Weber*. New York: Oxford University Press.

Gilligan, C. (1982). *In a different voice: Psychological theory and women's development*. Cambridge, MA: Harvard University Press.

Gilman, C. (1898). *Women and economics*. Boston: Small, Maynard.

Gilman, C. (1910). *The home: Its work and influence*. New York: Charlton.

Glick, P. C. (1947). The family cycle. *American Sociological Review, 12*, 164–174.

Goelman, H., & Pence, A. (1987). Effects of child care, family, and individual characteristics on children's language development. In D. Phillips (Ed.), *Quality child care* (pp. 89–104). Washington, DC: NAEYC.

Goffman, E. (1959). *Presentation of self in everyday life*. New York: Doubleday.

Goffman, E. (1974). *Frame analysis: An essay on the organization of experience*. New York: Harper & Row.

Goldner, V. (1993). Feminist theories: Application. In P. Boss, W. Doherty, R. LaRossa, W. Schumm, & S. Steinmetz (Eds.), *Sourcebook of family theories and methods: A contextual approach* (pp. 623–625). New York: Plenum Press.

Goldscheider, F., & Goldscheider, C. (1999). *Changing transition to adulthood: Leaving and returning home*. Thousand Oaks, CA: Sage.

Goode, W. (1959). Sociology of the family: Horizons in family theory. In R. Merton, L. Broom, & L. Cottrell (Eds.), *Sociology today* (Vol. 1, pp. 178–197). New York: Basic Books.

Goode, W., Hopkins, E., & McClure, H. (1971). *Social systems and family patterns: A propositional inventory.* Indianapolis, IN: Bobbs-Merrill.

Gordon, L. (1979). The struggle for reproductive freedom: Three stages of feminism. In Z. Eisenstein (Ed.), *Capitalist patriarchy and the case for socialist feminism* (pp. 107–136). New York: Monthly Review Press.

Gottman, J. M. (1979). *Marital interaction: Experimental investigations.* New York: Academic Press.

Gottman, J. M. (1993). A theory of marital dissolution and stability. *Journal of Family Psychology, 7,* 57–75.

Gottman, J. M. (1994). *What predicts divorce: The relationship between marital processes and marital outcomes.* Hillsdale, NJ: Lawrence Erlbaum.

Gottman, J. M., Coan, J., Carrere, S., & Sawnason, C. (1998). Predicting marital happiness and stability from newlywed interactions. *Journal of Marriage and the Family, 60,* 5–22.

Gottman, J. M., & Krokoff, L. (1989). Marital interaction and marital satisfaction: A longitudinal view. *Journal of Consulting and Clinical Psychology, 57,* 47–52.

Gottman, J. M., & Levenson, R. (1992). Marital processes predictive of later dissolution: Behavior, physiology and health. *Journal of Personality and Social Psychology, 5,* 295–318.

Gottman, J. M., Markman, H., & Notarius, C. (1977). The topography of marital interaction: A sequential analysis of verbal and non-verbal behavior. *Journal of Marriage and the Family, 39,* 461–478.

Gottman, J. M., & Notarius, C. I. (2000). Decade review: Observing marital interaction. *Journal of Marriage and the Family, 62,* 927–947.

Gottman, J. M., & Porterfield, A. (1981). Communicative competence in the nonverbal behavior of married couples. *Journal of Marriage and the Family, 43,* 817–824.

Greenstein, T. N. (1993). Maternal employment and child behavioral outcomes. *Journal of Family Issues, 14,* 323–354.

Greenstein, T. N. (1996). Gender ideology and perceptions of the fairness of the division of household labor: Effects on marital quality. *Social Forces, 74,* 1029–1042.

Gubrium, J., & Holstein, J. (1990). *What is family?* Mountain View, CA: Mayfield.

Gubrium, J., & Holstein, J. (1993). Phenomenology, ethnomethodology, and family discourse. In P. Boss, W. Doherty, R. LaRossa, W. Schumm, & S. Steinmetz (Eds.), *Sourcebook of family theories and methods: A contextual approach* (pp. 651–672). New York: Plenum.

Gwartney-Gibbs, P. (1986). The institutionalization of premarital cohabitation: Estimates from marriage license applications, 1970 and 1980. *Journal of Marriage and the Family, 48,* 423–434.

Haack, S. (1998). *Manifesto of a passionate moderate: Unfashionable essays.* Chicago: University of Chicago Press.

Habermas, J. (1970). *Knowledge and human interests* (J. Shapiro, Trans.). Boston: Beacon.

Hall, A., & Fagan, R. (1956). Definition of systems. *General Systems, 1,* 18–28.

Hannan, M., & Freeman, J. (1984). Structural inertia and organizational change. *American Sociological Review, 49,* 149–164.

Harding, S. (1987). The instability of the analytic categoire of feminist theory. In S. Harding & J. F. O'Barr (Eds.), *Sex and scientific inquiry.* Chicago: University of Chicago Press.

Hardy, G. (1908). Mendelian proportions in mixed populations. *Science, 28,* 49–50.

Haveman, R., & Wolfe, B. (1994). *Succeeding generations.* New York: Russell Sage.

Havighurst, R. (1948). *Developmental tasks and education.* Chicago: University of Chicago Press.

Hawkins, A., Marshall, C., & Allen, S. (1998). The orientation toward domestic labor questionnaire: Exploring dual-earner wives' sense of fairness about family work. *Journal of Family Psychology, 12,* 244–258.

Hawley, A. (1986). *Human ecology: A theoretical essay.* Chicago: University of Chicago Press.

Hechter, M. (1987). *Principles of group solidarity.* Berkeley: University of California Press.

Hempel, C. G. (1952). *Fundamentals of concept formation in empirical science.* Chicago: University of Chicago Press.

Henley, N., Meng, K., O'Brien, D., McCarthy, W., & Sockloskie, R. (1998). Developing a scale to measure diversity of feminist attitudes. *Psychology of Women Quarterly, 22,* 317–348.

Hill, R. (1949). *Families under stress.* New York: Harper & Brothers.

Hill, R. (1951). Review of current research on marriage and the family. *American Sociological Review, 16,* 694–701.

Hill, R. (1966). Contemporary developments in family theory. *Journal of Marriage and the Family, 28,* 15–27.

Hill, R. (1971, August). *Payoffs and limitations of contemporary strategies for family theory systematization.* Paper presented at National Council on Family Relations, Estes Park, CO.

Hill, R., & Hansen, D. (1960). The identification of conceptual frameworks utilized in family study. *Marriage and Family Living, 22,* 299–311.

Hill, R., & Rodgers, R. H. (1964). The developmental approach. In H. Christensen (Ed.), *Handbook of marriage and the family* (pp. 171–211). Chicago: Rand McNally.

Hinckley, A. (1976). *Applied ecology.* New York: Macmillan.

Hobbes, T. (1947). *Leviathan.* New York: Macmillan. (Original work published 1651)

Hochschild, A., & Machung, A. (1989). *The second shift: Working parents and the revolution at home.* New York: Viking Press.

Hogan, D. (1978). The variable order of events in the life course. *American Sociological Review, 43,* 573–586.

Holman, T. B., & Burr, W. R. (1980). Beyond the beyond: The growth of the family theories in the 1970's. *Journal of Marriage and the Family, 42,* 729–742.

Homans, G. C. (1961). *Social behavior: Its elementary forms.* New York: Harcourt, Brace & World.

Homans, G. C. (1964). Bringing men back in. *American Sociological Review, 29,* 809–818.

Homans, G. C. (1967). *The nature of social science.* New York: Harcourt, Brace & World.

Howard, R. L. (1981). *A social history of American family sociology, 1865-1940.* Westport, CT: Greenwood.

Jackson, D. D. (Ed.). (1974). *Communication, family, and marriage.* Palo Alto, CA: Science and Behavior Books.

James, W. (1975). *Pragmatism: A new name for some old ways of thinking.* London: Longmans.

Johnson, M. P., & Ferraro, K. J. (2000). Research on domestic violence in the 1990s: Making distinctions. *Journal of Marriage and the Family, 62,* 948–963.

Kahneman, D., & Tversky, A. (1979). Prospect theory: An analysis of decision under risk. *Econometrica, 47,* 263–289.

Kahneman, D., & Tversky, A. (1984). Choices, values, and frames. *American Psychologist, 39,* 341–350.

Kantor, D., & Lehr, W. (1975). *Inside the family: Toward a theory of family process.* San Francisco: Jossey-Bass.

Kaplan, A. (1964). *The conduct of inquiry.* San Francisco: Chandler.

Kaplan, L., & Hennon, C. (1992). Remarriage education: The Personal Reflections Program. *Family Relations, 41,* 127–134.

Kirkpatrick, C. (1936). The construction of a belief pattern scale for measuring attitudes toward feminism. *Journal of Social Psychology, 7,* 421–437.

Klein, D. M. (1994, November). *Theory as data: An investigation of ourselves.* Paper presented at the National Council on Family Relations, Theory Construction and Research Methodology Workshop, Minneapolis, MN.

Klein, D. M., & Aldous, J. (1979). Three blind mice: Criticisms of the "family life cycle" concept. *Journal of Marriage and the Family, 41,* 689–691.

Klein, D. M., & Aldous, J. (Eds.). (1988). Social stress and family development. New York: Guilford.

Klein, D. M., Borne, H., Jache, A., & Sederberg, N. (1979, August). *Family chronogram analysis: Toward the development of new methodological tools for assessing the life cycles of families.* Paper presented at the National Council on Family Relations, Theory Construction and Research Methodology Workshop, Boston.

Klein, D. M., & Janning, M. Y. (1997). Philosophies of family scientists. *Family Perspective, 30,* 483–502.

Knapp, S. J. (1997). Knowledge claims in the family field: A hermeneutical alternative to the representational model. *Family Perspective, 30,* 369–428.

Kourany, J., Sterba, J., & Tong, R. (Eds.). (1999). *Feminist philosophies: Problems, theories and applications* (2nd ed.). Upper Saddle River, NJ: Prentice Hall.

Kuhn, M. (1964). Major trends in symbolic interaction theory in the past twenty-five years. *Sociological Quarterly, 5,* 61–84.

Kuhn, T. (1970). *The structure of scientific revolutions.* Chicago: University of Chicago Press.

Kumagai, F. (1984). The life cycle of the Japanese family. *Journal of Marriage and the Family, 46,* 191–204.

Laibson, D., & Zeckhauser, R. (1998). Amos Tversky and the ascent of behavioral economics. *Journal of Risk and Uncertainty, 16,* 7–47.

LaRossa, R., & LaRossa, M. (1981). *Transition to parenthood: How infants change families.* Beverly Hills, CA: Sage.

LaRossa, R., & Reitzes, D. C. (1993). Symbolic interactionism and family studies. In P. Boss, W. Doherty, R. LaRossa, W. Schumm, & S. Steinmetz (Eds.), *Sourcebook of family theories and methods: A contextual approach* (pp. 135–163). New York: Plenum.

Lavee, Y., & Dollahite, D. (1991). The linkage between theory and research in family science. *Journal of Marriage and the Family, 53,* 361–373.

Lemert, C. (Ed.). (1993). *Social theory: The multicultural and classical readings.* Boulder, CO: Westview.

Levenson, R., & Gottman, J. (1983). Marital interaction: Physiological linkage and affective exchange. *Journal of Personality and Social Psychology, 45,* 587–597.

Levinger, G. (1965). Marital cohesiveness and dissolution. *Journal of Marriage and the Family, 27,* 19–28.

Levinger, G. (1966). Sources of marital dissatisfaction among applicants for divorce. *American Journal of Orthopsychiatry, 32*, 803–807.

Levinger, G. (1982). A social exchange view on the dissolution of pair relationships. In F. Nye (Ed.), *Family relationships: Rewards and costs* (pp. 97–122). Beverly Hills, CA: Sage.

Levi-Strauss, C. (1969). *The elementary structures of kinship*. Boston: Beacon.

Levy-Schiff, R. (1994). Individual and contextual correlates of marital change across the transition to parenthood. *Developmental Psychology, 30*, 591–601.

Lewin, K. (1935). *A dynamic theory of personality*. New York: McGraw-Hill.

Lewis, R., & Spanier, G. (1979). Theorizing about the quality and stability of marriage. In W. R. Burr, R. Hill, F. I. Nye, & I. Reiss (Eds.), *Contemporary theories about the family* (Vol. 2, pp. 1–41). New York: Free Press.

Lively, C. E. (1932). *The growth cycle of the farm family* (Bulletin No. 51). Wooster: Ohio Agricultural Experiment Station.

Loomis, C. P. (1936). The study of the life cycle of families. *Rural Sociology, 1*, 180–199.

Lorber, J. (1998). *Gender inequality: Feminist theories and politics*. Los Angeles: Roxbury.

Lorenz, K. (1966). *On aggression*. New York: Harcourt, Brace & World.

Lüscher, K., & Pillemer, K. (1998). Intergenerational ambivalence: A new approach to the study of parent–child relations in later life. *Journal of Marriage and the Family, 60*, 413–425.

Lyotard, J. (1984). *The post-modern condition* (G. Bennington & B. Massumi, Trans.). Minneapolis: University of Minnesota Press. (Original work published 1979)

Lyotard, J. (1992). *The postmodern explained*. Minneapolis: University of Minnesota Press.

Magrabi, F. M., & Marshall, W. H. (1965). Family developmental tasks: A research model. *Journal of Marriage and the Family, 27*, 454–461.

Malthus, T. (1872). *An essay on the principle of population* (7th ed.). London: Reeves & Turner. (Original work published 1798)

Marini, M. M. (1984). Age and sequencing norms in the transition to adulthood. *Social Forces, 63*, 229–244.

Marks, N. F., & Lambert, J. D. (1998). Marital status continuity and change among young and midlife adults. *Journal of Family Issues, 19*, 652–686.

Marks, S. (1977). Multiple roles and role strain: Some notes on human energy, time, and commitment. *American Sociological Review, 42*, 921–936.

Marks, S., & MacDermid, S. M. (1996). Multiple roles and the self: A theory of role balance. *Journal of Marriage and the Family, 58*, 417–432.

Martindale, D. (1960). *The nature and types of sociological theory*. Boston: Houghton Mifflin.

Marx, K. (1913). *The eighteenth brumaire of Louis Bonaparte*. Chicago: C. H. Kerr.

Marx, K., & Engels, F. (1965). *The German ideology*. London: Lawrence & Wishart. (Original work published 1845–1846)

Marx, K., & Engels, F. (1971). *The communist manifesto*. New York: International Publishers. (Original work published 1867)

Maslow, A. (1966). *The psychology of science: A reconnaissance*. Chicago: Henry Regnery.

Mattessich, P., & Hill, R. (1987). Life cycle and family development. In M. B. Sussman & S. K. Steinmetz (Eds.), *Handbook of marriage and the family* (pp. 437–469). New York: Plenum.

Mauss, M. (1954). *The gift* (I. Cunnison, Trans.). New York: Free Press.

McKenzie, R. (1924). The ecological approach to the study of the human community. *American Journal of Sociology, 30*, 287–301.

McLain, R., & Weigert, A. (1979). Toward a phenomenological sociology of the family: A programmatic essay. In W. R. Burr, R. Hill, F. I. Nye, & I. Reiss (Eds.), *Contemporary theories about the family* (Vol. 2, pp. 160–205). New York: Free Press.

Mead, G. H. (1934). *Mind, self, and society* (C. Morris, Introduction and Ed.). Chicago: University of Chicago Press.

Mead, M. (1928). *Coming of age in Samoa*. New York: Morrow.

Mead, M. (1930). *Growing up in New Guinea*. New York: Blue Ribbon Books.

Mead, M. (1935). *Sex and temperament in three primitive societies*. New York: Mentor Books.

Mead, M. (1955). *Male and female*. New York: Mentor Books.

Mehrabian, A. (1972). *Nonverbal communication*. Chicago: Aldine-Atherton.

Mehrabian, A., & Wiener, M. (1968). *Language within language: Immediacy, a channel in verbal communication*. New York: Appleton-Century-Crofts.

Menaghan, E. (1983). Marital stress and family transitions: A panel analysis. *Journal of Marriage and the Family, 45,* 371–386.

Menaghan, E. (1989). Role changes and psychological well-being: Variations in effects by gender and role repertoire. *Social Forces, 67,* 693–714.

Menaghan, E., & Parcel, T. (1990). Parental employment and family life: Research in the 1980's. *Journal of Marriage and the Family, 52,* 1079–1098.

Mendel, G. (1965). *Experiments in plant hybridisation*. London: Oliver & Boyd. (Original work published 1865)

Mesarovic, M. (1970). *Theory of hierarchical multi-level systems*. New York: Academic Press.

Miller, J. G. (1978). *Living systems*. New York: McGraw-Hill.

Millet, K. (1970). *Sexual politics*. New York: Doubleday.

Minuchin, S. (1974). *Families and family therapy*. Cambridge, MA: Harvard University Press.

Mishler, E. G., & Waxler, N. E. (1968). *Interaction in families: An experimental study of family processes and schizophrenia*. New York: John Wiley.

Mitchell, J. (1972). *Women's estate*. New York: Pantheon Books.

Modell, J. (1980). Normative aspects of marriage timing since World War II. *Journal of Family History, 5,* 210–234.

Moen, P., Elder, G. H., Jr., & Lüscher, K. (Eds.). (1995). *Examining lives in context: Perspectives on the ecology of human development*. Washington, DC: American Psychological Association.

Morris, C. (1934). Introduction. In G. H. Mead (Ed.), *Mind, self and society*. Chicago: University of Chicago Press.

Mullins, N. (1973). *Theories and theory groups in contemporary American sociology*. New York: Harper & Row.

Nelson, H. L. (Ed.). (1997). *Feminism and families*. New York: Routledge.

Neuman, W. L. (1994). *Social research methods: Qualitative and quantitative approaches*. Needham Heights, MA: Allyn & Bacon.

Nock, S. L. (1979). The family life cycle: Empirical or conceptual tool? *Journal of Marriage and the Family, 41,* 15–26.

Noller, P. (1984). *Nonverbal communication and marital interaction*. Elmsford, NY: Pergammon.

Noller, P., & Fitzpatrick, M. (1993). *Communication in family relationships*. Englewood Cliffs, NJ: Prentice Hall.

Norris, C. (1989). Philosophy, theory and the "Contest of Faculties": Saving deconstruction from the pragmatists. In Rajnath (Ed.), *Deconstruction: A critique* (pp. 67–82). London: Macmillan.

Nye, F. I. (Ed.). (1976). *Role structure and analysis of the family*. Beverly Hills, CA: Sage.

Nye, F. I. (1978). Is choice and exchange theory the key? *Journal of Marriage and the Family, 40*, 219–233.

Nye, F. I. (1979). Choice, exchange, and the family. In W. R. Burr, R. Hill, F. I. Nye, & I. Reiss (Eds.), *Contemporary theories about the family* (Vol. 2, pp. 1–41). New York: Free Press.

Nye, F. I. (1980). Family mini-theories as special instances of choice and exchange theory. *Journal of Marriage and the Family, 42*, 479–489.

Nye, F. I., & Berardo, F. (1981). *Emerging conceptual frameworks in family analysis*. New York: Praeger. (Original work published 1966)

Nye, F. I., White, L., & Frideres, J. (1969, October). *A partial theory of marital stability*. Paper presented to the National Council on Family Relations, Washington, DC.

Ogburn, W. F., & Nimkoff, M. F. (1955). *Technology and the changing family*. New York: Houghton Mifflin.

Okin, S. M. (1989). *Justice, gender, and the family*. New York: Basic Books.

Olson, D. H. (1972). Empirically unbinding the double-bind: Review of research and conceptual reformulations. *Family Process, 11*, 69–94.

Olson, D. H. (1995). Family systems: Understanding your roots. In R. Day, K. Gilbert, B. Settles, & W. Burr (Eds.), *Research and theory in family science* (pp. 131–153). Pacific Grove, CA: Brooks/Cole.

Oppenheimer, V. (1988). A theory of marriage timing. *American Journal of Sociology, 94*, 563–591.

Osmond, M. (1987). Radical-critical theories. In M. Sussman & S. Steinmetz (Eds.), *Handbook of marriage and the family* (pp. 103–124). New York: Plenum.

Osmond, M., & Thorne, B. (1993). Feminist theories: The construction of gender in families and society. In P. Boss, W. Doherty, R. LaRossa, W. Schumm, & S. Steinmetz (Eds.), *Sourcebook of family theories and methods: A contextual approach* (pp. 591–622). New York: Plenum.

Paolucci, B., Hall, O., & Axinn, N. (1977). *Family decision making: An ecosystem approach*. New York: John Wiley.

Park, R. (1925). The urban community as a spatial pattern and a moral order. Publications of the *American Sociological Society, 20*, 1–14.

Park, R., & Burgess, E. (1921). *Introduction to the science of sociology*. Chicago: University of Chicago Press.

Parsons, T. (1951). *The social system*. Glencoe, IL: Free Press.

Patterson, G., & Reid, J. (1970). Reciprocity and coercion: Two facets of social systems. In C. Neuringer & J. Michaels (Eds.), *Behavior modification in clinical psychology* (pp. 133–177). New York: Appleton-Century-Crofts.

Pearson, K. (1909). *The scope and importance to the state of science of national eugenics*. London: Dulau.

Peirce, C. S. (1905). What pragmatism is. *Monist, 5*, 411-436.

Perry-Jenkins, M., Repetti, R. L., & Crouter, A. C. (2000). Work and family in the 1900's. *Journal of Marriage and the Family, 62*, 981–998.

Peterson, W. (1969). *Population* (2nd ed.). New York: Macmillan.

Piaget, J. (1952). *The origins of intelligence in children* (M. Cook, Trans.). New York: Norton.

Pina, D., & Bengtson, V. (1993). The division of household labor and wives' happiness: Ideology, employment, and perceptions of support. *Journal of Marriage and the Family, 55*, 901–912.

Poduska, B. (1993). *For love and money: A guide to finances and relationships*. Pacific Grove, CA: Brooks/Cole.

Popper, K. (1959). *The logic of scientific discovery*. New York: Basic Books.

Powers, W. (1974). *Behavior: The control of perception*. Chicago: Aldine.

Price, S., McKenry, P., and Murphy, M. (2000). *Families across time: A life course perspective*. Los Angeles: Roxbury.

Prigogine, I., & Stengers, I. (1984). *Order out of chaos*. New York: Bantam.

Pyke, K., & Coltrane, S. (1996). Entitlement, obligation, and gratitude in family work. *Journal of Family Issues, 17*, 60–82.

Rabuzzi, K. A. (1982). *The sacred and the feminine: Toward a theology of housework*. New York: Seabury.

Rapp, R. (1982). Family and class in contemporary America: Notes toward an understanding of ideology. In B. Thorne et al. (Eds.), *Rethinking the family* (pp. 168–187). New York: Longman.

Raush, H., Barry, W., Hertel, R., & Swain, N. (1974). *Communication, conflict and marriage*. San Francisco: Jossey-Bass.

Renick, M., Blumberg, S., & Markman, H. (1992). The Prevention and Relationship Enhancement Program (PREP): An empirically based preventive intervention program for couples. *Family Relations, 41*, 141–147.

Rodgers, R. H. (1973). *Family interaction and transaction: The developmental approach*. Englewood Cliffs, NJ: Prentice Hall.

Rodgers, R. H., & White, J. M. (1993). Family development theory. In P. Boss, W. Doherty, R. LaRossa, W. Schumm, & S. Steinmetz (Eds.), *Sourcebook of family theories and methods: A contextual approach* (pp. 225–254). New York: Plenum.

Rodgers, R. H., & Witney, G. (1981). The family cycle in twentieth century Canada. *Journal of Marriage and the Family, 43*, 727–740.

Rodman, H. (1967). Marital power in France, Greece, Yugoslavia and the United States. *Journal of Marriage and the Family, 29*, 320–324.

Rollins, B., & Feldman, H. (1970). Marital satisfaction over the family life cycle. *Journal of Marriage and the Family, 32*, 20–27.

Rosenblatt, P. C. (1994). *Metaphors of family systems theory: Toward new constructions*. New York: Guilford.

Rossi, P., & Berk, R. (1985). Varieties of normative consensus. *American Sociological Review, 50*, 333–347.

Rudner, R. S. (1966). *Philosophy of social science*. Englewood Cliffs, NJ: Prentice Hall.

Russell, C. (1993). Family development theory as revised by Rodgers and White: Implications for practice. In P. Boss, W. Doherty, R. LaRossa, W. Schumm, & S. Steinmetz (Eds.), *Sourcebook of family theories and methods: A contextual approach* (pp. 255–257). New York: Plenum.

Russo, N. F. (1998). Measuring feminist attitudes: Just what does it mean to be a feminist? [Editorial]. *Psychology of Women Quarterly, 22*, 313–316.

Sabatelli, R. M. (1988). Exploring relationship satisfaction: A social exchange perspective on the interdependence between theory, research, and practice. *Family Relations, 37*, 217-222.

Sabatelli, R. M., & Shehan, C. L. (1993). Exchange and resource theories. In P. Boss, W. Doherty, R. LaRossa, W. Schumm, & S. Steinmetz (Eds.), *Sourcebook of family theories and methods: A contextual approach* (pp. 385–411). New York: Plenum.

Scanzoni, J. (1970). *Opportunity and the family*. New York: Free Press.

Scanzoni, J. (1972). *Sexual bargaining*. Chicago: University of Chicago Press.

Scanzoni, J., & Szinovacz, M. (1980). *Family decision-making: A developmental sex role model*. Newbury Park, CA: Sage.

Schoen, R. (1992). First unions and the stability of first marriages. *Journal of Marriage and the Family, 54,* 281–284.

Schram, R. W. (1979). Marital satisfaction over the life cycle: A critique and a proposal. *Journal of Marriage and the Family, 41,* 7–14.

Schuham, A. (1967). The double-bind hypothesis a decade later. *Psychological Bulletin, 68,* 409–416.

Schutz, A. (1967). *The phenomenology of the social world.* Evanston, IL: Northwestern University Press.

Scott, J. W. (1988). *Gender and the politics of history.* New York: Columbia University Press.

Sexton, C., & Perlman, D. (1989). Couple's career orientation, gender role orientation, and perceived equity as determinants of marital power. *Journal of Marriage and the Family, 51,* 933–941.

Shannon, C. E., & Weaver, W. (1949). *The mathematical theory of communication.* Urbana: University of Illinois Press.

Shaw, S. M. (1988). Gender differences in the definition and perception of household labor. *Family Relations, 37,* 333–337.

Shelton, B. A., & John, D. (1986). The division of household labor. *Annual Review of Sociology, 22,* 299–322.

Simmel, G. (1904). The sociology of conflict. *American Journal of Sociology, 9,* 490–525.

Simmel, G. (1950). The sociology of Georg Simmel (Kurt Wolff, Trans.). Glencoe, IL: Free Press.

Smith, D. E. (1992). Sociology from women's experiences: A reaffirmation. *Sociological Theory, 10,* 88–98.

Spanier, G. B., Sauer, W., & Larzelere, R. (1979). An empirical evaluation of the family life cycle. *Journal of Marriage and the Family, 41,* 27–38.

Spencer, H. (1880). *First principles.* New York: A. C. Burt.

Sprey, J. (1979). Conflict theory and the study of marriage and the family. In W. R. Burr, R. Hill, F. I. Nye, & I. Reiss (Eds.), *Contemporary theories about the family* (Vol. 2, pp. 130–159). New York: Free Press.

Stets, J. (1992). Interactive processes in dating aggression: A national study. *Journal of Marriage and the Family, 54,* 165–177.

Straus, M. (1994). State-to-state differences in social inequality and social bonds in relation to assaults on wives in the United States. *Journal of Comparative Family Studies, 25,* 7–24.

Stryker, S. (1964). The interactional and situational approaches. In H. Christensen (Ed.), *Handbook of marriage and the family* (pp. 125–170). Chicago: Rand McNally.

Stryker, S. (1968). Identity salience and role performance: The relevance of symbolic interaction theory for family research. *Journal of Marriage and the Family, 30,* 558–564.

Stryker, S. (1980). *Symbolic interactionism: A social structural version.* Menlo Park, CA: Benjamin/Cummings.

Stryker, S. (1987). Identity theory: Developments and extensions. In K. Yardley & T. Honess (Eds.), *Self and identity: Psychological perspectives* (pp. 89–103). London: Wiley.

Stryker, S. (1989). Further developments in identity theory: Singularity versus multiplicity of self. In J. Berger, M. Zelditch, & B. Anderson (Eds.), *Sociological theories in progress: New formulations* (pp. 35–57). Newbury Park, CA: Sage.

Sryker, S. (1991). Exploring the relevance of social cognition for the relationship of self and society: Linking the cognitive perspective and identity theory. In

J. A. Howard & P. L. Callero (Eds.), *The self-society dynamic: Cognition, emotion, and action* (pp. 19–41). New York: Cambridge University Press.

Stryker, S., & Serpe, R. T. (1994). Identity salience and psychological centrality: Equivalent, overlapping, or complementary concepts. *Social Psychological Quarterly, 57,* 16–35.

Sweet, L., Bumpass, L., & Call, V. (1988). *The design and content of the National Survey of Families and Households.* Madison: University of Wisconsin, Center for Demography and Ecology.

Szinovacz, M. (1987). Family power. In M. Sussman & S. Steinmetz (Eds.), *Handbook of marriage and the family* (pp. 651–694). New York: Plenum.

Taylor, D. (1997). The uneasy relationship between motherhood and feminism. In A. Jetter, A. Orleck, & D. Taylor (Eds.), *The politics of motherhood* (pp. 349–351). Hanover, MA: University Press of New England.

Teachman, J. D., Paasch, K., & Carver, K. (1997). Social capital and the generation of human capital. *Social Forces, 75,* 1343–1359.

Teachman, J. D., & Polonko, K. (1990). Cohabitation and marital stability in the United States. *Social Forces, 69,* 207–220.

Teachman, J. D., Tedrow, L. M., & Crowder, K. D. (2000). The changing demography of America's families. *Journal of Marriage and the Family, 62,* 1234–1246.

Thibaut, J. W., & Kelley, H. H. (1959). *The social psychology of groups.* New York: John Wiley.

Thomas, D. L., & Kleber, J. E. (1981). Comment on marital quality: A review of the seventies. *Journal of Marriage and the Family, 43,* 780–781.

Thomas, D. L., & Wilcox, J. E. (1987). The rise of family theory: A historical and critical analysis. In M. B. Sussman & S. K. Steinmetz (Eds.), *Handbook of marriage and the family* (pp. 81–102). New York: Plenum.

Thomas, W. I., & Thomas, D. S. (1928). *The child in America: Behavior problems and programs.* New York: Knopf.

Thompson, L. (1992). Feminist methodology for family studies. *Journal of Marriage and the Family, 54,* 3–18.

Thompson, L., & Walker, A. J. (1995). The place of feminism in family studies. *Journal of Marriage and the Family, 57,* 847–865.

Tiedje, L., Wortman, C., Downey, G., Emmons, C., Biernat, M., & Lang, E. (1990). Women with multiple roles: Role-compatibility perceptions, satisfaction, and mental health. *Journal of Marriage and the Family, 52,* 63–72.

Touliatos, J. (Ed.). (1994). *Inventory of marriage and family literature* (Vol. 19: 1992/93). Minneapolis, MN: National Council on Family Relations.

Toulmin, S. (1972). *Human understanding. Vol. 1: General introduction and part 1.* Oxford, UK: Oxford University Press.

Troost, K., & Filsinger, E. (1993). Emerging biosocial perspectives on the family. In P. Boss, W. Doherty, R. LaRossa, W. Schumm, & S. Steinmetz (Eds.), *Sourcebook of family theories and methods: A contextual approach* (pp. 677–710). New York: Plenum.

Tuana, N., & Tong, R. (Eds.). (1995). *Feminism and philosophy.* Boulder, CO: Westview.

Tuma, N., & Hannan, M. (1984). *Social dynamics.* New York: Academic Press.

Turner, J. (1991). *The structure of sociological theory* (5th ed.). Belmont, CA: Wadsworth.

Turner, J. (1998). *The structure of sociological theory* (6th ed.). Belmont, CA: Wadsworth.

Turner, R. H. (1970). *Family interaction.* New York: John Wiley.

Turner, R. H. (1980). Strategy for developing an integrated role theory. *Humboldt Journal of Social Relations, 7,* 123–139.

Turner, R. H., & Colomy, P. (1987). Role differentiation: Orienting principles. *Advances in Group Processes, 5,* 1–47.

van den Berghe, P. (1979). *Human family systems.* New York: Elsevier North-Holland.

van Leeuwen, L. T. (1981). Early family sociology in Europe: Parallels to the United States. In R. L. Howard (Ed.), *A social history of American family sociology, 1865–1940* (pp. 95–139). Westport, CT: Greenwood.

Vannoy, D., & Phillber, W. (1992). Wife's employment and quality of marriage. *Journal of Marriage and the Family, 54,* 387–398.

von Bertalanffy, L. (1968). *General systems theory.* New York: George Braziller.

von Glasersfeld, E. (1987). *Constructivism: Wissen ohne erkenntnis and Declaration of the American Society for Cybernetics* (Working paper No. 87-1). Center for Systems Research, University of Alberta, Canada.

Voydanoff, P. (1987). *Work and family life.* Newbury Park, CA: Sage.

Voydanoff, P., & Donnelly, B. W. (1999). Multiple roles and psychological distress: The intersection of the paid worker, spouse, and parent role with the role of the adult child. *Journal of Marriage and the Family, 61,* 725–735.

Walker, A. J., & Thompson, L. (1984). Feminism and family studies. *Journal of Family Issues, 5,* 545–570.

Wallace, W. (Ed.). (1968). *Sociological theory: An introduction.* Chicago: Aldine.

Walster & Walster (1978). *Equity: Theory and research.* Boston: Allyn & Bacon.

Watt, D., & White, J. M. (1999). Computers and the family: A family development perspective. *Journal of Comparative Family Studies, 30,* 1–15.

Watzlawick, P., Beavin, J., & Jackson, D. (1967). *Pragmatics of human communication.* New York: Norton.

Weinberg, W. (1908). Uber den nachweis der vererbung beim menschen. *Jh. Ver. Vaterl. Naturk. Wurttemb, 64,* 368–382.

Westney, O. (1993). Human ecology theory: Implications for education, research and practice. In P. Boss, W. Doherty, R. LaRossa, W. Schumm, & S. Steinmetz (Eds.), *Sourcebook of family theories and methods: A contextual approach* (pp. 448–450). New York: Plenum.

Westoff, C. (1978). Marriage and fertility in the developed countries. *Scientific American, 239,* 51–57.

Whitchurch, G., & Constantine, L. (1993). Systems theory. In P. Boss, W. Doherty, R. LaRossa, W. Schumm, & S. Steinmetz (Eds.), *Sourcebook of family theories and methods: A contextual approach* (pp. 325–352). New York: Plenum.

White, H. (1963). *An anatomy of kinship.* Englewood Cliffs, NJ: Prentice Hall.

White, J. M. (1984). Not the sum of its parts. *Journal of Family Issues, 5,* 515–518.

White, J. M. (1987). Researching developmental careers: The career conformity scale. *Journal of Family Issues, 8,* 306–318.

White, J. M. (1991). *Dynamics of family development: The theory of family development.* New York: Guilford.

White, J. M. (1997). Family theory, science, and the problem of certainty. *Family Perspectives, 30,* 445–454.

White, J. M. (1998). The normative interpretation of life course event histories. *Marriage and Family Review, 3/4,* 211–235.

White, J. M. (1999). Work-family stage and satisfaction with work-family balance. *Journal of Comparative Family Studies, 30,* 163–175.

White, J. M., & Mason, L. K. (1999). Post-positivism and positivism: A dialogue. *Family Science Review, 12,* 1–21.

White, L. K., & Booth, A. (1991). Divorce over the life course: The role of marital happiness. *Journal of Family Issues, 12,* 5–21.

Whitehead, A. (1929). *Process and reality.* New York: Macmillan.

Wiener, N. (1948). *Cybernetics*. New York: John Wiley.

Wilkinson, M. (1977, October). *Yes, Virginia, propositions can be derived from systems theory*. Paper presented to the National Council on Family Relations, Theory Construction and Methodology Workshop, San Diego, CA.

Wilson, E. O. (1975). *Sociobiology: The new synthesis*. Cambridge, MA: Harvard University Press.

Winton, C. A. (1995). *Frameworks for studying families*. Guilford, CT: Dushkin.

Wollstonecraft, M. (1792/1975). *A vindication of the rights of woman*. Baltimore, MD: Penguin.

Wood, J. T. (1995). Feminist scholarship and the study of relationships. *Journal of Social and Personal Relationships, 12*, 103–120.

Ylló, K., & Straus, M. (1990). Patriarchy and violence against wives: The impact of structural and normative factors. In M. Straus & R. Gelles (Eds.), *Physical violence in American families: Risk factors and adaptations to violence in 8,145 families* (pp. 383–399). New Brunswick, NJ: Transaction Books.

Zimmerman, C. C. (1947). *Family and civilization*. New York: Harper.

# Index

# About the Authors

**James M. White** is Professor in the School of Social Work and Family Studies at the University of British Columbia and is known internationally for his previous book, *Dynamics of Family Development,* which has been published in both the United States (1991) and in Japan (1994). Besides his interest in researching family development, he is also interested in marital interaction and communication. He is the author of numerous journal articles appearing both in sociology journals and such journals as *Journal of Family Issues, Journal of Social and Personal Relationships,* and *Journal of Marriage and Family.* He has authored chapters for books, including the chapter he coauthored with R. H. Rodgers on family development in the *Sourcebook of Family Theories and Methods: A Contextual Approach* (1993). He has served as referee for numerous journals in family relations and public health and is an Associate Editor for *Canadian Journal of Public Health, Journal of Comparative Family Studies,* and *The International Encyclopedia of Family Relationships.* He is past President of the Northwest Council on Family Relations, the membership of which includes academics, practitioners, and therapists from the states and provinces of the Pacific Northwest. He resides with his wife and three daughters in Vancouver, Canada.

**David M. Klein** is Associate Professor and Director of Graduate Studies in the Department of Sociology, University of Notre Dame. A graduate of the University of Washington (BA) and the University of Minnesota (PhD), he has taught and written on family theory throughout his career. Much of his work has dealt with family research methods, metatheory, and the history of family studies. His substantive areas of research have included family problem solving, intergenerational relations, and premarital assessment, among others. He is Associate Editor of *Journal of Marriage and Family* and *Journal of Family Issues* and has served as Chair and Archivist of the Theory

Construction and Research Methodology Workshop, Treasurer of the National Council on Family Relations, and Chair of its Research and Theory Section. His previous books include *Social Stress and Family Development* (with Joan Aldous) and *Changing Societal Institutions* (with Maureen T. Hallinan and Jennifer L. Glass).